GW00370786

# AAT UNITS 21, 22 AND 23

## UNIT 21
### Working with Computers

## UNIT 22
### Contribute to the Maintenance of a Healthy, Safe and Productive Working environment

## UNIT 23
### Achieving Personal Effectiveness

### Plus The IT sections of Units 1–4
*Foundation (NVQ/SVQ Level 2)*

**British Library Cataloguing-in-Publication Data**

A catalogue record for this book is available from the British Library.

We are grateful to the Association of Accounting Technicians for permission to reproduce past assessment materials. The solutions have been prepared by Kaplan Publishing.

Published by
Kaplan Publishing UK
Unit 2 The Business Centre
Molly Millars Lane
Wokingham
Berkshire
RG41 2QZ

ISBN 978-1-84710-613-1

© Kaplan Financial Limited, April 2008

Printed and bound in Great Britain.

All rights reserved. No part of this publication may be reproduced, stored in a retrieval system, or transmitted, in any form or by any means, electronic, mechanical, photocopying, recording or otherwise, without the prior written permission of Kaplan Publishing.

# CONTENTS

*We have included the IT aspects of Units 1 to 4 in this book because the AAT's Unit 21 simulation includes the IT aspects of these units.

KAPLAN PUBLISHING

# CONTENTS

**WORKBOOK**

KAPLAN PUBLISHING

# PREFACE

This is a study text and workbook for the following units of the AAT Foundation Standards of Competence NVQ/SVQ Level 2 in Accounting.

**Unit 21** – Working with computers
**Unit 22** – Contribute to the maintenance of a healthy, safe and productive working environment
**Unit 23** – Achieving personal effectiveness

It also includes the IT knowledge and understanding and performance criteria from **Units 1 to 4**.

---

### STUDY TEXT

The study text is written in a practical and interactive style:
· key terms and concepts are clearly defined
· all topics are illustrated with practical examples with clearly worked solutions

---

### WORKBOOK

The workbook comprises two main elements
(a) A question bank of key techniques to give additional practice and reinforce the work covered in each chapter. The questions are divided into their relevant chapters and students may either attempt these questions as they work through the study text, or leave some or all of these until they have completed the study text as a sort of final revision of what they have studied.
(b) Four mock simulations which closely reflect the type of simulation they may expect.

KAPLAN PUBLISHING

# STANDARDS OF COMPETENCE

## Unit 21 Working with Computers

### Unit commentary

This unit is about your ability to use a computer system safely and effectively. For the first element, you will need to demonstrate that you are fully aware of your responsibilities when using a computer system and the software packages you will need. For the second element you will be required to show an understanding of the need to keep data confidential and secure.

| Elements contained within this unit are: |
| --- |
| **Element 21.1** |
| **Use computer systems and software** |
| **Element 21.2** |
| **Maintain security of data** |

## Knowledge and Understanding

To perform this unit effectively you will need to know and understand

| **General Information Technology** | | **Chapters** |
|---|---|---|
| 1 | The importance of carrying out simple visual safety checks on hardware and correct powering up and shutting down procedures (Element 21.1) | 1 |
| 2 | The purpose of passwords (Element 21.2) | 1 |
| 3 | How to save, transfer and print documents (Element 21.1) | 1 |
| 4 | How to take back up copies (Element 21.1) | 1 |
| 5 | Causes of difficulties, necessary files which have been damaged or deleted, printer problems, hardware problems (Element 21.1) | 1, 2 |
| 6 | Different types of risk, viruses, confidentiality (Element 21.2) | 2 |
| 7 | Relevant security and legal regulations, data protection legislation, copyright, VDU legislation, health and safety regulations, retention of documents (Element 21.1) | 2 |

**The Organisation**

| | | |
|---|---|---|
| 8 | Location of hardware, software and back up copies (Elements 21.1 and 21.2) | 1 |
| 9 | Location of information sources (Element 21.1) | 1,2 |
| 10 | The organisation's procedures for changing passwords, and making back ups (Element 21.1) | 1 |
| 11 | House style for presentation of documents (Element 21.1) | 1,2 |
| 12 | Organisational security policies (Element 21.2) | 2 |

## Element 21.1  Use computer systems and software

### Performance Criteria
In order to perform this element successfully you need to

| | | |
|---|---|---|
| A | Perform initial **visual safety checks** and power up the **computer system** | 1 |
| B | Use **passwords** to gain access to the **computer system** where limitations on access to data is required | 1 |

KAPLAN PUBLISHING

**Chapters**

| C | Access, save and print data files and exit from relevant software | 1 |
|---|---|---|
| D | Use appropriate file names and save work | 1 |
| E | Back up work carried out on a computer system to suitable storage media at regular intervals | 1 |
| F | Close down the computer without damaging the **computer system** | 1 |
| G | Seek immediate assistance when **difficulties occur** | 1 |

**Range statement**
Performance in this element relates to the following contexts

**Visual safety checks**
· Hardware components
· Plugs
· Cables
· Interfaces

**Computer system**
· Stand alone PC
· Networked system

**Passwords**
· System
· Software

**Difficulties**
· Hardware failure
· Software failure
· Corruption of data

## Element 21.2  Maintain the security of data

**Performance Criteria**
In order to perform this element successfully you need to

| A | Ensure passwords are kept secret and changed at **appropriate times** | 2 |
|---|---|---|
| B | Ensure computer hardware and program disks are kept securely located | 2 |
| C | Identify **potential risks** to data from different **sources** and take steps to resolve or minimise them | 2 |

**Chapters**

| | | |
|---|---|---|
| D | Maintain **security** and **confidentiality** of data at all times | 2 |
| E | Understand and implement relevant **legal regulations** | 2 |

**Range statement**
Performance in this element relates to the following contexts

**Appropriate times**
· On a regular basis
· If disclosure is suspected

**Potential risks**
· Corruption
· Loss
· Illegal copying

**Sources**
· Internal
· External
· Viruses
· Poor storage facilities
· Theft

**Security**
· Back up copies
· Secure storage

**Confidentiality**
· Passwords

**Legal regulations**
· Data protection legislation
· VDU regulations
· Health and safety
· Document retention

KAPLAN PUBLISHING

# STANDARDS OF COMPETENCE

## Unit 22 Contribute to the Maintenance of a Healthy, Safe and Productive Working Environment

**Unit commentary**

This unit is about monitoring your working environment and making sure it meets requirements for health, safety, security and effective working conditions. **You must show that you can achieve this standard of health, safety and security in all areas of your work.**

| Elements contained within this unit are: |
| --- |
| **Element 22.1** |
| **Monitor and maintain a safe, healthy and secure working environment** |
| **Element 22.2** |
| **Monitor and maintain an effective and efficient working environment** |

## Knowledge and Understanding

To perform this unit effectively you will need to know and understand

| | **Health, safety and security at work** | **Chapters** |
|---|---|---|
| 1 | The importance of health, safety and security in your workplace (Element 22.1) | 3, 4 |
| 2 | The basic requirements of the health and safety and other legislation and regulations that apply to your workplace (Element 22.1) | 3, 4 |
| 3 | The person(s) responsible for health, safety and security in your workplace (Element 22.1) | 3, 4 |
| 4 | The relevant up-to-date information on health, safety and security that applies to your workplace (Element 22.1) | 3 |
| 5 | The importance of being alert to health, safety and security hazards (Element 22.1) | 3 |
| 6 | The common health, safety and security hazards that affect people working in an administrative role and how to identify these (Element 22.1) | 3, 4 |
| 7 | Hazards you can put right yourself and hazards you must report (Element 22.1) | 3 |
| 8 | The importance of warning others about hazards and how to do so until the hazard is dealt with (Element 22.1) | 3 |
| 9 | Your organisation's emergency procedures (Element 22.1) | 3 |
| 10 | How to follow your organisation's emergency procedures and your responsibilities in relation to these (Element 22.1) | 3 |
| 11 | How to recommend improvements to health and safety (Element 22.1) | 3 |
| 12 | Health and safety records you may have to complete and how to do so (Element 22.1) | 3 |

**Effectiveness and efficiency at work**

| | | |
|---|---|---|
| 13 | How the conditions under which you work can affect your effectiveness and efficiency and the effectiveness and efficiency of those around you (Element 22.2) | 5 |
| 14 | How to organise your own work area so that you and others can work efficiently (Element 22.2) | 5 |

KAPLAN PUBLISHING

**Chapters**

## Element 22.1  Monitor and maintain a safe, healthy and secure working environment

### Performance Criteria
In order to perform this element successfully you need to

| A | Make sure you read, comply with and have up-to-date information on the health, safety and security requirements and procedures for your workplace | 3, 4 |
|----|----|----|
| B | Make sure that the procedures are being followed and report any that are not to the relevant person | 3, 4 |
| C | Identify and correct any hazards that you can deal with[1] safely, competently and within the limits of your authority | 3, 4 |
| D | Promptly and accurately report any hazards that you are not allowed to deal with[2] to the relevant person and warn other people who may be affected | 3, 4 |
| E | Follow your organisation's **emergency procedures** promptly, calmly and efficiently | 3, 4 |
| F | Identify and recommend opportunities for improving health, safety and security to the responsible person | 3, 4 |
| G | Complete any health and safety records legibly and accurately[3] | 3, 4 |

## Range Statement
Performance in this element relates to the following contexts

**Emergency procedures**
· Illness
· Accidents
· Fires
· Other reasons to evacuate the premises[4]
· Breaches of security

## Element 22.2  Monitor and maintain an effective and efficient working environment

### Performance Criteria
In order to perform this element successfully you need to

| A | Organise the work area you are responsible for, so that you and others can work efficiently[5] | 5 |
|---|---|---|
| B | Organise the work area you are responsible for, so that it meets your organisation's requirements[6] and presents a positive image of yourself and your team | 5 |
| C | Identify conditions around you that interfere with effective working[7] | 5 |
| D | Put right any conditions that you can deal with[8] safely, competently, within the limits of your authority and with the agreement of other relevant people | 5 |
| E | Promptly and accurately report any other conditions[9] to the relevant person | 5 |
| F | Use and maintain equipment in accordance with manufacturer's instructions and your organisation's procedures[10] | 5 |

### Range Statement
There are no additional contextual requirements for this element

---

**Explanations or examples of terms used**

[1]  For example, trailing cables, filing cabinet drawers left open or windows being left unsecured when the premises are left unattended
[2]  For example, frayed cables, broken windows or a suspicious stranger on the premises
[3]  For example, accident reports
[4]  For example, bomb threats
[5]  For example, having your most used filing cabinet within easy reach of your desk
[6]  For example, respecting your organisation's guidelines on displaying posters, pictures or photographs
[7]  For example, bright sunlight, office temperatures too hot or too cold, or the layout of the office that may not support efficient working
[8]  For example, adjusting the heating
[10]  For example, reporting that the heating or air conditioning is not working
(For guidance only, not part of the standards)

KAPLAN PUBLISHING

# STANDARDS OF COMPETENCE

## Unit 23  Achieving Personal Effectiveness

### Unit commentary

This unit is concerned with the personal and organisational aspects of your role. In the first element you need to show that you plan and organise your work effectively and also demonstrate that you prioritise your activities. The second element requires you to demonstrate that you work effectively with others by offering assistance, resolving difficulties, meeting deadlines, etc. In the final element in this unit you need to show that you develop yourself through learning and acquiring new skills and knowledge.

| Elements contained within this unit are: |
| --- |
| **Element 23.1** |
| **Plan and organise your own work** |
| **Element 23.2** |
| **Maintain good working relationships** |
| **Element 23.3** |
| **Improve your own performance** |

## Knowledge and Understanding

To perform this unit effectively you will need to know and understand

| | The Business Environment | Chapters |
|---|---|---|
| 1 | Relevant legislation<br>· Copyright<br>· Data protection<br>· Equal opportunities | 7<br>7<br>7 |
| 2 | Sources of legal requirements<br>· Data protection<br>· Companies acts | 7<br>6, 7 |
| 3 | Where to access information about new developments relating to your job role | 8 |
| 4 | Employee responsibilities in complying with the relevant legislation | 6 |

**Methods**

| | | |
|---|---|---|
| 5 | Work methods and practices in your organisation | 6, 7 |
| 6 | Handling confidential information | 7 |
| 7 | Establishing constructive relationships | 7 |
| 8 | Why it is important to integrate your work with other people's | 7 |
| 9 | Ways of identifying development needs | 8 |
| 10 | Setting self-development objectives | 8 |
| 11 | Development opportunities and their resource implications | 8 |
| 12 | Ways of assessing own performance and progress | 8 |
| 13 | Maintaining good working relationships, even when disagreeing with others | 7 |
| 14 | The scope and limit of your own authority for taking corrective actions | 6, 7 |
| 15 | Use of different styles of approach in different circumstances | 7 |
| 16 | Target setting, prioritising and organising work | 6 |
| 17 | Work planning and scheduling techniques and aids | 6 |
| 18 | Time management | 6 |

KAPLAN PUBLISHING

**Chapters**

| | | |
|---|---|---|
| 19 | Team working | 6 |
| 20 | Seeking and exchanging information, advice and support | 7 |
| 21 | Handling disagreements and conflicts | 7 |
| 22 | Showing commitment and motivation towards your work | 6, 7 |
| 23 | Deadlines and timescales | 6 |
| 24 | Dealing with changed priorities and unforeseen situations | 6 |
| 25 | Informing and consulting with others about work methods | 7 |
| 26 | Negotiating the assistance of others | 7 |
| 27 | Coordinating resources and tasks | 7 |

**The Organisation**

| | | |
|---|---|---|
| 28 | The organisational and department structure | 6 |
| 29 | Own work role and responsibilities | 6 |
| 30 | Colleagues' work roles and responsibilities | 6 |
| 31 | Reporting procedures | 6, 7 |
| 32 | Procedures to deal with conflict and poor working relationships | 7 |
| 33 | Where to access information that will help you learn including formal training courses | 7, 8 |
| 34 | The people who may help you plan and implement learning you may require | 7, 8 |

## Element 23.1  Plan and organise your own work

### Performance Criteria

In order to perform this element successfully you need to

| | | |
|---|---|---|
| A | Identify and prioritise **tasks** according to organisational procedures and regulatory requirements | 6, 7 |
| B | Recognise changes in priorities and adapt resources allocations and work plans accordingly | 6 |

**Chapters**

| | | |
|---|---|---|
| C | Use appropriate **planning aids** to plan and monitor work progress | 6 |
| D | Identify, negotiate and coordinate relevant assistance to meet specific demands and deadlines | 6 |
| E | Report anticipated difficulties in meeting deadlines to the **appropriate person** | 6 |
| F | Check that work methods and activities conform to legal and regulatory requirements and organisational procedures | 6 |

**Range Statement**
Performance in this unit relates to the following contexts

**Tasks**
· Routine
· Unexpected

**Planning aids**
· Diaries
· Schedules
· Action plans

**Appropriate person**
· Line manager
· Project manager
· Colleague(s) relying on the completion of your work

## Element 23.2 Maintain good working relationships

**Performance Criteria**
In order to perform this element successfully you need to

| | | |
|---|---|---|
| A | **Communicate** with other people clearly and effectively, using your organisation's procedures | 7 |
| B | Discuss and agree realistic objectives, resources, working methods and schedules and in a way that promotes good working relationships | 7 |
| C | Meet commitments to colleagues within agreed timescales | 7 |
| D | Offer **assistance and support** where colleagues cannot meet deadlines, within your own work constraints and other commitments | 7 |
| E | Find workable solutions for any conflicts and dissatisfaction which reduce personal and team effectiveness | 7 |

KAPLAN PUBLISHING

**Chapters**

| | | |
|---|---|---|
| F | Following organisational procedures if there are **difficulties in working relationships** that are beyond your authority or ability to resolve, and promptly refer them to the appropriate person | 7 |
| G | Treat others courteously and work in a way that shows respect for other people | 7 |
| H | Ensure data protection requirements are followed strictly and also maintain confidentiality of information relating to colleagues. | 7 |

**Range Statement**
Performance in this unit relates to the following contexts

**Communicate**
· Face-to-face
· By telephone
· By fax
· By e-mail
· By creating word processed documents

**Other people**
· Those familiar with the subject matter
· Those not familiar with the subject matter

**Assistance and support**
· Personal
· Practical

**Difficulties in working relationships**
· Personality
· Working style
· Status
· Work demands

## Element 23.3  Improve your own performance

**Performance Criteria**
In order to perform this element successfully you need to

| | | |
|---|---|---|
| A | **Identify your own development needs** by taking into consideration your current work activities and also your own career goals | 8 |
| B | Define your own development objectives and, where necessary, agree them with the appropriate person | 8 |
| C | Research appropriate **ways of acquiring new skills and knowledge** | 8 |

**Chapters**

| D | Ensure that development opportunities are realistic and achievable in terms of resources and support from relevant persons | 8 |
|---|---|---|
| E | **Review and evaluate your performance and progress** and also to agreed timescales | 8 |
| F | Monitor your own understanding of developments relating to your job role | 8 |
| G | Maintain and develop your own specialist **knowledge** relevant to your own working environment | 8 |
| H | Undertake learning that will help you improve your performance | 8 |

**Range Statement**
Performance in this unit relates to the following contexts

**Identify your own development needs**
· Through training
· Through discussions
· Self-study of relevant materials

Performance and progress are reviewed and evaluated
· By self
· In conjunction with others

**Ways of acquiring skills and knowledge**
· Courses
· Internet
· Journals/trade publications
· Books
· Through colleagues
· Observation

KAPLAN PUBLISHING

# 1

# USING COMPUTER SYSTEMS AND SOFTWARE

## INTRODUCTION

Element 21.1 requires you to make visual checks before turning on the computer, to use passwords and access, save and print data. You should be able to take back up copies and close down the computer safely, seeking assistance when difficulties occur. In this first part of this chapter we will be describing the hardware and software that you are likely to come across in your work. We will also be covering the checking, powering up, using passwords and closing down of the system and looking at some of the difficulties that might occur.

## KNOWLEDGE & UNDERSTANDING

- The importance of carrying out simple visual safety checks on hardware and correct powering up and shutting down procedures (Item 1)
- The purpose of passwords (Item 2)
- How to save, transfer and print documents (Item 3)
- How to take back up copies (Item 4)
- Causes of difficulties, necessary files which have been damaged or deleted, printer problems, hardware problems (Item 5)
- Location of hardware, software and back up copies (Item 8)
- Location of information sources (Item 9)
- The organisation's procedures for changing passwords and making back ups (Item 10)
- House style for presentation of documents (Item 11)

## CONTENTS

1 Computer hardware and software
2 Networks and communications
3 Getting started
4 Accessing data files
5 Files and folders
6 Backing up
7 Printing and distributing reports
8 Difficulties

**PERFORMANCE CRITERIA**
· Perform initial visual safety checks and power up the computer system (Item A in Element 21.1)
· Use passwords to gain access to the computer system where limitations on access to data is required (Item B in Element 21.1)
· Access, save and print data files and exit from relevant software (Item C in Element 21.1)
· Use appropriate file names and save work (Item D in Element 21.1)
· Back up work carried out on a computer system to suitable storage media at regular intervals (Item E in Element 21.1)
· Close down the computer without damaging the computer system (Item F in Element 21.1)
· Seek immediate assistance when difficulties occur (Item G in Element 21.1)

# 1   Computer hardware and software

### 1.1  Computer hardware

Computer systems consist of hardware and software and, in many cases, telecommunications links.

Hardware is the generic term for the equipment, circuits and machinery which come in boxes and containers; that is, physical objects that can be seen and touched. It consists of central processing units and peripheral equipment, and (in systems using the telecommunications network) modems. Peripheral equipment is used for input and output and for external data storage.

> ☐ **DEFINITION**   ☐☐☐☐
>
> **Software** is the term used for the instructions, represented or stored electronically in the machine itself, to control and co-ordinate the operations of the components in the system. The instructions endow the machinery with the ability to process data.

Of course, the sizes of computer can differ greatly from supercomputers down to laptops, and there will be choices as to the types of input, output and backing store devices used.

KAPLAN PUBLISHING

## 1.2  Basic components of a PC

All information systems require computer hardware and software to make them operate effectively. The diagram shown below can represent all computers. Data is entered through input devices, data may be used from the backing store, and output is produced. Records on the backing store may also be updated.

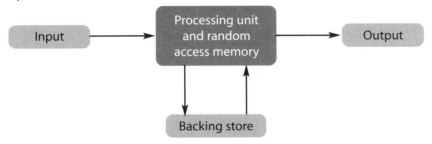

A picture of the basic components of a personal computer system appears below.

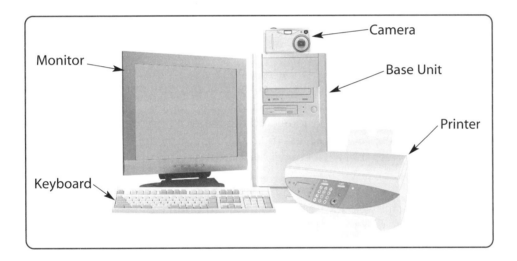

The basic components of a computer's hardware consist of a central processor (CPU), input devices, storage devices (for filing data), and output devices (which display data). Peripheral devices are those connected to the computer system and controlled by it, but that are not part of the CPU or main memory. Examples of peripherals are printers, disk drives and scanners.

All computers need some way of allowing the user to give instructions or feed in information (keyboard, mouse, modem, scanner, TV tuner, microphone), and some way of showing what is going on (monitor, speakers). Other important parts are a place where information can be stored (floppy disks, hard disk), the electronic chips which do the calculations (CPU or Central Processing Unit) and other electronic chips which hold the information while it is being worked on (Random Access Memory or RAM). These chips and other important circuitry are installed on a large printed circuit board (motherboard) and this, together with the hard disk is hidden away inside the computer's case (Base unit or System Box). You also need a means of making the data accessible to people who don't have a computer (printer). Modern personal computers also have many extras e.g. a CD-ROM drive which is used to input information stored on compact disk; a modem, used to communicate with other computers and the Internet via the telephone line; a sound card used to generate electronic music and play back real sounds.

**Base unit or System box** – this houses the power supply, motherboard, CPU chip, memory, the hard disk drive, video card, floppy disk drive, CD-ROM drive and all sorts of other hardware devices. System boxes come in two basic configurations – the desktop model and the tower configuration. The front of the computer case provides access to any of the floppy drives, CD-ROM drives and any other drives that a user may have (such as an internal ZIP drive). These drives fit in bays.

The power switch is also located at the front although older cases may have it on the side or even at the rear of the computer. The reset switch can be used to restart the computer in the event of the computer 'crashing'. Using the reset switch is equivalent to turning the computer off and then on again. To the left of the reset switch are the indicator lights, one to indicate the computer is on and receiving power and the other lights up when there is hard drive activity.

When a computer is operational, the rear of the case is generally a huge tangle of power leads and other plug in cables. The system box has one power cord that gets plugged into the wall and all sorts of connection points called 'ports' for the peripherals to get plugged into.

**Monitor** – this is rather like a television set, although it does not function in quite the same way. Its display is the computer's way of telling you what is going on and show you what you are doing while you input information. It is often referred to as the *Visual Display Unit or VDU*.

**Keyboard** – this has a layout similar to that of a typewriter but it has several extra keys. To the right and the left of the big Spacebar are two keys marked ALT and CTRL. These are the *Alternate* and *Control* keys. Across the top of the keyboard is a row of *Function keys* each marked with an F and a number. To the

KAPLAN PUBLISHING

right of the typewriter keys are four keys bunched in a triangle with arrows on them. Above these is a block of six more. Together these ten keys comprise the *Cursor Control keys*. On the far right is a numerical keypad, made out in the form of an electronic calculator. The keyboard is used to send instructions to the computer and to input information or data.

**Printer** – this is not actually part of the computer, but it is the most common addition to one. It enables you to transfer letters and documents you have prepared in the computer onto paper as *hard copy* so that they are in a more portable form.

**Modem** – this is actually both an input and an output device. Its function is to enable a computer to communicate with other computers by means of a telephone line. Modems can be used to send faxes and electronic mail (E-mail), to connect to office computers from home or when travelling and to 'surf' the Internet's *World Wide Web*. This is a worldwide network of computers containing all types of information.

### 1.3  Input devices

Examples of input hardware devices are:

#### Keyboard and mouse
A keyboard and mouse are commonly used input devices in office systems, in conjunction with a visual display screen (VDU); the mouse is used to control a pointer on the screen and to select from menu options or icons.

#### Touch screen
A touch screen is a device, which allows the user to make a selection by touching a menu option or icon on the screen. The browser in many libraries uses a touch screen. When choosing from selections of authors or titles on the screen, touching the screen over the required name or title acts the same as clicking on it with a mouse.

#### Bar code reader

A bar code is a pattern of black and white stripes representing a code, often an inventory item code. The code is read by a scanner or light pen, which converts the bar code image into an electronic form acceptable to the computer. Bar codes are used widely at checkout points in supermarkets and shops.

#### Plastic cards/Smart cards
Plastic swipe cards hold data in electronic form on a magnetic strip on the card. Smart cards or other items such as badges might hold data in electronic form in an electronic chip. These can be read by a special reading device and fed into the computer system. The uses of plastic cards should be very familiar to you: they are used in banking systems, credit cards, security passes and so on.

### Scanner

A scanner is a device that can read any form of image and convert it into an electronic form for acceptance by a computer system. Scanners can therefore be used to input diagrams and pictures, signatures and other visual images, as well as images of text. Scanners are widely used in the publishing industry, for the processing of diagrams and other pictures in books, magazines and newspapers.

### Optical mark reader (OMR)

Optical mark readers (OMR) - use standard forms on which marks are made with a marker (pencil, ballpoint pen) in predetermined positions. OMR is used widely by educational establishments to evaluate multiple-choice examination papers.

### Optical character recognition (OCR)

With optical character recognition (OCR), a reader can recognise hand-written characters from their shape, and convert them into electronic data format. OCR applications have included meter-reading forms for electricity and gas meters. The person reading the meter records the meter reading in boxes on a standard form, and the form is then input into the processing system through an OCR reader.

### Magnetic ink character recognition (MICR)

With MICR, a special reader can detect characters on a standard form in 'magnetic ink' characters. The use of MICR is uncommon, although its most well known use is the automatic reading of characters on bank cheques.

### Electronic funds transfer at the point of sale (EFTPOS)

Many retailers use electronic funds transfer at the point of sale. The terminal is used with a customer's credit or debit card to pay for goods or services. The credit card account or bank account is debited automatically.

### Voice recognition

This type of device uses software to convert speech into computer-sensible form via a microphone provided users speak clearly and slowly.

---

▷ **ACTIVITY 1** ▷ ▷ ▷ ▷

What type of input mechanism is used to read your choice of numbers on a UK National lottery ticket?

[Answers on p. 37]

---

### 1.4  Storage devices

Storage devices are required for holding data or information (and programs) in electronic form. They are used for both input of data into a computer system and for output of data and information for storage. A distinction is made between:

· internal storage within the central processing unit, and
· external storage, which refers to all other electronic storage.

### Internal storage

Data and programs can be stored in the internal RAM of the computer, or in a hard disk as **ROM (Read Only Memory)**.

**RAM (Random Access Memory**, is volatile memory (the contents are lost when the computer is turned off) but it is accessible directly by the computer.

**Hard disks** provide the permanent storage in a computer. The contents of memory remain intact without the need for power supply.

### External (backing) storage

The function of external storage is to maintain files of data and programs in a form intelligible to the computer. The principal requirements of external storage are that:

· sufficient storage capacity exists for the system to function adequately
· the stored data can be quickly input to the computer when required
· the stored data can be quickly and accurately amended when necessary and the updated files are easily created.

There are numerous types of backing storage and the type used will depend to a large extent on the sort of programs run on the computer system.

**Magnetic disks** – are currently the most important type of external or backing store although CD/RW and DVD are also being used more on new machines. The main types of disks are:

· **Floppy disks** – are held in a rigid plastic case, which has a sliding cover to allow access to the disk. They hold about 1.4Mb each. Floppy disks can easily be inserted and removed from the computer's disk drive. They are used for taking copies of files and are often used for the supply of new software. They are slow to read and write, and are not normally used as main backing store.

· **Compact disks (CDs)** – These disks look like ordinary audio CDs and are similarly robust. They can hold about 650Mb of data, which makes them ideal for multimedia applications where video and audio data is very space consuming. Rewriteable CD storage (CD/RW) is also available.

· **Digital versatile disks (DVDs)** – are used as storage devices on newer computers. These offer enhanced capacity (up to 17 Gb).

**Memory Sticks** – These are used to carry information around from work to home for example, in a small, easy to carry stick or drive.

### 1.5  Output devices

Output from a computer system is often stored, in which case the output is transferred to a storage device. Data can also be output onto microfiche or microfilm (for which a computer output on microfilm or COM device is needed). The other most common forms of output are printers and screen displays.

### Printers

Different types of printer are available. The most commonly used are now either:

· ink-jet printers for smaller computers and low-volume output, and
· laser printers, which are capable of faster output and so can handle much higher print volumes, with high print quality.

Printers can be used for the output of diagrams and pictures as well as text, and have widespread applications in business. In some computer systems, output can be printed on the standard pre-printed stationery, to produce documents such as sales invoices and statements.

### VDU screen

Output to a VDU screen is temporary, whereas printed output is more permanent. However, many computer systems rely on output to VDU, where the computer user can simply read the information provided. There are many examples of VDU output, but examples are:

· e-mail messages, which can be printed out but are more usually read on screen
· customer service centres, where customer sales orders and queries by telephone can be handled by a customer service representative with access to central computer records through keyboard, mouse and VDU screen.

The choice of output will be influenced by such factors as outlined below.

· **Cost and volumes** – A small business producing 200 invoices a day and processing payroll once a week is likely to want a relatively small, cheap printer to service this modest workload. A loan company producing 10,000 statements a month, together with reminder letters and default notices, will require a fast printer capable of producing multipart documents of good quality at speed, as well as visual displays for quick and easy reference.

· **Handling requirements** – Some output is long-lived and required for reference (e.g. a printout of balances in the financial ledger); some output is required to be multipart for legal reasons e.g. invoices (for VAT purposes). Certain output requires to be printed but is used for a limited period of time e.g. daily balance listings prepared by a bank.

· **Speed of system response** – A customer requesting a balance at a cash point wants a swift response. A telephone clerk employed by a credit card company wants to be able to give an instant validation or rejection of a transaction. There is not the same degree of urgency for producing, say, an aged list of balances for control purposes.

### 1.6 Computer software

Computer software is the term used to describe collections of instructions to the computer hardware. Without instructions or commands a computer cannot do anything. With an appropriate set of instructions a computer can perform numerous tasks both simple and complicated. Such a set of instructions is called a program.

When creating programs different *programming languages* are used. The average computer user will not need to create programs but will use ready-made application programs created by professional or keen amateur programmers. When running a program it is not apparent to the user which language was used to create it. Some programming languages commonly in use are: Visual BASIC, Pascal, Delphi, C++ and Assembler. Each has its own pre-defined set of commands and a set of rules on how each command can be used.

There are different types of software available for computers:
· operating systems
· utilities – tools designed to improve the way in which the operating system works.
· bespoke applications
· off-the-shelf applications.

**Operating systems software**
The operating system is the most important piece of software in any computer system, as without it the system will not work at all. It enables the following functions:
· communication between the operator and the computer
· control of the processor and storage hardware
· the management of files
· the use of peripherals such as printers and modems.

**□ DEFINITION**                                          □ □ □ □

When the computer is multi-tasking, and running several application programs simultaneously, the **operating system** allocates internal storage space to each application, chooses which programs should be run in which order of priority and decides how much CPU time to give to each application.

Microsoft Windows is the most popular operating system for PCs and small networks.

**WYSIWYG** is an acronym meaning 'what you see is what you get'. It refers to the technology that enables users to see images on-screen exactly as they will appear when printed out. As screen and printer fonts have become more sophisticated, and as GUIs have improved their display, people have come to expect everything to be WYSIWYG.

**▷ ACTIVITY 2**                                          ▷ ▷ ▷ ▷

What is the difference between computer hardware and computer software?
[Answers on p. 37]

## 2    Networks and communications

### 2.1  Stand-alone or networked?

In recent years, personal computers (PCs) have become the most widespread and commonly used computer resource. Their versatility and cheapness, combined with the wide variety of software that is available, allow their use in almost every business.

PCs may be used on a stand-alone basis, or they may be linked with other computers. A stand-alone system is not linked with any other IT system. It can be based on any operating system and consist of a PC with or without a hard disk, Unix workstation or Apple Macintosh.

---

**□ DEFINITION**                                                              □□□□

**Networks** are groups of computers, printers, and other devices that are connected together with cables.

---

Information travels over the cables, allowing users to exchange documents and data with each other, print to the same printers, and generally share any hardware or software that is connected to the network. The 'heart' of the network is the server. Most networks include one or more computers that are designated as file servers. A file server is a computer whose hard disk is accessible to other computers on the network. Its job is to 'serve' data and program files to these other machines via cables or other network connections.

The file server stores all of the network's shared files. It also:

·    manages the hard drive(s)
·    ensures that multiple requests (especially write requests) do not conflict with each other
·    protects data
·    prevents unauthorised access
·    maintains lists of rights/authorisation associated to data files.

The advantages of having networked rather than stand-alone computers include the following:

- expensive resources such as high quality printers can be shared
- software can be stored on a shared hard disk instead of being duplicated on individual computers
- files of data which are stored on a shared hard disk can be accessed freely
- incompatible hardware, such as PCs and Macs, can be linked by means of the network and files passed between them
- data is less likely to be lost or accidentally erased because formal housekeeping procedures are normally instituted e.g. making regular backups
- memos and other messages can be passed from one machine to another, providing a fast, and low cost, messaging system. This is called electronic mail, or Email for short
- information stored on remote computers can be accessed e.g. sales, inventory and other internal information in the case of internal systems, or financial and economic information in the case of public systems
- the network can be gradually extended as the organisation grows. Each new machine brings with it additional processing power
- if one machine breaks down, the others can continue working – provided the file server has not stopped.

## 2.2 Types of network

Systems can be linked in various ways:
- **A local area network (LAN)** links microcomputers within an office or building. Cables rather than telecommunication lines link the parts of the network. Each device can communicate with every other device, allowing people to exchange email and transfer files from one computer to another.
- **A wide area network (WAN)** links two or more separate locations together using telecommunication lines and satellites. This permits multiple users to have access to a remote computer.

When a network is set up an internal website (intranet) is often established to enable employees to share data, documents and internal web pages, which cannot be accessed by outsiders.

The illustration below shows a local and a wide area network where the processing power is spread throughout the organisation over a number of individual or departmental systems. It also shows how the organisation can be linked to the Internet.

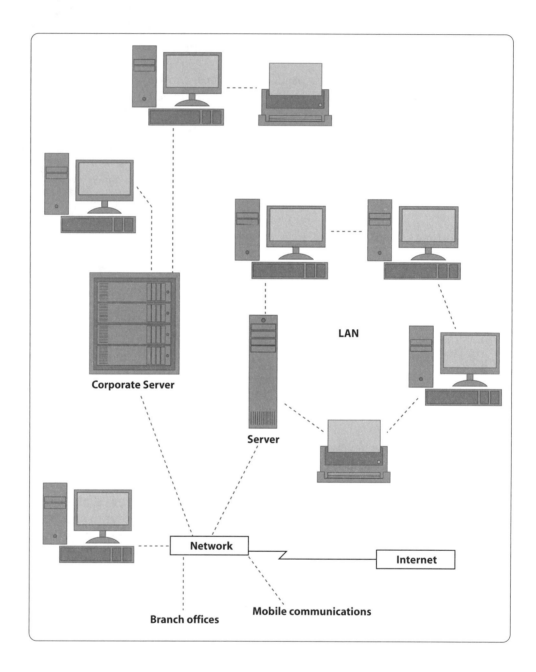

## 3 Getting started

### 3.1 Using Microsoft Windows

The AAT standards for this unit do not specify the type of computer system or software packages you are expected to use. As we have already noted, the most popular operating system used today is Microsoft Windows and for this reason we will be using it in our explanations and examples.

### 3.2 Static electricity

As we walk around the office, the library, or home, our bodies are apt to build up a charge of static electricity (especially in winter). These charges are discharged as small 'lightning bolts' when we come in contact with a ground. The ground may be a filing cabinet, a colleague, or the inside of the computer you plan to start up. It's the latter case that can prove to be disastrous, at least as far as the delicate electronics inside the computer are concerned. (A static discharge that spans one centimetre represents approximately 25,000 volts of electricity). An important safeguard is to routinely discharge any static electricity in your body before touching any computer component – do this, preferably, by holding on to a ground while touching the computer, or at least immediately before. A good ground might be a radiator, filing cabinet or metal desk.

### 3.3 Visual safety checks on hardware

Before switching on your PC, there are a few quick safety checks that you can do:

· **Hardware components** – make sure they are not damaged or wet. Remove any unnecessary items from your PC and monitor e.g. flower pots, coffee cups or other items that may contain liquids. Check that the computer case is not too close to the wall.
· **Plugs** – check that they are not overloaded and that there are no trailing cables that could trip someone up.
· **Cables** – verify cables and peripherals are connected correctly to the computer.
· **Interfaces** – make sure the cables are firmly pushed in to their slots and all peripherals are turned on.

In a stand alone system the main processing unit – the system box – should be connected to a variety of devices such as the mouse, keyboard, monitor, printer, scanner, back up devices e.g. zip drive and the Internet connection. A quick check will ensure all these devices are securely plugged in.

If you are working on a network system some of the peripheral devices, such as the printer, will not be connected directly to your machine and may not be near your desk. You will be able to check their status on screen when your computer is up and running.

As well as the visual checks outlined above, you need to check your positioning at your desk and VDU. We will look at this area in more detail in a later chapter.

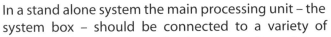

### 3.4 Powering up the computer system

Once you have visually checked the equipment, you can turn on your computer. To do this:

> Turn on the power – many systems are set up so that all the components are plugged into a single power strip and powering up means only having to switch this on. Other systems require the monitor to be switched on separately in which case:
>
> Turn on the monitor by pushing the button in the lower right corner – a green or amber light will be visible on the lower right corner of the screen.
>
> Push the power button on the front of the CPU – a green light will be visible on the CPU.
>
> Let the computer go through its start-up script.

At this stage you might be looking at the 'Desktop' with an array of the programs available to access or you might need to press start and access the programs from the pull down menu.

If you have ever left a floppy disk in the drive when you restarted your computer, you have probably seen this message.

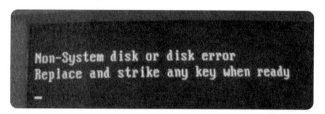

This is the message you get if a floppy disk is in the drive when you restart your computer. The system has tried to boot the computer from the floppy disk left in the drive. Since it did not find the correct system files, it could not continue. Of course, this is an easy fix. Simply pop out the disk and press a key to continue.

### 3.5 Purpose of passwords

The British Computer Society's definition of a password is 'a sequence of characters that must be presented to a computer system before it will allow access to the system or parts of that system'. Password protected systems require users attempting to access the system to enter a string of characters. If what is entered matches the password held on file for that authorised user, the system permits entry. Otherwise access is denied. Passwords may be allocated to a person (a username), a terminal, to a system function or to an individual file.

**System passwords** – may be built into a system to limit access to a workstation on a network. They can operate at a variety of levels to prevent people from getting beyond an initial screen or to prevent them accessing specific confidential parts of the system.

**Software passwords** – are aimed at restricting access to certain programs.

KAPLAN PUBLISHING

### 3.6 Logging on (or logging in)

When you have switched the computer on, you may be asked to log on using your password. As you type it in a series of *******s appear in the box. If you get the password wrong, the computer will either display a message or beep at you telling you the password is invalid if you press OK or 'Enter'. If you make a mistake entering the password you can use the 'Delete' key to go back and start again.

You might have to go through a similar procedure to access the software that you need e.g. if you are opening an accounting package, such as Sage, then a password might be required before it allows you to access the files.

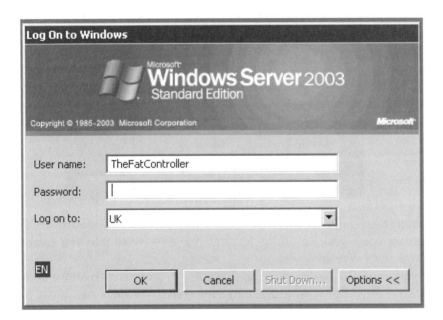

If the PC you are using is operating under Windows, when it is switched on you will see icons on a screen. This initial screen is called the Desktop. Pointing to the desired program you can open it by clicking the left button on the mouse twice.

Alternatively, you can click on Start in the bottom left hand corner of your Window, then slide the pointer up to All Programs, and then select the required application.

### 3.7 Shutting down procedures

It is important to understand that before you turn off your computer, you need to 'shut down' Windows the right way.

One by one close the programs and files that are still active by using their Exit options, remembering to save any work you wish to keep. In software designed for use with Microsoft Windows, you can close each window by clicking on the X symbol in the top right hand corner.

Once all the files and programs are closed, you can shut down the computer by clicking on START and then selecting Shut Down. Later versions have different options e.g. for Windows XP you may first need to Log Off and then Turn Off Computer as shown below.

Turning off the computer this way brings up the following options:
- Standby – puts your computer in a low power state so that you can quickly resume your Windows session
- Turn off – shuts down Windows so that you can safely switch off the computer
- Restart – shuts down Windows and then starts Windows again

**Logging off** – if you need to log off a network:
- Click on the Start button
- Select the Log Off option
- Confirm that you want to Log Off

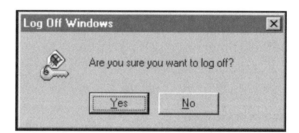

Before switching off using earlier versions of Windows you have to wait for the message 'It is now safe to switch off your computer' and then switch off using the on/off switch. PCs running Windows XP switch themselves off without further intervention. If you turn the computer off without shutting down the system, information stored in the computer's memory may be lost before it can be written to the hard drive, and the information stored on your hard drive may become corrupt.

## 4 Accessing data files

### 4.1 Organisational requirements

There are two areas to be aware of when starting up an application:
· security and confidentiality, and
· maintenance.

**Security and confidentiality** – the system that you are using (particularly if you are one of many users on a network or mainframe) may contain confidential information. Think of it as a filing cabinet full of documents. If it were a filing cabinet you would want to lock it. The computer equivalents of locking the cabinet include:
· using passwords to restrict access
· restricting user access to certain parts of the system only
· storing confidential information in a particular directory (a directory is like a drawer in the filing cabinet)

**Maintenance** – it is important to keep your computer clean if it is to work properly. There are special products available to clean the machine. *Never* use ordinary household cleaning products. The screen should be wiped with a special anti-static screen-wipe. The keyboard should be kept free from dust with a keyboard brush. Any marks on the computer casing should be removed with a special cleaner.

### 4.2 Passwords

> **□ DEFINITION**　　　　　　　□□□□
>
> **Passwords** are effectively software 'keys'. They usually consist of a short combination of alphabetic and/or numeric characters, as well as symbols, which the terminal user must enter into the computer and have verified by it (against a central file of valid passwords) before he or she is permitted access to specific data or programs.

To be effective, the password needs to keep out unauthorised access. However, there are problems with password confidentiality:

· An authorised user may divulge their password to an unauthorised user possibly to bypass the administrative 'hassle' of getting new identities on the system.
· Most passwords chosen by authorised users have some form of association for them (National Insurance number, birth date, names or nicknames) or are extremely simple to form (common words or names found in a dictionary) and can be discovered by intelligent experimentation.
· If you assign people random combinations of letters and numbers, which are far more difficult to crack, you come up against the problem that they are also far more difficult to remember. Most users will write their password down either on the terminal itself or nearby, making the task of discovering it easy.

KAPLAN PUBLISHING

The system administrator needs to provide a number of options by which the end-user can generate their own password such that it will be easily remembered but difficult for anyone, even personal colleagues of the end-user, to decipher from their knowledge of the end-user. Examples might include dates of birthdays plus personal initials of some sort and symbols like $, *, or #. Some systems include an automatic password generator, but experience has shown that, where these are used, users tend to write them down, as they are virtually impossible to remember.

In any event, all passwords should be changed on a regular basis (e.g. quarterly). Repeated attempts to log in using incorrect passwords should be noted and reported on the system so that users who have problems in this area can be given specific assistance.

### 4.3  Location of information sources

After data has been input to a computer system and the source documents have been filed, there will still be many occasions when you want to access files and look up an item of information for example to answer queries from staff about their pay, or to respond to customer queries about their accounts. The first step is to access the appropriate applications package. Click on Start in the bottom left hand corner of your Window, then slide the pointer up to Programs, and then select the required application. Using typical Windows applications:

- to locate letters or other written documents select the [W] Microsoft Word application

- to locate a spreadsheet worksheet, such as a budgeted cashflow amount, select the [X] Microsoft Excel application

- to locate a database, such as the holiday allowance for an employee, select the [P] Microsoft Access application

- to locate customer accounts, select the accounting package used, e.g. Sage Line 50 or Pegasus Capital Gold.

Once you have accessed the package, then you must identify the file you need. By clicking on **File** (top left in Window), then **Open**, you can search for the file that you need.

### ○ EXAMPLE   ○○○○

A customer, Mr M G Jones of 14 Ash Way, Chester, has a code number 1048972. He is complaining that his son, also Mr M G Jones, is receiving communications that are not his, even though he is also a customer. His son's number is 1048973.

If you wanted to find all the entries throughout your system for Mr M G Jones – letters, sales, receipts – you could do a search using the customer code and also a search using his name. Doing two searches would

KAPLAN PUBLISHING

eliminate the chances of missing an entry and also identify mistakes that may have been made.

For this search you would look through all the files for Mr M G Jones and then compare them with all the entries under his code number 1048972. From the Start button, go to the Find and then the Files or Folders.

This will bring up the Find box where you can specify the location, the type of file or folder and the text.

When you click on **Find Now**, the computer will search through the specified files for the entries that you need and display the file names where there are entries that match your requirements.

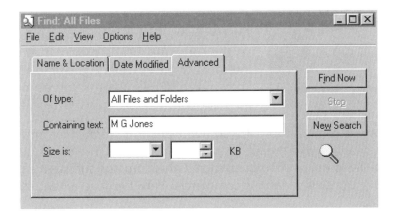

Retrieval of the data required, so that you can display it on screen or print it out, varies with different packages.

Automatic search facilities are provided by most commercial application packages, e.g. clicking on **Edit** and **Find** in Word will give you a prompt to type in the name or word you are looking for. The finder will highlight each entry of your item in turn or display a message if it is unable to find the entry.

In a typical accounts package, you could check an item in a particular supplier's account by first selecting the **Purchase Ledger** option on the main menu, and then the **Accounts Enquiries** or **Transactions History** option on the Purchase Ledger menu. The screen display will then prompt you to specify the unique reference code for the supplier's account before displaying the details on the screen.

### 4.4 Web browsers

The Internet and the World Wide Web are terms that are frequently associated with access to vast amounts of information. The Internet (an abbreviation for International Network) is a global interconnected network of networks. 'The NET' is a colloquialism for the Internet.

The World Wide Web (or WWW, W3 or 'The Web') refers to the body of information, which is accessed by means of 'web browsing' software such as Netscape Navigator or Microsoft Internet Explorer. These allow users to move through the Web and incorporate search engines, which allow searches to be made on the basis of keywords. It is also possible to access other search engines such as Yahoo and Lycos.

Once key words are entered the search software will return a list of all Web sites that refer to those words. Users can read a brief description of the site and choose whether or not to visit it. Hyperlinks can provide links to other pages in the site or to other related sites.

If an organisation wants to provide information through the Web it must set up a Web site. A Web site consists of space on a computer, which has communication links and a unique address that can be used to find the Web site. Often, the space on the computer will be provided by one of the Internet Service Providers. The unique address is known as a URL (uniform resource locator) and has a format such as: http://www.aat.org.uk

http://www is common for all Web addresses. The remainder of the address becomes specific to the organisation – here it is the AAT. The 'org.uk' suffix means that it is a UK not-for-profit organisation. Other common suffixes are 'com', which means that the organisation is commercial, 'gov' for government and 'edu' for educational.

### 4.5 Using manual search facilities

There may be occasions when you want to search manually through records. For example, you might wish to find the price of an item in stock, a customer account in a list of accounts or a specific invoice in a list of invoices raised in the period.

This type of manual search through material on the screen is called scrolling and browsing.

There are different ways of moving about the screen. You can scroll up and down through material on screen by using the arrow keys or the PgUp (page up) and PgDn (page down) buttons on the keyboard.

A faster way is to point to and move the scroll bar in the middle on the right side of the screen. Alternatively, you can move one of the directional triangles or double arrows, also on the right side of the screen.

KAPLAN PUBLISHING

## 5 Files and folders

### 5.1 Basic terms

**Files** – each document, whether it is a ▤ plain text file or a ▥ letter in Word or ♫ music or ▭ the directions for a program, is called a file. The first part of a file's name (before the dot) is called the filename. The part of a filename after the dot is called the **extension**. So together it looks like: **filename.extension**. An application may recognise certain extensions automatically. For example, MS Word documents use the extension **doc**. Excel spreadsheets use **xls**. Every file must have a name and you generally try to make the name as descriptive of the contents of the file as you can.

Spaces, letters, and numbers are always allowed in long file names, but some symbols are still not allowed. The following are not allowed \ / : * ? " < > | You will get an error message if you try to use these characters in a name.

Windows treats lower case and upper case as the same. So the name **picture.bmp** is the same as **Picture.bmp** and **PICTURE.BMP**. But some other operating systems, like UNIX, treat those names as different.

There are practical limits to the length of a file name:

- The longer the name, the longer it takes to type.
- The longer the name, the more chances to mistype.
- Long names may not fit in the display space in a dialog box – choose the first 10 or so characters so that if the rest of the name is chopped off in the display, you will still have some idea of what the file is about.

**Folders** – files are grouped together in ▭ folders, also called directories when using other operating systems like DOS. Folders are used to organise the information on the hard disk of your PC and are arranged in levels like a family tree – the top level normally being the Hard Disk Drive C. Folders and sub-folders are then created below this level. Folders can contain documents, programs and other folders (sub-folders).

A thoughtful choice of folder names can help organise your work and save a lot of time hunting for the right document. How you do this will depend on how you work and whether you need to share files with others.
Files can be grouped by task or by type or by author or by where they are going. You could put all the files having to do with this part of the course into a single folder called **Unit 21**.

**Drive** – your files and folders are stored on a ▭ hard disk on your computer or on a ▭ network drive, or on some kind of removable media like ▭ a floppy disk or ▭ CD. Drives are named with letters. The floppy drive is normally A: The hard drive is normally C: if you only have one hard drive. Network drives are usually further down the alphabet, like M: or O:

**Path** – the drive and folders you must go through to get to the folder or file that you want is called the path. A path always starts with a drive letter. The path C:\Program Files\Internet Explorer leads to the folder that holds Internet Explorer's files.

### 5.2  Working with files and folders in Windows

**Windows Explore** – can be used to manage folders and files. To start Windows Explore – right click when your pointer is situated over the Start Button, then click where it says Explore.

There are two panes in an Explore window. The left pane contains the folder tree, which shows visually how the drives and folders are related to each other. It shows all of the computer's drives and folders in a nested arrangement.

A small plus sign ⊞ marks drives and folders that contain other things. Clicking this symbol expands this branch of the folder tree.

A minus sign ⊟ marks something that is already expanded to show its contents. Clicking it will collapse this branch of the folder tree.

The right pane shows the contents of the drive or folder that is selected on the left. The name of the selected drive or folder is at the top of the right pane. In the case of a folder, the icon will change to 📂 an open folder.

The display for the right pane can be changed to use any of the views that My Computer windows used: Large Icons, Small Icons, List, Details and Web. The new view affects the right pane only.

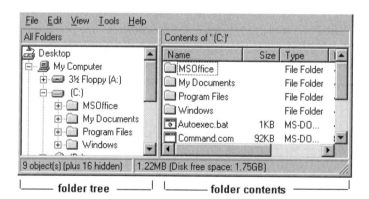

If you want to create a new folder:
- From the folder tree, select the disk drive or folder where your new folder will go.
- Click File then New and then Folder. A New Folder item will appear on the right side of the window.
- Next click on the name and change it to whatever you want.
- Press the Enter key and the new folder name will be confirmed.

KAPLAN PUBLISHING

·   Make sure when you name a folder it does not contain any of these characters:

\ / : * ? " < > | as they are not allowed.

**Renaming** – files and folders can be renamed by highlighting the file to be renamed, selecting 'Rename' from the File menu and entering the new file or folder name.

## O EXAMPLE                                              O O O O

You can create a new folder for all the information regarding AAT.

Click on Start with the right hand button on your mouse and select 'Explore'. Click on the local disk (it may be C). From the 'File' menu select 'New' and then 'Folder'. A new folder will be displayed and you can rename it to AAT. If you then double click on this new folder, you can then create some files. From the 'File' menu select 'New' and then 'Microsoft Word Document'.

The new folder will be displayed, which you can call Contacts or Courses or Addresses. If you choose a file name that already exists, Windows will warn you of your error and you must choose another name or add a number to it e.g. Courses 02.

If you plan to create a series of files you can number them 1, 2, 3 etc. but if you have over 10 they will be sorted in the order 1, 10, 2, 3 etc. To avoid this, number the earlier ones 01, 02 etc. Once files and folders have been set up, they can be copied and moved.

### Deleting a folder:

·   From the folder tree, select the folder you want to delete.
·   Press the delete key on your keyboard.
·   A box will pop up asking if you are sure you want to delete it. Click yes.
·   **Retrieving** – under Windows, when you delete a file it is sent to the 'Recycle Bin'. This is equivalent of placing a piece of paper in a waste-bin, from where it can be retrieved so long as the waste-bin has not been emptied. To retrieve the file, open the recycle bin, highlight the file to be restored and access the Restore command from the File menu.

You should get into the habit of saving your work every 10 to 15 minutes even if it contains errors or is incomplete. Computers will crash at times when you do not expect them to, so make sure you save your work often.

### 5.3  House style – creating or amending a document

House style is a standard format and set of layout rules that are applied to documents produced by an organisation e.g. the preferred spelling of certain words when there is more than one way to spell them and whether or not full stops should be used with abbreviations. It basically details your organisation's preferred way of presenting information so that you have consistency within documents or across a number of communications that you may produce. It can apply to items such as text styles, logo position/size/colour, margin settings, paper colour, and contents of headers/footers.

A House Style can be used to identify an organisation and also allows the organisation to have control over documents being produced and presented by their employees; hence the image they want to project of themselves.
To create a document template or use an existing style go to FILE, then New and then choose either a blank document or an existing template. The example below shows the templates available for a report.

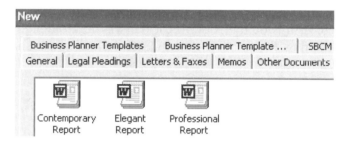

When amending an existing document, if a house style applies to it then you should familiarise yourself with the rules that apply to that document.

### 5.4  Saving a file

Once you have created or amended a document, you must save it if you wish to use it in the future. If you try to Exit or click on the X symbol before saving the following message will appear

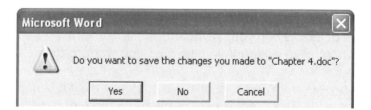

To save a new document file i.e one that has not been named:

·  From the FILE menu choose the **SAVE AS** option.
·  A dialogue box will appear.
·  If necessary, use the DRIVE drop down menu to select the relevant drive; if you are saving to floppy disk, it is generally the 'a:' or 'b:' drive.
·  In the **FILE NAME** text box type in the name you wish to use (up to eight characters). All spreadsheet packages automatically add a three-digit extension to your filename. In Word it will be doc. In Lotus it will begin with wk and in Excel it will begin with xl.
·  Click on the **OK** button.

KAPLAN PUBLISHING

When you have saved a file once, you do not need to choose the **SAVE AS** option again, but simply choose **SAVE** from the **FILE** menu or click on the icon on the tool bar (picture of a floppy disk).

### 5.5 Transferring a file

Transferring a file means moving or copying it to another area.

· To move a file or folder (drag it from window to window), locate the file or folder you wish to move by double clicking on the appropriate drive and folders until you reach the location. Highlight – by single clicking on the file or folder - and, holding the left button of the mouse down, drag and drop the highlighted items where you want it to be. Release the mouse button to complete the procedure.

· Copies can be made from folder to folder or from disk to disk using the copy and paste function, but you will not be allowed two files with the same name in the same folder. To copy, place the mouse pointer over the file or folder you want to copy. Hit the combination Ctrl + C to copy the file to your computer's clipboard and then put your cursor over the location you wish to copy to and select Ctrl +V to paste the contents of the clipboard. Alternatively, you can use the commands in the Edit menu by choosing Copy and then Paste.

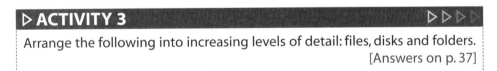

> **ACTIVITY 3** ▷ ▷ ▷ ▷

Arrange the following into increasing levels of detail: files, disks and folders.
[Answers on p. 37]

### 5.6 Deleting files

Before files are deleted you must be very certain that they are not needed, either by you or someone else. If you do not know what a file is for, or who uses it, do not delete it.

However, it usually becomes necessary to delete files at some point because hard disks are filled eventually. Many of the files will be unused and may represent earlier versions of current files. If you are going to delete files you should carefully consider whether it might not be a good idea to take archive copies so that files could be retrieved again in the future.

As well as deleting files on the hard disk, it is important to keep control of floppy disks and CDs. As more and more copies and back-ups can be taken, the security of the system can be adversely affected, and control of these many disks will become more difficult. Once control is lost you will be frightened to delete any file in case it turns out to have been important.

It is better to keep relatively few well-controlled disks and files with carefully documented contents than keep many uncontrolled files where you are not sure of their contents and have run out of space in the proper disk boxes.

### 5.7 Closing a file/Quitting

When you have finished working on a document and you have saved it, you will need to close it down. You can do this by either pressing the button at the top right hand side of the worksheet with a cross on it or by choosing the CLOSE or EXIT option from the FILE menu.

If you only want to exit an application briefly and prefer not to close down the whole package you can switch to another application or back to the Windows Program Manager by pressing <Alt><Tab> repeatedly. This allows you to step through all the opened applications in rotation.

If you have changed the file, you will be asked if you wish to save the changes you made before closing. Click on the appropriate button.

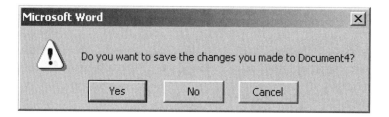

### 5.8 Safeguards

Because vital records are stored on magnetic media, if files are lost or damaged it may leave an organisation in a serious position. All computer storage media are highly vulnerable to a number of dangers, e.g:
· operator mishandling
· machine malfunction
· incorrect environmental conditions (dust, humidity).

Consequently, safeguards have to be established to prevent loss of files, e.g:
· standards and procedures for users
· standby facilities to use another computer or alternative facilities in the event of a breakdown
· temperature and humidity controls.

### 5.9 Care of disks and CDs

Whether you are using floppy disks or compact disks, you must store them in a clean, dry place, such as a disk box (a specially designed plastic tray). If you leave them lying on your desk they may have something put on top of them or have coffee spilt on them.

Keep the disks away from electrical equipment as this may scramble the information on the disk.

KAPLAN PUBLISHING

If you are using floppy disks, do not write on labels that are already stuck to the disks as the pressure from the pen may damage the disk.

Precautions can be taken to ensure that you do not lose the material on disks, e.g. software that has been purchased, or data that you cannot recreate. Floppy disks have a small tab in one corner that slides across. The machine will check the tab before over-writing the contents of the disk.

## 6 Backing up

### 6.1 Why back up?

Accidents happen – the server goes down, computers freeze, and sometimes our brains just momentarily shut off. Backing up your work is one of the smartest things you can do to prepare for those worst-case scenarios.

The phrase 'back up' is often loosely used to refer to a copy of the original document. Specifically, it refers to either:
· the copying or moving of a file or folder onto another disk or location
· the creation of an archive of one or more files and folders.

An archive is a single file usually containing many separate files that are compressed together for easy storage and transferability. A special program like WinZip is needed to create an archive and to retrieve files from an archive.

There are many benefits to backing up files and folders. Three of the most common benefits are:
· preserve the original format of a document
· protect document data in case working document is lost or corrupted
· protect multiple documents and data in case workstation hard drive stops working.

### 6.2 Backing up files

There is no set rule about when you should back up files, but it should be at least at the end of every day and preferably when you have completed a long run of inputting. Some information is held on disk for reference purposes only, whilst other information, such as accounting records, record current transactions and balances. The reference data will not change often and therefore will need to be backed up infrequently. Because accounting data changes every day, it needs frequent back-ups.

If you are working on a network, files will be saved to your workstation's hard disk and also to the server. With a stand-alone system, the back up files will probably be saved to some form of storage device - this might be the disk drive in the workstation itself or may be an external drive.

Data is archived for several different reasons. One reason is to comply with legislation and regulations. Another is to provide the ability to recover business critical data in the event of a site-wide data loss, such as a fire or flood. Another reason is to provide a secure repository for point-in-time, snapshot data, for baseline reference in programming, design, custom manufacturing, etc.

Many large companies keep weekly archives off-site for a period of one month, and monthly archives for one year. Yearly archives are retained for the required legal period. In the event of a site-wide disaster, such as a fire, the maximum amount of data lost would be one week.

### 6.3 Various back-up options

There are many ways in which files and folders can be backed up. Within the Windows environment there are five commonly used options:

(i) **Save as – saving a file to another folder or drive** – this is a quick an easy way to save an additional copy of a document to another location.

(ii) **Copying a file to a floppy, zip disk or memory stick** – sometimes copying your files and folders to a removable disk can add extra security to preserving documents and data. The floppy and zip disks are the most popular used. However, burnable CD-ROMs and DVDs are rapidly becoming standard features on new PCs, many people now use memory sticks to store files and folders.

(iii) **Dragging and dropping files to another location** – for individuals who do not like to use the drop down and popup menus, dragging and dropping is another viable option for copy files to a different location.

(iv) **Sending files to another location** – a unique feature that is now part of the Windows environment is the Send To option on the popup menu.

(v) **WinZip** – is a program that allows users to quickly create archives by compressing files. These files are commonly called zipped files (not to be confused with the zip drives and disks). Using WinZip for backing up files is a time saving method for its ease of use and functionality.

### 6.4 Three-tier back-up system

Backing up files is a safety net that cannot be emphasised enough. Having a plan or system set up to ensure regular backing up of files is one way to ensure that the most current versions of documents and data are being backed up. Below is a three-tier back-up system – sometimes called Grandfather/Father/Son – that makes backing up relatively easy. It also helps set up a regular schedule on your calendar.

| | |
|---|---|
| 1st back-up | first week (or month) use first disk; label as 1st with date |
| 2nd back-up | next period back up using a different disk; label accordingly |
| 3rd back-up | next period back up using a different disk; label accordingly |
| 4th back-up | use the first disk and start the rotation over again |

For example, when the third back-up is made, the third disk is written leaving the previous two disks unchanged. In the next updating run, the first disk is used again and becomes the 4th back-up.

The principle is that, at any point in time there are three back-ups:
· The 'son' is the most recent and holds all data.
· The 'father' is the back-up before the son but does not hold the data of the most recent period.
· The 'grandfather' is the back-up before the father but does not hold the data of the two most recent periods.

### 6.5 Organisation's backing up policy

An organisation may have back-up procedures in place for all aspects of their information system.

**Data back-up** – users of computer systems must be aware that the medium on which data is stored everyday can fail and it is important that controls are put in place to ensure that the risks of loss are minimised. The form of data back-up depends on the type of application that accesses and updates the data.

Where the data is maintained by batch processing, the Grandfather/Father/Son method of backing up will be used.

More likely, where the data is maintained on-line, data will be backed up each day, so that if the normal storage medium fails, the information is available for the system to be restored to the last point of data entry prior to the back-up being taken.

Copies of all data files should be taken on a frequent and regular basis and kept off-site or in a fireproof safe. The data can then be restored in case of data loss or corruption.

Most organisations will have a policy for backing up its data. It should include the following:
· Back-up disks held off the premises
· Back-up held on more than one set of disks
· periodic dumping stored securely.

Disks should be replaced regularly (perhaps every three months) as they wear out and the data can become corrupted.

**Software back-up** – copies of system software and applications should also be taken and stored off-site so that the computer system can be re-created on new hardware if the building is damaged or destroyed. Software can also be restored if it becomes corrupted or accidentally deleted.

**Hardware back-up** – the type of policy employed might be one or more of the following:

· **Additional hardware** to that required for every day use may be bought and kept in case of breakdown. A replacement can be quickly substituted without loss of operating time.

· **Mutual support** – where organisations have similar installations, a number have formed associations such that should one lose its facilities, the others will provide sufficient capacity for processing to re-commence within a given timescale.

· **Bureau/Manufacturer support** – all major hardware manufacturers provide various 'disaster-recovery' services as part of their maintenance offerings. These include mobile computer facilities through to virtual 'Hot' Centre environments.

In-house hardware back-up may take the form of a 'hot centre' standby system (where the hardware is powered up and ready for immediate use) or a 'cold centre' standby (where equipment is stored away and must be connected up before use). A 'hot centre' is maintained as a virtual duplicate of the normal site, including all current data. If the main site 'goes down', the hot centre can take over immediately without any noticeable difference in service to the end-users. Alternatively, the 'cold centre' is a location that does not contain any computer equipment but which can be turned very quickly into a live site based on a well thought out, disaster-recovery plan.

Hot standby systems are often used by organisations such as banks, where the system is essential to the operation of the business. In such a system data would automatically be backed up to the standby machine on a continuous basis.

## 7 Printing and distributing reports

### 7.1 House style presentation

Before printing any reports, you should check with your supervisor that the correct house style (layout and format) is set up on your computer and the correct paper is loaded into the printer. Remember that when you send a report or document internally you should always include your name and the identity of the report on it.

If the report is confidential put it in a suitable envelope, seal the envelope and mark it *private and confidential.*

When sending documents to customers or suppliers follow the procedures of your organisation.

The printing and distributing options are given by clicking on **File** in Microsoft Word:

The **Page Setup** allows you to select from the following options and shows a preview of your choice:

The **Print Preview** gives you a view of the contents of the page that would be printed.

Clicking on **Print** allows you to choose the range and the number of copies.

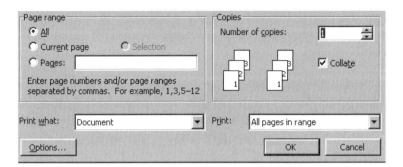

The **Properties** button gives you the chance to choose the paper size, the orientation of the sheet (the option of having the print in landscape or portrait mode) and the resolution of the graphics.

The **Send To** option (depending on the version of Word you are working with) will allow you to route the selected document to everyone on a mailing list, a fax list or an e-mail list.

This could be over the organisation's LAN, via a fax modem or over the Internet. With e-mail you can send many types of file as 'attachments' e.g. word processing, database and spreadsheet files from one computer to another. Documents such as orders and invoices can be generated on the computer and sent by e-mail attachment to suppliers and customers.

You can select an **Exchange Folder** to copy the file to. This allows you to use Exchange or Microsoft Outlook to view, group, categorise, or sort files by their properties.

By clicking on **Microsoft PowerPoint**, the package assumes that the selected document will form part of a presentation.

### 7.2 Using the printer

Before using your printer (as with all electrical equipment), read the manual carefully. Look out for these procedures in particular:
· Connecting the printer to the computer.
· Switching the printer on.
· Checking that the printer is on-line (i.e. ready to print).
· Aligning the paper.
· Advancing the paper to the top of the next page.
· Stopping the printer safely (e.g. to unblock a paper jam).

Before you can print out your first report you will probably have to select the type of printer used from a list provided by the package.

The **Print** command will normally be part of the package you are using.

## 8 Difficulties

### 8.1 Getting help

When something goes wrong it should be fixed as soon as possible. You should not try to do this yourself unless you know what to do. If you cannot deal with it, you should know where to get help. Consult your help desk representative or supervisor.

There are many types of hardware and software problems that you might encounter – some of them will be easier to fix than others. For example, when you start your computer, if you get the message Non-system disk or disk error, then probably a floppy disk has been left in the drive.

Remove the floppy and press any key to continue.

No matter what weird behaviour your computer displays, do the obvious first:

· Stay calm it is only a computer and you are smarter than it is.
· Check all cables and power cords.
· Pay attention to error messages and write them down word-for-word. If you call technical support, this is essential information.
· Read the instructions that came with the software or peripheral.
· If you change something and it does not solve the problem change it back. You do not want to make your problems worse.
· Take one step at a time and document everything so you can undo everything if necessary.
· Remember what you were doing when it happened - what software package were you using at the time? Word? Excel? Netscape? What were you trying to do? Print? Save? Access something you haven't accessed before? When was the last time you did this successfully? Or is this the first time you've tried it?
· Find out if anyone near you has the same problem – e.g. if there is a problem with the print server then other people will be having the same problem.
· Restart - often problems can fix themselves if you close down the program you are having the problems with and then open it again – save your work first!
· More extreme problems can often sort themselves out if you close all your programs (save your work!) then close down your machine completely, then start it up again.
· Delete unnecessary files - .tmp files, cookies, cache files, file000.chk files, and Temporary Internet files can be eliminated easily and should be cleaned out at least once a month.

### 8.2 Hardware problems

There are many problems you can experience when working with computers. The following problems and solutions are the most common:

(i)   Computer won't start – check the following:
  ·   Check all connections.
  ·   Is the computer plugged in? Plug something else into the outlet and see if it works.
  ·   Is there a Surge Protector switch to turn on?
  ·   Is there a Master Wall Switch that controls the outlet?
  ·   Turn the system off and wait 30 seconds and then try again.
  ·   Reach behind the machine and see if you feel air blowing out of the power supply. If you do, then you know the machine is getting some power.
  ·   Look at the keyboard for the indicator lights being lit up as the machine starts up.

(ii)  Computer locks-up or 'freezes'. The cursor is stuck on the hourglass and won't let you do anything.

Usually a PC locks up due to hardware or software conflicts. You can tell if it's a hardware conflict if the lock-ups occur while using the same combination of equipment (e.g. printing while downloading something off the Web). More commonly, a lock-up is due to software conflicts. These are harder to troubleshoot, since they could appear randomly. Most times, this is due to a lack of memory.
  ·   Try to close the offending program by holding down the Ctrl and Alt keys and then press Delete. This will bring up the Close Program dialog box. You will see a list of all tasks (programs) currently running. You may notice one program has 'Not Responding' instead of 'Running' listed next to it. Select this task and click the End Task button.
  ·   If [Ctrl] [Alt] [Delete] has no effect (a hard lock-up) the only option is to completely shut down the computer by pressing the power button. Leave it for 15-30 seconds then restart the computer.

(iii) You have run out of disk space on your computer - to check for disk space:
  ·   Open 'My Computer'. Right click on the C: drive and select Properties from the shortcut menu. A pie chart will appear telling you the used and free space.
  ·   Try running the Disk Cleanup Wizard. This utility can tell you whether you are running out of room and help you clear away some space. Click the Start button and choose Programs | Accessories | System Tools | Disk Cleanup. Choose the disk to clean up (C:) and let the wizard do the work.
  ·   Empty the recycle bin - right click on the recycle bin and select 'Empty Recycle Bin'.
  ·   Delete all files with .tmp extension - these files are temporary files that are not needed.


### 8.3  Monitor problems

Monitor problems include the following:
(i)   You can't see anything on your computer screen:
  ·   Is the computer turned on? If the computer is on, the light on the CPU will be lit.

- Is the computer plugged in? Check to see if ALL plugs are secure.
- Is the power turned on?
- Is the monitor on? If the monitor is on, the light will be lit.
- If it is turned on, check the contrast and brightness buttons to see if they have been tampered with.
- Is the computer in Power Save or Sleep mode? Move the mouse or press any key on the keyboard to see if the computer will 'wake-up'
- Are all peripherals plugged in? Check all cables and cords leading in to and out of your computer

(ii) The screen is too bright or too dark – check if the brightness or contrast control is at the appropriate position, not at the maximum or minimum.

### 8.4 Keyboard and mouse problems

After switching on your computer, if it gives off a constant beeping noise, it is telling you that your keyboard is not connected or not working. Check the plug to make sure it is connected securely. Try unplugging it and re-plugging it again.

If there is no response, check the indicator light on the keyboard. Is it on? Do the lights respond when you press the caps lock or the num lock key? If not, maybe your keyboard is broken.

Is there a key stuck? Gently pry off the cover and clean it with alcohol. Make sure it is not connected to your machine when you are cleaning it.

If your mouse starts acting strangely, it could be an insufficient memory problem. Switch your computer off and then on again and see if that corrects the problem. If it will only move one way, either vertically or horizontally, it may need cleaning. Shut down your machine and unplug your mouse from the computer. Open the underside of the mouse and remove the ball. If the ball is a rubber ball, do not clean it with alcohol. Clean it with a soft cloth. There should be no lubricant placed on a mouse ball. Clean the roller in the body of the mouse with a cotton swab that is slightly damp with alcohol. Replace the ball when the rollers are dry and replace the bottom portion.

### 8.5 Printer problems

When using the printer it can be frustrating when you have problems. Here are some of the more common problems with some of the possible reasons. This is not an exhaustive list and you should always read the manual before dealing with a fault. Alternatively, you should seek immediate assistance when difficulties occur.

KAPLAN PUBLISHING

(i)  Printer does not print out when command is given
- Printer not switched on.
- Printer not connected to computer.
- Printer not on-line.
- Wrong command used.

(ii)  'Load A4' message – the printer may be out of paper or may be set up to print from a different paper tray. Check that the printer is not expecting to use paper loaded in the manual feed tray.

(iii)  'Load letter' message – settings are probably set to Letter paper size rather than A4. To change the settings choose File and Page Setup then select A4 as the paper size.

(iv)  Output is not as expected (e.g. characters used, characters wrong size, spacing incorrect)
- Wrong printer type selected.
- Printer incompatible with software.
- Printer cable faulty.
- Printer using incorrect fonts.
- Fonts have not been downloaded correctly from computer to printer.

(v)  Quality poor, characters faint – ribbon or cartridge needs replacing.

(vi)  Paper jam – could be either wrong paper used or paper damaged.

(vii) Printed crooked on paper – paper not aligned properly.


### 8.6  Problems with data files that have been damaged or deleted

There are many different causes of data loss that will require data recovery of some sort. The most common problems with data files are caused when a file that you are using becomes corrupted, gets accidentally overwritten by an older version of the file, wiping out what you may have done or is deleted by accident. There are various different methods of deleting information from data media, for example with deletion commands, by formatting, with power glitches or viruses, by overwriting or by destroying the data medium. Some of these situations can be solved easily by undoing the move by pressing on the Undo Typing button, relying on back up files or with software, while other situations require help to recover the data. For example, to recover a file from the recycle bin:
- Double click recycle bin icon
- Select file to be restored
- Right mouse click select restore
- The file will be restored to the original location.

Some software still has many bugs that cause files to crash – which might mean that you have lost everything entered since the last time you saved your work.  In Windows XP when an application package crashes it shows the following dialogue box.

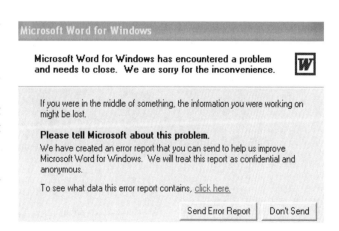

This gives users with an Internet connection the opportunity to let Microsoft know about possible bugs so that they can be corrected in future versions.

To try to retrieve the file, open the folder containing it and look for the latest tmp file (see below). You can click on this to open it and, if the content contains the latest entries or amendments, you can copy it to another file.

~WRL3982.tmp
TMP File
722 KB

Sometimes you may have problems opening files because you are not sure what software to use to open the file. For example, you might receive an e-mail attachment with an unusual file extension part of the file name – zip, xls, jpg, gif, avi or bmp. To open a zip file you must first unzip it using software such as WinZip or PKZip. The opened (extracted) files will than show their extensions and can be viewed using the appropriate software e.g. a file with a .doc extension is a Microsoft word document. A file ending in .xls is a spreadsheet that can be opened using Microsoft excel. The extension .avi is a video clip that you can see using Real Player or Windows Media Player. Paint shop or an alternative image manipulation file can open files with the jpg, gif or bmp extensions.

## 9 Test your knowledge

1 What are the basic components of a computer's hardware?

2 List seven input devices.

3 Name three computer programming languages.

4 What type of product is Microsoft Excel?

5 Briefly describe a stand-alone system.

6 What does the file server do?

7 What are the two main advantages of having networked rather than stand-alone computers?

8 Why is static electricity a problem in a computer environment?

9 Describe five visual safety checks that you must perform when starting up a computer system.

10 Describe three problems with password confidentiality.

11 What is 'standby'?

[Answers on p. 37]

## 10 Summary

This initial chapter introduced the basics of computer hardware and software, including networks and communications, stressing the importance when getting started of carrying out simple visual safety checks on hardware and the correct powering up and shutting down procedures. When accessing data files, we discussed the purpose of passwords and showed how to save, transfer and print documents using your organisation's procedures for changing passwords and making back ups and its house style for presentation of documents. We identified possible causes of difficulties e.g. files which have been damaged or deleted, printer problems, hardware problems and ways of dealing with them or obtaining assistance when difficulties occur.

### Answers to chapter activities & 'test your knowledge' questions

#### △ ACTIVITY 1

The system is based on optical mark readers to automatically read the data and print the official ticket.

#### △ ACTIVITY 2

Computer hardware is the equipment that makes up the computer system. It comprises the main processing unit, a screen, monitor, mouse and peripherals.

Computer software comprises the programs such as word processing, spreadsheets, databases and accounting programs that run through the operating system on the hardware.

#### △ ACTIVITY 3

Disks are divided into folders and the folders contain a collection of files.

**Test your knowledge**

1   The basic components of a computer's hardware consist of a central processor (CPU), input devices, storage devices (for filing data), and output devices (which display data). Peripheral devices are those connected to the computer system and controlled by it, but that are not part of the CPU or main memory

2   Keyboard, mouse, VDU, image or document scanner, optical character recognition, optical mark reader, MICR reader, bar code, plastic card, microphone.

3   Some programming languages commonly in use are: Visual BASIC, Pascal, Delphi, C++ and Assembler.

4   Microsoft Excel is a spreadsheet program.

5   A stand-alone system is not linked with any other computer system. It can be based on any operating system, run on any platform, and consist of a PC with or without a hard disk, Unix workstation or Apple Macintosh. The system can possess floppy disks and CD drives, a hard disk, a mouse and other peripheral components.

6   The file server stores all of the network's shared files. It also:
    · manages the hard drive(s)
    · ensures that multiple requests (especially write requests) do not conflict with each other
    · protects data
    · prevents unauthorised access
    · maintains lists of rights/authorisation associated to data files.

7   Advantages
    · Expensive resources can be shared
    · Software can be stored centrally
    · Files can be stored centrally and accessed freely
    · Data easily backed up
    · Memos and emails can be sent to members of network easily
    · Network can easily be expanded
    · If one machine breaks down other machines can continue working.

8   Static electricity is a problem in a computer environment if the computer acts as a ground and the static discharge damages its electronics.

9   Before switching on your PC, there are a few quick safety checks that you can do:
    · Hardware components – make sure they are not damaged or wet. Remove any unnecessary items from your PC and monitor e.g. flower pots, coffee cups or other items that may contain liquids. Check that the computer case is not too close to the wall.
    · Pl ugs – check that they are not overloaded and that there are no trailing cables that could trip someone up.
    · Cables – verify cables and peripherals are connected correctly to the computer.
    · Interfaces – make sure the cables are firmly pushed in to their slots and all peripherals are turned on.

10  To be effective, the password needs to keep out unauthorised access. However, there are problems with password confidentiality:
    · An authorised user may divulge their password to an unauthorised user possibly to bypass the administrative 'hassle' of getting new identities on the system.
    · Most passwords chosen by authorised users have some form of association for them (National Insurance number, birth date, names or nicknames) or are extremely simple to form (common words or names found in a dictionary) and can be discovered by intelligent experimentation.

· If you assign people random combinations of letters and numbers, which are far more difficult to crack, you come up against the problem that they are also far more difficult to remember. Most users will write their password down either on the terminal itself or nearby, making the task of discovering it easy.

11 Working with Windows, Standby puts your computer in a low power state so that you can quickly resume when you are ready to return to it.

KAPLAN PUBLISHING

# MAINTAIN THE SECURITY OF DATA

## INTRODUCTION

Element 21.2 requires you to appreciate the need to change passwords at appropriate times and keep program disks securely located. You should be able to identify and minimise potential risks to data.

This chapter identifies some of the major risks to the security of computer systems and data, and discusses some controls available to reduce or eliminate those risks. We will outline the importance of storing back up copies safely and of keeping passwords confidential and changing them on a regular basis, or if disclosure is suspected.

All organisations have a legal obligation regarding information and its storage, processing and retrieval. Because of the responsibility for the security of information systems and their products, managers and employees involved with these systems must be aware of the legal issues and current legislative framework.

## KNOWLEDGE & UNDERSTANDING

- Different types of risk, viruses, confidentiality (Item 6)
- Relevant security and legal regulations, data protection legislation, copyright, VDU legislation, health and safety regulations, retention of documents (Item 7)
- The organisation's procedures for changing passwords and making back ups (Item 10)
- Organisational security policies (Item 12)

## CONTENTS

1 Security
2 Protecting data from risks
3 Legislative requirements
4 Health and safety regulations

## PERFORMANCE CRITERIA

- Ensure passwords are kept secret and changed at appropriate times (Item A in Element 21.2)
- Ensure computer hardware and program disks are kept securely located (Item B in Element 21.2)
- Identify potential risk to data from different sources and take steps to resolve or minimise them (Item C in Element 21.2)
- Maintain security and confidentiality of data at all times (Item D in Element 21.2)
- Understand and implement relevant legal regulations (Item E in Element 21.2

## 1　Security

### 1.1　Security risks

> **□ DEFINITION** ▢▢▢▢
>
> **Security** is defined by the British Computer Society as 'the establishment and application of safeguards to protect data, software and computer hardware from accidental or malicious modification, destruction or disclosure'.

There are five basic types of security risk to an organisation.

1.  **Physical intrusion** leading to theft or damage of assets. Theft includes loss and illegal copying.

2.  **Physical damage** to hardware or computer media – malicious damage, poor operating conditions, natural disasters and simple wear and tear can physically damage machinery and storage media such as disks, tapes and diskettes. These carry a triple threat – the cost of repair or replacement of hardware; the danger of damaged data or program files; and the cost of computer down time. The loss of accounting records could be sufficient to cause the company to fail. Most non-technical users of systems would be surprised that there is an inherent risk to any computer system. Systems failure can mean that data is lost or physical damage can occur in a manner that is virtually impossible to guard against in a cost-effective way.

3.  **Damage to data** – hackers, viruses, program bugs, hardware and media faults can all damage data files. The havoc caused by damaged data is made worse if it is not detected and rectified quickly. Hacking activities can:
    -   generate information which is of potential use to a competitor organisation
    -   provide the basis for fraudulent activity
    -   cause data corruption by the introduction of unauthorised computer programs and processing onto the system, otherwise known as 'computer viruses'
    -   alter or delete the files.

4.  **Operational mistakes**, due to innocent events such as running the wrong program, or inadvertently deleting data that is still of value to the organisation, can cause significant problems, ranging from the need to resuscitate files and repeat computer runs, to the possibility of losing customers. Links to the Internet bring extra security risks. Examples include the following:
    -   corruptions such as viruses can spread through the network
    -   disaffected employees can do deliberate damage to data or systems
    -   hackers may be able to steal data or to damage the system.
    -   employees may download inaccurate information or imperfect or virus-ridden software from an external network

KAPLAN PUBLISHING

- information sent from one part of an organisation to another may be intercepted
- the communications link itself may break down.

5. **Industrial espionage/fraud** – can lead to loss of confidentiality with sensitive information being obtained by outsiders or non-related employees. Industrial espionage and sabotage can yield significant advantages to competitors, and fraud and blackmail is a significant threat.

## 1.2 Software security risks

The effects of poor security on software could be:

- **Deliberate physical attacks**, including theft or damage to installation in general – with files being taken. This threat can come from inside and outside the organisation e.g. access by unauthorised personnel could result in theft, piracy, vandalism.
- **Malicious damage** can also involve individuals from within or outside the organisation (such as hackers), damaging or tampering with data or information in order to disrupt the organisation's activity for malevolent reasons.
- **Fraudulent attacks** by employees or management or fraudulent transactions by altering programs. Fraudsters can divert funds from an enterprise to their own pockets or can attempt to hold employing companies to ransom by the threat of sabotage to vital computer systems.
- **Loss of confidentiality** – sensitive information obtained by outsiders or non-related employees.

## 1.3 Risks to information

The increasing use of computers in all aspects of business has led to a lot of information about individuals being kept by various organisations.

Information can be damaged, lost or stolen the same as equipment and other assets can. There are certain types of information that must be protected because of its confidentiality or value to competitors, for example:

- **Personal and private information** about employees and customers – there is a risk that some of this information is inaccurate which could cause serious problems for the individual concerned (e.g. being refused a loan if they have the wrong credit rating). The Data Protection Acts of 1984 and 1998 were introduced to help reduce this risk. The Acts stipulate that only legitimate parties can access data, and information must be secured against alteration, accidental loss or deliberate damage. Furthermore, the Act states that data must be obtained fairly, to precise specifications and must not be kept for longer than required. Individuals can find out information held about themselves by writing to the organisation and asking for a copy.
- **Critical information** about the business and its products/services, its marketing plans and legal or financial details of intended mergers, takeovers or redundancies. The importance of the organisation's commercial and trade information cannot be underestimated. The leaking of a company's

trade secrets, such as its production processes, to its competitors may seriously affect its performance and its profits.

· **Details related to the security** of the organisation such as access codes, passwords and banking schedules.

There are also risks associated with copyright and copying, transmitting, sending and destroying confidential information without authorisation and appropriate security measures.

Remember e-mail is neither secure nor confidential.

### 1.4 Computer viruses

> **□ DEFINITION**                                  □□□□
>
> A **computer virus** is a piece of software that piggybacks on real programs and seeks to infest a computer system, hiding and automatically spreading to other systems if given the opportunity.

For example, a virus might attach itself to a program such as a spreadsheet program. Each time the spreadsheet program runs, the virus runs, too, and it has the chance to reproduce (by attaching to other programs) or wreak havoc. A computer virus passes from computer to computer like a biological virus passes from person to person.

Viruses can be classified using multiple criteria: origin, techniques, types of files they infect, where they hide, the kind of damage they cause, the type of operating system or platform they attack, etc.

A single virus, if it is particularly complex, may come under several different categories. And, as new viruses emerge, it may sometimes be necessary to redefine categories or, very occasionally, create new categories

Types of virus/infection include:

· **File infectors** – this type of virus infects programs or executable files (files with an .EXE or .COM extension). When one of these programs is run, directly or indirectly, the virus is activated, producing the damaging effects it is programmed to carry out. The majority of existing viruses belong to this category, and can be classified depending on the actions that they carry out.

· **Overwrite viruses** – this type of virus is characterised by the fact that it deletes the information contained in the files that it infects, rendering them partially or totally useless once they have been infected. Infected files do not change size, unless the virus occupies more space than the original file because, instead of hiding within a file, the virus replaces the file's content. The only way to clean a file infected by an overwrite virus is to delete the file completely, thus losing the original content.

KAPLAN PUBLISHING

· **E-mail viruses** – an e-mail virus moves around in e-mail messages, and usually replicates itself by automatically mailing itself to dozens of people in the victim's e-mail address book.

· **Trap doors** – undocumented entry points to systems allowing normal controls to be bypassed

· **Logic bombs** – are triggered on the occurrence of a certain event.

· **Time bombs** – which are triggered on a certain date e.g. Friday 13th.

· **Worms** – are not strictly viruses, as they do not need to infect other files in order to reproduce. They have the ability to self-replicate, and can lead to negative effects on the system and most importantly they are detected and eliminated by anti-viruses.

· **Trojans** – are examples of malicious code, which unlike viruses do not reproduce by infecting other files, nor do they self-replicate like worms. They appear to be harmless programs that enter a computer through any channel. When that program is executed (they have names or characteristics which trick the user into doing so), they install other programs on the computer that can be harmful. A Trojan may not activate its effects at first, but when it does, it can wreak havoc on your system. They have the capacity to delete files, destroy information on your hard drive and open up a back-door to your system. This gives them complete access to your system allowing an outside user to copy and resend confidential information.

Most computer viruses have three functions – avoiding detection, reproducing themselves and causing damage. The damage caused may be relatively harmless and amusing ('Cascade' causes letters to 'fall' off a screen), but are more often severely damaging.

The potential for the damage a virus can cause is restricted only by the creativity of the originator. Given the mobility between computerised systems and the sharing of resources and data, the threat posed by a viral attack is considerable.

Once a virus has been introduced, the only course of action may be to regenerate the system from back up. However, some viruses are written so that they lie dormant for a period, which means that the back ups become infected before the existence of the virus has been detected; in these instances restoration of the system becomes impossible.

## 1.5 Fraudulent activities

Fraud is criminal deception – essentially it is theft involving dishonesty. It may be opportunistic or organised. The dishonesty may involve suppliers, contractors, competitors, other third parties, employees and ex-employees and, increasingly, organised crime and senior managers. Many frauds involve collusion and sophisticated methods of concealment. With an ever-increasing amount of business being carried out electronically (via 'e-commerce') the opportunities for cybercrime and computer fraud are also growing exponentially.

Fraud normally involves staff removing money from the company but other methods of fraud that might affect the data held on a computer system include:

- the creation of fictitious supplier accounts and submission of false invoices, usually for services rather than goods, so that payments are sent to the fictitious supplier
- corruption and bribery, particularly where individuals are in a position of authority as regards making decisions on suppliers or selecting between tenders
- misappropriation of incoming cheques from bona fide customers
- giving unauthorised discounts to customers
- stock losses, including short deliveries by driver
- fictitious staff on the payroll.

## 2 Protecting data from risks

### 2.1 Security measures

Computer security can be divided into a number of separate functions with different aims:

- **Threat avoidance:** this might mean changing the design of the system.
- Prevention: it is practically impossible to prevent all threats in a cost-effective manner.
- **Deterrence:** the computer system should try to both prevent unauthorised access, and deter people from trying to access the system. Controls to prevent and detect access include passwords and hardware keys. As an example, computer misuse by personnel can be grounds for dismissal.
- **Detection:** if the computer system is accessed without authorisation, there should be controls to sense the access and report it to the appropriate personnel. Detection techniques are often combined with prevention techniques. Controls will therefore include control logs of unauthorised attempts to gain access and manual reviews of amendments made to program and data files.
- **Recovery:** if the threat occurs, its consequences can be contained e.g. by the use of checkpoint programs. Procedures should be in place to ensure that if the computer system was destroyed, or compromised by a virus, then processing could continue quickly. A basic control procedure would be a complete backup of all data.
- **Correction:** any unauthorised changes made to the computer systems are corrected as soon as possible. This means that complete backups of all data are available and that staff are properly trained in the procedures necessary for recovery and re-installing of data in an emergency situation.

### 2.2 Physical security

Physical security includes protection against natural and man-made disasters, e.g. fire, flood, etc. Examples of measures to avoid physical damage to the system include:

· Fire precautions, e.g. smoke and heat detectors, training for staff in observing safety procedures and alarms.
· Devices to protect against power surges.

Physical security also includes protection against intruders and theft. As computers and other hardware become smaller and portable, they are more likely to be taken from the organisation. Burglar alarms should be installed and a log of all equipment maintained. People with official access to the equipment who are taking it off-site should book it out with the appropriate authorisation.

Access to the building may be controlled by security guards, closed circuit TV monitoring access, other mechanical devices such as door locks and electronic devices, e.g. badge readers and card entry systems.

## 2.3 Data security

Guidelines for data security include keeping files in fireproof cabinets, shredding computer printouts if they include confidential information, controlling access to the data, (e.g. passwords and physical access controls) and taking back-ups of data to minimise the risks of destruction or alteration.

To offset the risk of fraudulent attacks there must be: adequate controls over input/processing/programs; strict division of duties; and regular internal audit review of systems and controls.

To prevent loss of confidentiality, there should be controls over input and output. With on-line systems there should be passwords issued only to authorised personnel, restricted access to files at the terminals and a computer log of attempted violations.

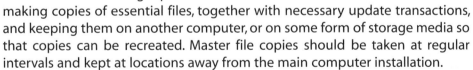

All disks containing important information must be backed up on a regular basis. Information on a computer is vulnerable: hard disks can fail, computer systems can fail, viruses can wipe a disk, careless operators can delete files, and very careless operators can delete whole areas of the hard disks by mistake. Computers can also be damaged or stolen. For these reasons backing up data is essential. This involves making copies of essential files, together with necessary update transactions, and keeping them on another computer, or on some form of storage media so that copies can be recreated. Master file copies should be taken at regular intervals and kept at locations away from the main computer installation.

Contingency plans for a disaster should include standby facilities, with a similar computer user or a bureau, being available to allow processing to continue.

## 2.4 Rules for using passwords

If passwords are used for authentication in a computer system, the safety of the access privileges will depend on their correct use and the following rules should be observed:

· It must not be possible to guess the password as easily as names, motor vehicle licence numbers, birth dates, or the like.

· The password should consist of at least one non-letter character (special character or number) and have at least six characters. The selection of trivial passwords (BBBBBB, 123456) must be prevented.

· Preset passwords (e.g. by the manufacturer at the time of delivery) must be replaced by individually selected passwords.

· The password must be kept secret and should only be known personally to the user.

· The password must be altered regularly, e.g. every 90 days. This will ensure that if an unauthorised person has obtained it, he or she will have limited use.

· The password should be altered if it has come to the knowledge of unauthorised persons.

· After any alteration of the password, previous passwords should no longer be used and reuse of previous passwords should be prevented by the IT system.

---

## ▷ ACTIVITY 1

You have been asked for suggestions for a checklist of control procedures to remind authorised users about password security in the computer department.

[Answers on p.58]

---

### 2.5  Controls to help prevent hacking

Hacking is the gaining of unauthorised access to a computer system. It may form part of a criminal activity or it may be a hobby, with hackers acting alone or passing information to one another. Hacking is often a harmless activity, with participants enjoying the challenge of breaking part of a system's defences, but severe damage can be caused.

Once hackers have gained access to the system, there are several damaging options available to them. For example, they may:

· gain access to the file that holds all the ID codes, passwords and authorisations

· discover the method used for generating/authorising passwords

· discover maintenance codes, which would render the system easily accessible.

By specifically identifying the risks that the hacker represents, controls can be designed that will help prevent such activity occurring. Examples include:

· **Physical security** – check that terminals and PCs are kept under lock and key, and ensure that, where dial-in communication links are in place, that a call-back facility is used. (In call-back, the person dialling in must request that the system calls them back to make the connection.

· Management often requires that the contents of certain files (e.g. payroll) remain confidential and are only available to authorised staff. This may be achieved by keeping tapes or removable disks containing the files in a locked cabinet and issuing them only for authorised use.

KAPLAN PUBLISHING

- **Passwords** – the controls over passwords must be stringently enforced and password misuse should represent a serious disciplinary offence within an organisation. Associated with the password is a list of files, and data within files, which the user is allowed to inspect. Attempts to access unauthorised files or data will be prohibited by the operating system and reported at the central computer. For example, an order clerk using a VDU would be allowed access to the stock file, but not to the employee file. Similarly, the clerk would be allowed access to the customer file for purposes of recording an order, but would not be able to inspect details of the account. For systems that use passwords and logging on techniques, the workstation should not be left in the middle of editing. A screensaver with password control can be used for short absences, which saves closing down the machine.
- **Data encryption** – files can be scrambled to render them unintelligible unless a decoding password is supplied. Data may be coded so that it is not understandable to any casual observer who does not have access to suitable decryption software. Encryption provides a double benefit. It protects against people managing to gain access to the system, and it protects against the tapping of data whilst being transmitted from one machine to another.
- **System logs** – every activity on a system should be logged and be subject to some form of exception reporting, e.g. unusual times of access could be reported.
- **Random checks** – the 'constable on the beat' approach checks who is doing what at random intervals on the system, and ensures that they are authorised for those activities.
- **Shielding of VDUs** – to protect against people with detection equipment being able to view remotely what is being displayed on VDUs, the units may be shielded to prevent the transmission of radiation that can be detected

## 2.6 Preventative steps against computer viruses

It is extremely difficult to guard against the introduction of computer viruses. Even seemingly harmless screen savers have been known to contain deadly viruses that destroy computer systems. You should not download from the Internet or open e-mails that have attachments unless you know the source of the e-mail and that you trust that source. If you are in doubt you should ask your line manager for permission to open documents.

Steps may be taken to control the introduction and spread of viruses, but these will usually only be effective in controlling the spread of viruses by well-meaning individuals. The actions of hackers or malicious employees are less easy to control. Preventative steps may include:
- anti-virus software to prevent corruption of the system by viruses. Although the focus of the program is to detect and cure known viruses; it will not always restore data or software that has been corrupted by the virus. As new viruses are being detected almost daily, it is virtually impossible for the virus detection software to be effective against all known viruses
- control on the use of external software (e.g. checked for viruses before use)
- use of only tested, marked disks within the organisation

· restricted access to floppy disks and CDs on all PCs/workstations
· passwords and user numbers can be used to limit the chances of unauthorised people accessing the system via the public communications network.

## 3 Legislative requirements

### 3.1 Introduction

Several Acts of Parliament, notably the Data Protection Act 1998, the Copyright, Designs and Patents Act 1988 and the Computer Misuse Act 1990 regulate the use of computers. Each Act identifies a number of prohibited actions, which if proven in a court of law may lead the perpetrator to face damages and/or a fine or imprisonment or both. Additionally, the use of software may also be subject to the terms of licensing agreements entered into by the organisation you work for, which are enforceable in the civil courts.

### 3.2 Data Protection Act 1998

People have been keeping records for centuries and it might be considered surprising that concern is only recently being voiced. It is mainly because of the amount of information that can be gathered and stored and the ease with which that information can be manipulated and exchanged. School records, banking records, itemised telephone bills, medical records, etc, are all now capable of being consolidated to show what purchases someone makes, where they travel, who they talk to and how well they are. It is well known that information is traded for mailing lists.

The exchange of information itself is not worrying. The concern lies in the use made of the information, or how it may be interpreted. It may be used to decide whether to give a person a job, or given credit or called to the police station for interrogation.

The 1998 Data Protection Act covers how information about living identifiable persons is processed and used. It is much broader in scope than the earlier 1984 act, in that ALL organisations that hold or process personal data MUST comply. This Act has implications for everyone who processes manual or electronic personal data. It applies to filing systems of records held on computer or manual sets of accessible records e.g. a database of customer names, addresses, telephone numbers and sales details.

Under the terms of the Act, the need for privacy is recognised by the requirements that all data should be held for clearly designated purposes. Accuracy and integrity must be maintained and data must be open to inspection. Only legitimate parties can access data and information must be secured against alteration, accidental loss or deliberate damage. Furthermore, the Act states that data must be obtained fairly, to precise specifications and must not be kept for longer than required. It reinforces the need for confidentiality in business dealings. A business should not reveal information about one customer to another or information about its employees without their permission. The Act gives a data subject, with some exceptions, the right to examine the personal data that a data controller is holding about him or her. Individuals may write to a data controller to ask whether they are the subject of personal data, and they are entitled to a reply.

The data controller may charge a nominal fee for providing the information, but is required to reply within a certain time.
Where personal data is being held, the data subject has the right to receive details of:
(i)   the personal data that is being held
(ii)   the purposes for which the information is being processed
(iii)  the recipients to whom the information might be disclosed.

The data subject is also entitled to receive this information in a form that can be understood. In practice, this usually means providing the data subject with a printout of the data, and an explanation of any items of data (such as codes) whose meaning is not clear.

Any individual who suffers damage as a result of improper use of the data by the data controller is entitled to compensation for any loss suffered.

The *Data Protection Registrar* keeps a register of companies who hold information on computer. Each company that falls into this category must register of its own accord. A copy of the Data Protection Register is held in all major libraries.

Any unregistered data user who holds personal data that is not exempt commits a criminal offence; the maximum penalty for which is an unlimited fine.

## 3.3  Retention of documents

All businesses need to keep certain records for legal and commercial reasons. The difficulty lies in knowing which documents must be kept and for how long. Your organisation will have a policy that states the retention (and disposal) policy for such documentation. It will outline minimum retention periods for different types of documents based on best practice and, where applicable, the minimum retention periods required by law. The Data Protection Act stipulates that personal data is kept securely and that it should be accurate.

Business records are normally stored for at least six years. Payroll data must be kept for three years. There are a number of legal reasons why financial data, which of course includes personal data, should be kept for this time. Accounting records need to be kept for at least six years in case they are required as evidence in a legal case. They should also be kept so that they can be inspected by HM Revenue and Customs (formerly called the Inland Revenue or HM Customs and Excise) in case there is a tax or VAT inspection.

Once information becomes out of date, it may be deleted or destroyed but you must be aware that throwing a piece of paper in the waste bin is not destroying it. Even when information is out of date it may still be damaging if it falls into the wrong hands.

---

### ▷ ACTIVITY 2                                                    ▷ ▷ ▷ ▷

A well-known customer telephones you and asks if you can look up on your screen and let him know if Joe Bloggs (another customer) is paying on time because he is having trouble getting money out of him and wonders whether he is going bust. Unfortunately, you know from your work that Joe Bloggs is not very good at paying his invoices. What should you say?

[Answers on p. 58]

---

### 3.4  Patent and copyright infringement

Copyright law covers books of all kinds, sound recordings, film and broadcasts, computer programs, dramatic and musical works. Copyright in general terms is the right to publish, reproduce and sell the matter and form of a literary, musical, dramatic or artistic work. The **Copyright Designs and Patents Act 1988** states that the copyright holder has the exclusive right to make and distribute copies. The Copyright (Computer Software) Amendment Act 1989 indicates that software is treated as literary work and provides the same protection to the authors of computer software as it does to literary, dramatic and musical works. An amendment to the 1988 Act made in 1992 allows you to make a copy for back-up purposes. . The Act makes it illegal to steal or to create copies of software. You are not allowed to make copies of software; make copies of manuals or allow copies to be made unless you have a licence from the owner of the copyright. It is also an offence to run the software on more than one computer at the same time unless that is covered in the licence.

Application packages will always contain an embedded serial number. If a pirate copy is found, the original purchaser can usually be determined. There are steep penalties for companies prosecuted for software theft – unlimited damages, legal costs and the cost of legitimising the software. However, most breaches of copyright law happen because business users do not know what the law is.

Where a package is intended for use by more than one person, for instance on a network, then a multi-user licence is normally purchased, and this sets a limit on the total number of users. An alternative to this is a site licence, but this can be restrictive if, say, a travelling salesperson or someone working from home connects to the network. Some software can be copied legally; this is shareware. The software can be loaded onto a computer and tested; however, if the user decides to keep the software, then a royalty payment is due to the author. Freeware is software that can be copied and used without charge, although the software author retains the copyright to that software. Finally, public domain software is freely available and sharable software that is not copyrighted.

KAPLAN PUBLISHING

Modern software packages are complex and costly to produce, but are often easy to copy and distribute. Manufacturers are increasingly bringing prosecutions to try to reduce the number of pirate copies of their software. Staff should be made aware of this. Master and back-up copies of packages (usually on diskette or CD-ROM) should be kept in a locked safe. Programs on LAN servers should be given 'execute only' protection to prevent them being copied, and physical access to the server should be restricted. Regular and automatic audits should be made of personal computers to check that they only contain authorised programs.

### 3.5  Why worry about copyright rules?

The 'moral' reasons for following copyright rules are:
·   copyright protection is essential to ensure that authors and publishers receive appropriate remuneration for their work
·   acknowledging source and ownership of materials is good academic practice.

The pragmatic reasons for following copyright rules are:
·   breaches of copyright can lead to civil prosecution and fines and, in worst cases, criminal prosecution
·   licensing bodies make regular checks on certain organisations to ensure rules are being followed.

Note also, that you can infringe copyright, and be prosecuted, not only for making illegal copies yourself, but also as an 'accessory' by providing resources or authorisation (e.g. within a company) for someone else to illegally copy or perform material.

### 3.6  Computer misuse

Data that has been stored on a computer is, potentially, easier to misuse than that stored on paper. Computer-based data can be altered without leaving an obvious trace that it has changed. For example, an exam score written in a mark book can be changed but you can usually tell that the mark has changed. A mark stored on a computer can be changed and it will look as if nothing has happened.

Malicious (harmful) programs can be introduced to a computer that can damage the data stored on it; copy the data and send it somewhere else; or simply change the stored data. The programs are named after the way the get onto different computers: viruses, worms and Trojan horses.

It is very easy to make copies of computer data without leaving a trace that it has been done. A photocopier will also make copies of paper-based data but electronic copies of data can be smuggled out easily on floppy disks, memory chips or over a network connection.

Many computers are connected to a network or the Internet. If someone is persistent enough it is possible to use this connection to gain access to the computer (and the data on it) from outside. Of course, someone is able to physically break into a room and read data from paper records, however, it is sometimes more difficult to trace someone who has broken into a computer over a network or the Internet.

**The Computer Misuse Act 1990** makes it a criminal offence to attempt to access, use or alter any computer data, program or service to which you have not been granted authorised access rights. Therefore any attempt to interfere with or bypass the security controls, to attempt to obtain information such as other people's password, or accessing or modifying other people's programs or files without permission are offences under the Act. Amongst other things, this Act makes illegal the activity of hacking and the introduction of viruses and worms.

The Act has created three new criminal offences.

(i) **Unauthorised access** – This refers to any hacker who knowingly tries to gain unauthorised access to a computer system. The crime is committed in attempting to gain access, regardless of whether the hacker is success-ful or not. It includes: using another person's identifier (ID) and password; creating a virus; laying a trap to obtain a password; or persistently trying to guess an ID and password.

(ii) **Unauthorised access with the intention of committing another offence** – This crime carries stricter penalties than the crime mentioned above. It seeks to protect against unauthorised entry with the intention of committing a further criminal act such as fraud. Examples include: gaining access to financial or administrative records: reading or changing confi-dential information.

(iii) **Unauthorised modification of data or programs** – This makes the intro-duction of viruses into a computer system a criminal offence. Guilt is assessed upon the intention to disrupt or in some way impair the normal operation and processes of the computer system. Examples include: destroying another user's files; modifying systems files; introducing a local virus; introducing a networked virus; or deliberately generating informa-tion to cause a system malfunction.

### 3.7 Enforcement of standards

Observance of standards is more a matter of attitude than policing. When people are aware of the purposes of standards, they are more likely to follow them than if they are just threatened. Training is the main element of enforce-ment. There are some cases where ignoring standards should automatically lead to disciplinary action:
(i) any standards to do with safety, e.g. dangerous positioning of cables, particularly power cables, or working alone in an electrically hazardous environment
(ii) standards with legal implications, e.g. ignoring a requirement of the Data Protection Act or using an illegal copy of a program

(iii)  actions which may affect a number of other people, e.g. running a program which might introduce a virus into a network

(iv)  attempted unauthorised entry, e.g. trying to find someone else's password or unauthorised copying of confidential files (e.g. salaries).

# 4    Health and safety regulations

## 4.1  The Health and Safety (Display Screen Equipment) Regulations 1992

Ensuring the workplace is safe and healthy for employees can sometimes lead to emphasis on the obvious hazards such as lifting and use of dangerous equipment. However, the health and safety implications of poorly designed workstations is extremely important in today's environment where more and more people are working at personal computers and desks for long periods of time.

In addition to the Workplace (Health, Safety and Welfare) Regulations there are the Health and Safety (Display Screen Equipment) Regulations, which relate directly to use of display screen equipment (DSE). In general these are in place to ensure that workstations and jobs are well designed for individuals and that the risks to health and safety are minimised. The regulations do not cover screens whose main purpose is to show television or film pictures. Workstation equipment includes:

· display Screen Equipment (DSE) e.g. Computers, Terminals and accessories such as printers
· desks
· chairs
· accessories – e.g. telephone, foot rests, document holders, wrist rests
· work environment & work organisation.

The Health and Safety (Display Screen Equipment) Regulations 1992 came into effect from January 1993 to implement an EC Directive. They require employers to minimise the risks in VDU work by ensuring that workplaces and jobs are well designed.

The Regulations apply where staff habitually use VDUs as a significant part of their normal work (three hours or more per day) – even if they work from home. Other people, who use VDUs only occasionally, are not covered by these Regulations, but their employers still have general duties to protect them under other health and safety at work legislation.

## 4.2  Hazards

There are hazards associated with the use of Display Screen Equipment (DSE). They include:
· upper limb disorders (musculoskeletal disorders) – aches and pains in the hands, wrists, arms, neck, shoulders, back, etc

- visual difficulties – eyes can become tired and existing conditions can become more noticeable
- repetitive strain injury (RSI) – appears to arise from making the same movements repeatedly and affects your hands and arms
- fatigue and stress
- headaches
- skin irritation
- back and neck strain.

The likelihood and extent of these harmful outcomes is related to the frequency, duration, pace and intensity of the tasks; the adequacy of the equipment and its arrangement; the physical environment; the workplace's organisational 'climate'; the characteristics of the individual; the posture of the user; and other factors.

It should be noted, however, that only a small percentage of users will experience problems as a result of DSE. Those problems that do occur are generally not due to the equipment itself but the way it is used. The majority of concerns can be prevented by effective workplace and job design, ensuring that workstations and work patterns are designed to suit the individual.

### 4.3 Problems with Display Screen Equipment (DSE)

If you are a user of display screen equipment:

- Problems with the task, the workstation or its environment that are increasing the risk to your health and safety, and that you cannot resolve yourself, must be reported to your manager.
- You might experience the early signs and symptoms of ill health and identify the cause and the preventative measures to prevent continuing ill health. You must report this to your manager to enable support to be given for the measures you are taking.
- Ill-health problems might have developed to a stage that causes suffering and incapacity from doing all or part of your normal work. This will need to be the subject of an Accident Report. The manager's investigation into the accident may need the assistance of a Display Screen Equipment assessor. A long-term remedy might be identified and a short-term adjustment to task, routine and/or workstation might be appropriate. A DSE assessor is not competent to diagnose health conditions or advise on treatment or therapy. If however your doctor recommends certain adaptation of the task or workstation to your condition the assessor might be able to help with implementation.
- In more serious cases the condition might be such that the manager will need to arrange a rehabilitation programme and 'reasonable adjustments' of the work and workstations.

## 5 Test your knowledge

1 Explain four types of security threat to an organisation.

2 Outline the types of critical information about the business that might be at risk.

3 What types of viruses are there?

4 Computer security can be divided into a number of separate functions with different aims. Outline three of them.

5 What are the guidelines for data security with regard to the theft of disks?

6 Explain five rules for using passwords.

7 Why must all disks containing important information be backed up on a regular basis?

8 Describe the controls that will help prevent hacking.

9 What type of legislation exists to protect individuals from misuse of information that other individuals or organisations may hold about them?

10 Outline the reasons why your organisation must follow copyright rules.

11 List the hazards associated with the use of Display Screen Equipment (DSE).

[Answers on p. 58]

## 6 Summary

There are many different risks in the IT environment, both to computer hardware and to the organisation's data and, after reading this chapter, you should be able to discuss the controls available to reduce or eliminate those risks. Other important security aspects include ensuring that back-up copies are stored safely and passwords are kept confidential and changed on a regular basis, especially if disclosure is suspected.

This chapter also looked at the legal issues and current legislative framework that regulates the use of computers and aims to protect users.

## Answers to chapter activities & 'test your knowledge' questions

### △ ACTIVITY 1 △△△△

Some of the suggestions that would be included in a checklist for password security are:

· Passwords are meant to be secret and not revealed to anyone else.
· Never write it down.
· Change your password regularly or if you suspect someone knows it.
· Do not choose an obvious password such as your name, or in the case of a PIN, your date or year of birth.
· Try to avoid onlookers seeing you key in your password.
· For keyboard passwords, choose keys that require both hands rather than one or two finger, easy runs along a pattern of the keys.

### △ ACTIVITY 2 △△△△

You should not divulge any confidential information about your customer Joe Bloggs. Apart from it being very unprofessional it would also be breaking the law. Under the Data Protection Act 1998 data should not be made available to outsiders without authorisation.

**Test your knowledge**  △ △ △

1 Security threats to an organisation include:
· Physical intrusion leading to theft or damage of assets. Theft includes loss and illegal copying.
· Physical damage to hardware or computer media including malicious damage, poor operating conditions, natural disasters and simple wear and tear can physically damage machinery and storage media such as disks, tapes and diskettes.
· Damage to data from hackers, viruses, program bugs, hardware and media faults can all damage data files.
· Operational mistakes, due to innocent events such as running the wrong program, or inadvertently deleting data that is still of value to the organisation, can cause significant problems, ranging from the need to resuscitate files and repeat computer runs, to the possibility of losing customers.
· Industrial espionage/fraud – can lead to loss of confidentiality with sensitive information being obtained by outsiders or non-related employees.

2 The types of critical information about the business that might be at risk include details of its products/services, its marketing plans and legal or financial details of intended mergers, takeovers or redundancies. The importance of the organisation's commercial and trade information cannot be underestimated. The leaking of a company's trade secrets, such as its production processes, to its competitors may seriously affect its performance and its profits.

3   There are many types of virus/infection. Examples are file infectors, over-write viruses, e-mail viruses, logic bombs, time bombs, Trojan horses and worms.

4   Computer security can be divided into a number of separate functions with different aims e.g. threat avoidance, prevention, deterrence, detection, recovery and correction.

5   Guidelines for data security include keeping files in fireproof cabinets, shredding computer printouts if they include confidential information, controlling access to the data, (e.g. passwords and physical access controls) and taking back-ups of data to minimise the risks of destruction or alteration.

6   Rules for using passwords include the following:
   · Do not use easy to guess passwords.
   · Use at least one non-letter character and have at least six characters.
   · Replace preset passwords.
   · Keep passwords secret.
   · Change passwords regularly, especially if someone might know it.
   · After alteration, do not use previous passwords.

7   All disks containing important information must be backed up on a regular basis because information on a computer is vulnerable: hard disks can fail, computer systems can fail, viruses can wipe a disk, careless operators can delete files, and very careless operators can delete whole areas of the hard disks by mistake. Computers can also be damaged or stolen. For these reasons backing up data is essential. This involves making copies of essential files, together with necessary update transactions, and keeping them on another computer, or on some form of storage media so that copies can be recreated. Master file copies should be taken at regular intervals and kept at locations away from the main computer installation.

8   Controls that will help prevent hacking include:
   · checking that terminals and PCs are kept under lock and key, and ensuring that, where dial-in communication links are in place, that a call-back facility is used
   · keeping tapes or removable disks containing sensitive or confidential information files in a locked cabinet and issuing them only for authorised use.
   · stringently enforcing controls over passwords and ensuring password misuse represents a serious disciplinary offence within the organisation
   · files can be scrambled using data encryption to render them unintelligible unless a decoding password is supplied. Encryption provides a double benefit. It protects against people managing to gain access to the system, and it protects against the tapping of data whilst being transmitted from one machine to another
   · every activity on a system should be logged and be subject to some form of exception reporting, e.g. unusual times of access could be reported

· checking to find out who is doing what at random intervals on the system, and ensuring that they are authorised for those activities
· shielding of VDUs – to protect against people with detection equipment being able to view them remotely.

9 Data protection legislation. In the UK the relevant Act is the Data Protection Act 1998.

10 The reasons your organisation must follow copyright rules are because breaches of copyright can lead to civil prosecution and fines and, in worst cases, criminal prosecution. Also, licensing bodies make regular checks on certain organisations to ensure rules are being followed.

11 The hazards associated with the use of Display Screen Equipment include upper limb disorders, visual difficulties, RSI, fatigue and stress, headaches, skin irritation and back and neck strain.

# HEALTH AND SAFETY IN THE WORKPLACE

**INTRODUCTION**

Every year in the United Kingdom there are thousands of accidents in the office, which result in injury. Typical hazards in an office might include desks/chairs too near to doors, trailing wires, cables and leads, unlit or poorly lit corridors and stairs, top-heavy filing cabinets, unmarked plate glass doors and wet floors.

The consideration, design and implementation of the working environmental factors will be governed by appropriate legal regulations. Although there are many statues, which affect the relationship between an organisation and its employees, the regulations that are relevant to the office environment are outlined in this chapter.

## CONTENTS

1  Health and safety in your workplace
2  Health and Safety legislation and regulations
3  Fire
4  Hazards in the office
5  Minimising hazards in the work area
6  Health and safety policy

## KNOWLEDGE & UNDERSTANDING

· The importance of health and safety in your workplace (Item 1)
· The basic requirements of the health and safety and other legislation and regulations that apply to your workplace (Item 2)
· The person(s) responsible for health, safety and security in your workplace (Item 3)
· The relevant up-to-date information on health and safety that applies to your workplace (Item 4)
· The importance of being alert to health and safety hazards (Item 5)
· The common health and safety hazards that affect people working in an administrative role and how to identify these (Item 6)
· Hazards you can put right yourself and hazards you must report (Item 7)
  The importance of warning others about hazards and how to do so until the hazard is dealt with (Item 8)
· Your organisation's emergency procedures (Item 9)
· How to follow your organisation's emergency procedures and your responsibilities in relation to these (Item 10)
· How to recommend improvements to health and safety (Item 11)
· Health and safety records you may have to complete and how to do so (Item 12)

**PERFORMANCE CRITERIA**
· Make sure you read, comply with and have up-to-date information on the health and safety requirements and procedures for your workplace (Item A in Element 22.1)
· Make sure that the procedures are being followed and report any that are not to the relevant person (Item B in Element 22.1)
· Identify and correct any hazards that you can deal with safely and competently and within the limits of your authority (Item C in Element 22.1)
· Promptly and accurately report any hazards that you are not allowed to deal with to the relevant person and warn other people who may be affected (Item D in Element 22.1)
· Follow your organisation's emergency procedures promptly, calmly and efficiently (Item E in Element 22.1)
· Identify and recommend opportunities for improving health and safety to the responsible person (Item F in Element 22.1)
· Complete any health and safety records legibly and accurately (Item G in Element 22.1)

# 1 Health and safety in your workplace

## 1.1 The importance of health and safety at work

The maintenance of safe working conditions and the prevention of accidents are most important. Top of your list of importance is obviously to protect yourself and others from dangers that might cause injury or sickness.

Health and safety is as important in an office as in a factory. Constant absenteeism through poor working conditions or accidents is costly for any organisation and people do not work as productively if they are ill, tired or in an unsatisfactory environment. It is therefore in the organisation's interests, as well as the employees', that health and safety procedures are observed. The costs of not having adequate measures to ensure health and safety include the following:

· Cash, cheques, equipment, machinery and stock may be destroyed or damaged. If the losses are serious the organisation may have to close down for a time. It may not be possible to complete orders on time, leading to a loss of customers and the consequent effect on profits and jobs.
· There may be serious injury to employees, customers and the general public, which could lead to claims for compensation and damage to the prestige of the organisation.
· Confidential records (e.g. correspondence and information on creditors, debtors and stock) may no longer be available.

Because health and safety at work is so important, there are regulations that require all of us not to put others or ourselves in danger. The regulations are also there to protect the employees from workplace danger.

## 2 Health and Safety legislation and regulations

### 2.1 The basic requirements

Health and safety in the workplace is mainly a matter of common sense but, of course, none of us is entirely sensible all the time. This means that we need to have policies, procedures and rules about making our workplaces safe and healthy so that we are not put at risk whilst working.

The basis of British health and safety law is the Health and Safety at Work etc Act 1974, which is enforceable by law. It provides the legal framework to promote, stimulate and encourage high standards. The Health & Safety Executive and Environmental Health Officers check to make sure that all the regulations currently in force are being complied with by employers and the self employed, so far as is reasonably practicable.

The Act sets out the general duties that employers have towards employees and members of the public, and employees have to themselves and to each other.

The provisions of the Act place a duty on the employer to take all reasonable and practicable steps and precautions to provide a working environment that is safe and free from health hazards. Such steps and provisions should include information regarding the employee's work procedures, operations and general environment and the promoting of instruction, training and supervision. The employer has an obligation to ensure that an employee follows recognised safety codes of practice and is not endangering himself/herself and/or other employees.

> Your employer has a duty to provide the following:
> · safe ways in and out of the place of work
> · a safe working environment
> · safe equipment and procedures
> · arrangements for the safe use, handling, storage and transport of articles and substances
> · adequate information, instruction, training and supervision
> · adequate investigation of accidents.

Failure to do so could result in a criminal prosecution in the Magistrates Court or a Crown Court. Failure to ensure safe working practises could also lead to an employee suing for personal injury or in some cases the employer being prosecuted for corporate manslaughter.

Your employer must also take out Employer's Liability Insurance and display the insurance certificate on the premises. This insurance will cover the employer for any accidents you might have at work.

But it is not only the employer who has a responsibility to make the workplace safe; the employee also has a responsibility to follow the safety rules and to protect both themselves and their colleagues from getting hurt. In some circumstances employers and employees can be prosecuted if they cause an accident by not following the health and safety regulations.

> You as an employee (or a self-employed person) must:
> · take care of your own health and safety in the workplace and not endanger the people you work with
> · co-operate with anyone carrying out duties under the Act (including the employer)
> · make sure you know what the health and safety rules of your employer are and keep these rules
> · correctly use work items provided by your employer including personal protective equipment in accordance with training or instructions, and
> · never interfere with or misuse anything provided for your health, safety or welfare.

As you can see, your employer has a duty to provide a safe working environment, but you, the employee, have a duty to look after yourself and other people within that environment.

### 2.2  Duties of employer – Consulting employees

Under the Health and Safety (Consultation with Employees) Regulations 1996, employers must consult either directly with their employees or through an elected representative on health and safety matters. This involves giving information to employees and listening to and taking account of their concerns before any health and safety decisions are taken. Issues could include:
· the planning of health and safety training
· changes to equipment or procedures which may substantially affect the health and safety of employees at work
· the consequences of introducing new technology.

### 2.3  Duties of employer – rules on safety procedures

It is always advisable for employers to have a written code of conduct, rules regarding training & supervision, and rules on safety procedures. This should include information on basic health and safety requirements.

Posters/leaflets (published by the HSE) with information relating to health, safety and welfare must be displayed in a prominent place in the work area.

They should include the following details:
· the name and address of the enforcing authority
· the address of the Employment Medical Advisory Service
· the persons responsible for health and safety management
· the name and location of trade union or other safety representatives and the groups they represent.

### 2.4  Duties of employer – Risk assessment

An employer should assess the level of risk as against the cost of eliminating that risk in deciding whether they have taken reasonable steps as far as they are able. Another requirement is for employers to carry out a risk assessment and assess the level of risk as against the cost of eliminating that risk in deciding whether they have taken reasonable steps as far as they are able. Employers with five or more employees need to record the significant findings of the risk assessment and identify any group of employees who are especially at risk. The objective is to minimise the risk the employees may face by taking whatever practical action is necessary, some of which may be required by statute.

Risk assessment should be straightforward in a simple workplace such as a typical office. It should only be complicated if it deals with serious hazards such as those on a nuclear power station, a chemical plant, laboratory or an oil rig.

*Risk Assessment should only be complicated if it deals with serious hazards*

This process is legally required for all work activities and operations and involves:

· **Identifying** any hazards within the business.
· **Deciding** who might be harmed by them.
· **Evaluating** those risks, the existing control measures and if any changes need to be made.
· **Recording** your findings (for five or more employees only).
· **Reviewing** and revising the assessment as changes in the business occur.

Besides carrying out a risk assessment, employers also need to:

· make arrangements for implementing the health and safety measures identified as necessary by the risk assessment
· appoint competent people (often themselves or company colleagues) to help them to implement the arrangements
· set up emergency procedures
· work together with other employers sharing the same workplace
· provide adequate first-aid facilities
· make sure the workplace satisfies health, safety and welfare requirements e.g. for ventilation, temperature, lighting and sanitary, washing and rest facilities
· ensure that appropriate safety signs are provided and maintained, and
· report certain injuries, diseases and dangerous occurrences to the appropriate health and safety enforcing authority

Other regulations require action in response to particular hazards, or in industries where hazards are particularly high.

### 2.5  Duties of employer – Policy statement

For organisations with more than five employees, there must be a written statement of the safety measures and the means used to implement them, which should be brought to the notice of all employees. Where there is a recognised trade union in the workplace, which has appointed a safety representative, that person must be consulted when drawing up the safety policy.

This document, outlining the company's rules, regulations and procedures, will include the following:

· details about how to report accidents
· where the accident book is kept
· the position of the first aid box
· details of qualified first-aid personnel
· the names and duties of the official safety representatives and the manager in charge of safety policy
· information on safe working practices throughout the organisation.

### 2.6 EU Regulations and Codes of Practice

The UK has incorporated certain European Union health and safety at work regulations into UK law. These were introduced to ensure that EU member states had the same standards to allow for fair competition between businesses working within the Union. The areas covered by the regulations are:

1. **Management of Health and Safety at Work Regulations (Management Regulations)** places an obligation on the employer to actively carry out a risk assessment of the work place and act accordingly. The assessment must be reviewed when necessary and recorded where there are five or more employees. It is intended to identify health and safety and fire risks.

2. **Workplace (Health, Safety and Welfare) Regulations** deals with any modification, extension or conversion of an existing workplace. The requirements include control of temperature, lighting, ventilation, cleanliness, room dimensions, etc. The regulations also provide that non-smokers should be allocated separate rest areas from smokers.

3. **The Provision And Use Of Work Equipment Regulations** deals with minimum standards for the use of machines and equipment with regard to suitability, maintenance and inspection.

4. **The Manual Handling Operations Regulations (Manual Handling Regulations)** deals with the manual handling of equipment, stocks, materials, etc. The term 'manual handling operations' means any transporting or supporting of a load (including the lifting, putting down, pushing, pulling, carrying or moving thereof) by hand or by bodily force. Where reasonably practicable an employer should avoid the need for his or her employees to undertake manual handling involving risk of injury.

5. **Personal Protective Equipment Work Regulations (PPE)** – the main requirement is that personal protective equipment is to be supplied – free of charge – and used at work wherever there are risks to health and safety that cannot be adequately controlled in other ways. The Directive applies to any device or appliance designed to be worn or held by an individual for protection against one or more health and safety hazards. It includes gloves, protective clothing, footwear, sunglasses, helmets and respiratory protective devices.

6.  **The Health & Safety (Display Screen Equipment) Regulations (Display Screen Regulations)** cover the use of VDUs and microfiches at work and introduced measures to prevent repetitive strain injury, fatigue, eye problems etc. in the use of technological equipment. Every employer should make a suitable and sufficient analysis of each workstation and surrounding work environment to ensure it meets the detailed requirements set out in the Regulations. This includes eyesight tests on request, breaks from using the equipment and provision of health and safety information about the equipment to the employee. The Health and Safety Executive advises that breaks should happen before tiredness sets in and affects productivity, and that short regular breaks are better than longer, occasional ones. Breaks should be part of the normal working day.

## 2.7 Management of Health and Safety at Work

Other relevant Regulations include:

·   **Working Time Directive and Working Time Regulations** – regulates the maximum working hours for workers, (including night workers) and free health assessments to assess suitability to work particular hours. It also governs rest periods and breaks.

·   **The Reporting of Injuries, Diseases and Dangerous Occurrences Regulations (RIDDOR)** – employers must notify the Health and Safety Executive or local authority about work accidents resulting in death, personal injury or sickness where an employee is off work for more than three days. Records must be kept of all such accidents at the workplace for at least three years. Accident books must be kept where an employer employs ten or more persons on the same premises. (If the employment is at a mine, quarry or factory, accident books must be kept regardless of the number of employees.)

·   **Electricity at Work Regulations** – place a duty on an employer to assess risks involved in work activities involving electricity, (this can even cover electrical appliances such as kettles). All such equipment must be properly maintained.

·   **Fire Precautions (Workplace) (Amendment) Regulations** – the fire authority should inspect all workplaces to check the means of escape, fire-fighting equipment and warnings and to issue a fire certificate. A breach of a fire certificate could lead to a prosecution of the employer or responsible manager or other staff member.

·   **The Health and Safety (First Aid) Regulations** state that there should be adequate and appropriate equipment, facilities and personnel to enable first aid to be given to an employee if they are injured or become ill at work. First aid means treating minor injuries at work and giving immediate attention to more serious casualties until medical help is available. An employer must provide a suitably stocked first aid box and appoint a person to take charge of first-aid arrangements.

·   **Employers Liability (Compulsory Insurance) Regulations** – employers must insure against liability for injury or disease sustained by an employee in the course of their employment. The sum to be insured is not less than £5 million.

·   **Noise at Work Regulations (Noise Regulations)** – imposes a duty on employers to reduce risk of damage to hearing of employees from exposure to noise.

Regulations made under the Act have the same scope and provide the potential to achieve clear and uniform standards. They cover areas such as the work environment, fire, first aid, VDUs, noise, stress, lifting loads manually and chemicals.

The Management of Health and Safety at Work Regulations 1999 place a legal obligation on all employers to provide staff with health and safety training. This training should form part of an induction process and there should also be regular reminder sessions.

During their induction, staff should be told about the organisation's overall approach and commitment to health and safety standards. Employees should be reminded that they have a legal duty to take care of themselves, fellow workers and anybody else they come into contact with while at work.

Training should focus on hazards that staff will come into contact with during an average working day. For example, they might need to know correct lifting procedures, or how to deal with a leak or spillage. If they use any hazardous equipment, they must get proper training before they are allowed to operate it.

During training, staff should be reminded of their duty to report accidents, hazards or safety defects, as well as any narrowly avoided accidents. Employers should take care to ensure that young or inexperienced staff have understood their training.

### 2.8  Workplace (Health, Safety and Welfare)

The Regulations cover many aspects of health, safety and welfare in the work-place and apply to nearly all places of work.

They set general requirements for employers in:
·   The working environment including: temperature; ventilation; lighting including emergency lighting; room dimensions; suitability of workstations and seating; and outdoor workstations (e.g. weather protection).
·   Safety including: safe passage of pedestrians and vehicles, windows and skylights (safe opening, closing and cleaning); glazed doors and partitions (use of safe material and marking); doors, gates and escalators (safety devices); floors (their construction, obstruction slipping and tripping hazards); falls from heights and into dangerous substances; and falling objects.
·   Facilities including: toilets, washing, eating and changing facilities; clothing storage, seating, rest areas (and arrangements in them for non-smokers); and rest facilities; cleanliness; and removal of waste materials.
·   Housekeeping including maintenance of the workplace, its equipment and facilities; cleanliness and removal of waste materials.

Equally, as an employee you must:

·    read instructions
·    understand and take note of warning signs – there are four types:

·    dress and behave safely
·    report any problems to your supervisor or to the health and safety officer.

If you think there is a health and safety problem in your workplace, you should first discuss it with your employer, supervisor or manager. You may also wish to discuss it with your safety representative, if there is one.

If you think your employer is exposing you to risks or is not carrying out legal duties, and you have pointed this out without getting a satisfactory reply, you can contact the enforcing authority for health and safety in your workplace. Health and Safety Inspectors can give advice on how to comply with the law. They also have powers to enforce it.

## 3    Fire

### 3.1  Introduction

It is not very likely that you will experience a fire or have to fight it but your employer should instruct you in the following on your first day at work:
·    where the fire-fighting equipment is
·    where the nearest fire alarm is
·    how to operate the alarm
·    what you have to do if the alarm sounds
·    where the nearest fire exit is
·    where you have to assemble once you are out of the building.

To guard as much as possible against fire there must be provided the means of:
(a)     warning
(b)     fighting the fire
(c)     escape.

### 3.2 Warning

The means of warning may be manual or automatic. Manual methods include breaking the glass on fire alarms, bells, rattles and sirens. Automatic methods include smoke and heat detectors. Some large organisations install personal computer based control systems, which monitor unusual occurrences such as fires, in addition to preventing unauthorised access.

Employers must make sure that, in the event of a fire, there are set procedures to follow, for example, for evacuating the building and contacting the emergency services. To make this easier, employees should be nominated to implement these measures and be trained accordingly. The premises must have sufficient fire exits for the number of staff employed. These exits must be clearly marked, lead as directly as possible to a safe area and be kept clear at all times. If routes require lighting, then there must be an emergency power supply in the event of the failure of the main system. To ensure that employees are aware of the evacuation procedures, fire drills must be held regularly, Fire Action notices (see HSE publication below) should be displayed prominently and all equipment must be well-maintained and checked to see that it is in good working order.

### 3.3 Fighting the fire

Under the Health and Safety at Work Act 1974, every employer has a duty to ensure that their workplace has appropriate fire-fighting equipment and is fitted with detectors and alarms.

Extinguishers, sand buckets, hosepipes and sprinklers must be examined regularly to check that they are in working order. In the event of a fire that cannot be put out quickly, the fire brigade must be called without delay.

Generally speaking, portable fire extinguishers can be divided into five categories according to the extinguishing medium they contain:
- water – use on fires involving freely burning materials, for example wood, paper, textiles and other carbonaceous materials
- foam – use on fires involving flammable liquids, for example petrol and spirits. NOT ALCOHOL OR COOKING OIL
- powder – use on fires involving flammable gases, for example propane and butane
- carbon dioxide – use on fires involving electrical equipment, for example photocopiers, fax machines and computers
- wet chemical – use on fires involving cooking oil and fat, for example olive oil and butter.

It is now compulsory for all fire extinguishers to have a sign in both text and icons explaining the extinguishers' uses.

They are not all suitable for every kind of fire. For example, water based extinguishers should not be used on electrical fires or on burning liquids. It is vital to use this type of equipment in accordance with the manufacturer's instructions. A zone of colour of up to 5% of the external area, positioned immediately above or within the section used to provide the operating instructions, may be used to identify the type of extinguisher.

The most useful form of fire-fighting equipment for general fire risks is the water-type extinguisher or hose reel. One such extinguisher should be provided for approximately each 200 square metres of floor space, with a minimum of one per floor.

Fire extinguishers should normally be located in conspicuous positions on escape routes, preferably near exit doors. Wherever possible, fire-fighting equipment should be grouped to form fire points. These should be clearly visible or their location clearly and conspicuously indicated so that fire points can be readily identified. Where workplaces are uniform in layout, extinguishers should normally be located at similar positions on each floor.
When using an extinguisher remember the phrase, '**PASS**.'

- **P**ull out the pin.
- **A**im the extinguisher nozzle at the base of the flames.
- **S**queeze the trigger while holding the extinguisher upright.
- **S**weep the extinguisher from side to side, covering the area of the fire with the extinguishing agent

Where hose reels are provided, they should be located where they are conspicuous and always accessible, such as in corridors.

Fire blankets should be located in the vicinity of the fire hazard they are to be used on, but in a position that can be safely accessed in the event of a fire. They are classified as either light-duty or heavy-duty. Light-duty fire blankets are suitable for dealing with small fires in containers of cooking oils or fats and fires involving clothing. Heavy-duty fire blankets are for industrial use where there is a need for the blanket to resist penetration by molten materials.

## ▷ ACTIVITY 1   ▷ ▷ ▷ ▷

Look at the two fire extinguishers illustrated below. Which one would you use in each of the following circumstances?

(a) Overloading of an electrical circuit leads to an outbreak of fire, spreading throughout the electrical installation concerned.

(b) A smouldering cigarette is dropped in amongst some discarded cloths and leads to an outbreak of fire in a wooden hut.

This activity covers performance criterion A in Element 22.1.

[Answer on p. 89]

### 3.4 Escape

The effectiveness of the means of escape depends on how and where they are situated. Escape routes must be labelled and signposted and ideally should have emergency lighting.

KAPLAN PUBLISHING

Fire exit doors must not be obstructed or locked from the outside.

You should ensure that you know where the fire exits are in your working environment.

### 3.5 Emergency procedures

Each organisation should plan, implement and communicate appropriate safety procedures in the case of an emergency. This might be a fire, bomb threat, explosion or armed intrusion.

The main points to remember are as follows:

| |
|---|
| adequately trained and briefed staff should be appointed to conduct evacuation or other procedures |
| all employees must know their fire drill: the escape routes, the location of the nearest fire exit and where they have to assemble when evacuating the building (for whatever reason) |
| fire alarms should be placed throughout the building so that everyone can hear them; they should be tested on a regular basis during working hours so that employees recognise the sound |
| fire doors must be kept closed and routes leading out of endangered areas should always be monitored with particular care to ensure they are free from obstruction |
| gangways and passages must be kept clear |
| rubbish should not be allowed to accumulate |
| 'No Smoking' area regulations must be observed |
| inflammable items must be stored away from anything that will cause them to ignite |
| waste paper baskets must not be used as ashtrays |
| damaged gas and electrical appliances must be reported immediately. |

Each individual in an organisation must know the procedure to follow in the event of a emergency. Make sure you know how to contact your first-aider, fire officer and security officer.

# 4 Hazards in the office

## 4.1 Being aware of hazards

A hazard is defined by the current health and safety legislation as something with the potential to cause harm (e.g. chemicals, electricity, working from ladders, etc). Risk is the chance, high or low, that someone will be harmed by the hazard. Risk assessment is actually the identification of hazards in the workplace and the quantifying of the risk that such hazards might cause harm. This means:

· looking for hazards
· deciding who might be harmed, and how
· evaluating the risks arising and deciding if existing precautions are adequate
· recording your findings
· reviewing your assessment periodically and revising as necessary.

Obviously an office does not have the same hazards as a building site or factory but, to be able to operate safely within the workplace, you need to be aware of what is potentially hazardous.

Become aware of any hazards around your own workstation. Is the area around you free from hazards, e.g. objects lying on the floor, overloaded electrical sockets, trailing leads, top-heavy bookcases, overloaded filing cabinets? This is known as good housekeeping and is vital if you are to protect yourself and others.

Some of these hazards can be dealt with easily e.g. you can close filing cabinet drawers or rearrange cables so that they are not trailing across gangways.

You must also be aware of the limits to your own authority in dealing with hazards. This is partly a matter of studying your organisation's published policy, but also boils down in many cases to common sense. Potential hazards that you cannot deal with yourself e.g. frayed cables or broken windows should be reported immediately to the person identified in company procedures.

## 4.2 Types of hazard

There are several categories that we could divide hazards into:

(i) **Housekeeping and premises** - relating to cleanliness, waste disposal, safe storage and stacking, clear exits and gangways, use of equipment such as ladders. There are a number of rules governing where you work in terms of warning signs, noise, temperature, ventilation, toilets, washing and eating facilities, machinery and equipment. The Regulations also require workers to be protected from loud noise. Employers must reduce noise levels as far as is reasonably possible. If having done this the daily noise exposure level is equivalent to the noise of a heavy lorry, workers must be provided with ear protectors and the area where they are to be used should be marked.

(ii) **Electrical equipment** – installations including plugs and cables, extension leads and portable equipment. Each year about 1,000 accidents at work involving electric shock or burns are reported to the HSE. They are caused by:

- damaged plugs or sockets
- faulty wiring and/or exposed wires
- overloading of electrical circuits
- liquids brought into contact with electrical circuits
- incorrect extraction of plugs from sockets. (You should first turn off the switch, then grasp the plug to remove it; do not just pull on the cord.)

It is important that you do not change fuses or plugs if not authorised to do so, overload electrical sockets, for example, using fan heaters from extension sockets or use equipment that is faulty or appears to be damaged.

If any electrical equipment is faulty or damaged it should be reported to the manager. Such equipment should not be used until it is repaired.

(iii) **Mechanical equipment** – use and care of protective equipment, noise and checking and maintenance of appliances. This category includes not just machine presses or other heavy manufacturing equipment, but also simple office equipment such as hole punches, scissors and paper knives, guillotines and staplers. Any machine with moving parts is a hazard if an individual gets his/her clothing tangled in it. Long hair can also be a hazard if you work with such equipment.

We have already looked at the hazards in the use of Display Screen Equipment. VDUs are now a common feature in every aspect of our work and a cause of increasing concern over recent years. However, if used as recommended it has been shown that they do not have properties which are inherently dangerous to health. Where problems do occur, they are generally caused by the way in which they are being used, rather than the VDUs themselves. The kinds of disorder that may arise are associated with the individual's posture while working at a VDU, the glare from the VDU screen and the repetitive nature of the tasks carried out at a VDU (e.g. inputting data via a keyboard).

(iv) **Dangerous substances** – some substances used at work, or which arise from a work activity, are considered to be hazardous. Equipment and machinery in use in offices may need liquid or powder additives containing corrosive or toxic chemicals. There may even be flammable substances, such as spirits, which give off fumes. Tippex, glue or other solvents are harmful if inhaled or swallowed or if they come into contact with your eyes. The Control of Substances Hazardous to Health Regulations require employers to control or prevent employees' exposure to such substances.

(v)  **Stress** – many people argue about the definition and sometimes even the existence of 'stress'. However, research has shown that whatever you choose to call it, there is a clear link between poor work organisation and subsequent ill health. Stress at work can be tackled in the same way as any other risk to health – by identifying the hazards, assessing who is at risk and the level of risk, deciding how to manage the risk and putting the plans into action. Hazards can include lack of control over the way you do your work, work over-load (or underload), lack of support from your managers, conflicting or ambiguous roles, poor relationships with colleagues (including bullying), or poor management of organisational change.

Typical hazards in an office might include:
(a)  desks/chairs too near to doors
(b)  unsafe electric plugs
(c)  trailing wires, cables and leads
(d)  torn carpets and other floor coverings
(e)  unlit or poorly lit corridors and stairs
(f)  top-heavy filing cabinets and drawers left open
(g)  untrained operators using machines such as guillotines
(h)  unmarked plate glass doors
(i)  projecting door and drawer handles
(j)  wet floors.

There are, of course, potentially many others; this list is not intended to be fully comprehensive.

## 5  Minimising hazards in the work area

### 5.1  Personal safety checklist

The following questions should be considered:

(a)  Do you know how to operate equipment properly?

(b)  Do you always ask for assistance when using dangerous machinery for the first time?

(c)  Do you always look at the manual before carrying out any unusual procedures (e.g. clearing paper jams from the inside of a photocopier)?

(d)  Do you always report hazards and leave any electrical work (e.g. repairing equipment) to qualified electricians?

(e)  Do you know how to move objects and equipment safely within the work environment?

(f)  Do you keep your back straight and bend your knees when you pick up objects?

(g)  Do you ask for help when you need it, e.g. when carrying heavy objects, or negotiating doors or stairs?

Much of this is common sense but you do need to be aware of it when in the working environment.

## 5.2    Office layout and organisation

Office layout is determined by economy of space, efficiency and security but the safety of the occupants should not be forgotten. Where there is insufficient space for people and equipment and movement is restricted, there may be safety hazards. Particular attention must be given to accessing emergency equipment and emergency exits. Some common sense measures for minimising hazards include the following:

- Arrange furniture, filing cabinets etc so as to promote a logical workflow and minimise the need for employees to walk to and fro throughout the day.
- Where possible, obstructions should be removed to prevent trips occurring. If it is not possible to remove an obstruction then suitable barriers and/or warning notices should be used.
- Floors should be checked for damage on a regular basis and maintenance carried out when necessary. Potential slip and trip hazards to look for include holes, cracks, and loose carpets and mats.
- Locate any activities needing light close to windows.
- Use the ground floor for activities involving heavy machinery or goods etc, so as to avoid any need for manoeuvring such objects up and down stairs
- Many accidents occur on stairways. Handrails, slip resistant covers to steps, high visibility and non-slip marking of the front edges of steps, and sufficient lighting can all help in preventing slips and trips on stairs. Other changes of level such as ramps are often difficult to see. They need to be well marked, with appropriate use of safety signs.
- Poor housekeeping and general untidiness are a major cause of slips and trips. The working environment should be kept clean and tidy, with floors and access routes kept clear of obstacles. Rubbish must be removed regularly so it does not build up.
- Ensure that secure ladders or other suitable equipment is available near to high shelving.
- Encourage each employee to arrange his/her workstation in a safe and efficient manner (e.g. keep heavy files within easy reach to avoid straining after them; keep drawers closed to avoid causing obstructions; adjust seats to achieve a comfortable posture).
- Avoid slippery or uneven floors.
- Ensure that cords, cables and leads are tidied away where they cannot cause an obstruction (e.g. use trip-guards or trunking on electrical cables, particularly for office equipment).
- Ensure that doors, passages and gangways are free of obstructions.

Although the possible safety hazards are exaggerated in the picture below, try to identify them and suggest appropriate action in accordance with the Health and Safety at Work legislation.

## ▷ ACTIVITY 2 ▷ ▷ ▷ ▷

Walk around your department or building and make a list of anything that is potentially dangerous. Things to look out for include:
(a)     piles of rubbish left near an entrance way
(b)     drawers to filing cabinets left open
(c)     fire extinguishers not maintained and inspected
(d)     fire doors jammed open
(e)     electric plugs overloaded.

[There is no answer to this activity]

Remember that you have a duty to look after yourself and others in your environment.

### 5.3  Lifting and moving loads manually

Lifting and moving loads manually is the biggest cause of injury, so it is important when lifting, to use the right method – following written instructions or procedures. These are likely to include the following:
·   Get close to the load and stand with the feet apart for stability.
·   Attempt to hold or manipulate loads with the hands as close as possible to the body.  An individual's capacity to manage loads reduces dramatically the further away from the body he places his hands.
·   use the correct posture when handling loads.  People dealing regularly with heavy loads should be given appropriate instruction as to the most suitable posture.
·   Bend the knees sufficiently to grasp the item and provide leverage.

KAPLAN PUBLISHING

· Use the strong muscles in the legs, not the back, to stand up and lift the load. Avoid lifting loads too high in a single movement, or carrying them over too long a distance.
· Lower the load using the same principles (bending the knees, keeping the load close, good grip).

### 5.4 Use of protective equipment

For many kinds of operation, particularly in manufacturing contexts, the use of protective equipment is clearly essential. It is the duty of the employer to decide in each case what equipment is needed and then to provide it (free of charge) to the employees concerned. It is also the employee's duty not to interfere with or misuse anything provided to protect their health, safety and welfare. Protective equipment may include items of clothing, such as aprons, gloves, footwear, helmets etc and other types of equipment, such as life jackets, safety harnesses or visors to protect the eyes.

### 5.5  The use of substances

Many kinds of manufacturing operations involve the use of substances but hazardous chemicals are also found in almost all modern offices, chemicals in photocopiers and printers being obvious examples.
The Control of Substances Hazardous to Health 2 Regulations (COSHH2) came into force to protect employees from noxious substances and require employers to:
· determine the hazard posed by substances
· assess the risk presented to people's health
· prevent anyone being exposed, or
· control the exposure to reduce the risk
· ensure controls are in place for the substance's proper use
· inform, instruct and train employees in the proper use of substances, and to
· monitor exposure to substances and conduct regular health surveillance.

### ▷ ACTIVITY 3          ▷ ▷ ▷ ▷

Jonty Sheds Ltd is a small family-run business involved in the manufacture of garden furniture, sheds and summerhouses. Shed panels or whole items of garden furniture are suspended in huge baths of industrial wood preservative before being manually removed by operatives. Recently there has been some suggestion that chemicals in the wood preservative may be carcinogenic.

(a)  What duties does Jonty Sheds Ltd have toward employees under the Health and Safety legislation?
(b)  What responsibilities do employees have to protect their own health and that of their colleagues?

This activity covers performance criteria A and B in Element 22.1.

[Answer on p. 90]

### 5.6 Hazards you can deal with yourself – working at a VDU

Employees who spend a large part of their working day working at a VDU risk various problems including eye strain, back problems and repetitive strain injury (RSI). RSI appears to arise from making the same movements over and over again and affects hands and arms.

To minimise the risk of problems, there are certain things you can do:

- Adjust your chair and VDU to find the most comfortable position for your work. As a broad guide, your forearms should be approximately horizontal and your eyes the same height as the top of the VDU. A space in front of the keyboard is sometimes helpful for resting the hands and wrists when not keying. Good posture can be easily achieved if the chair and desk area are well set up for the tasks in hand.

 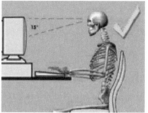

- Make sure there is space under your desk to move your legs freely. Move any obstacles such as boxes or equipment. Avoid excess pressure from the edge of your seat on the backs of your legs and knees. A footrest may be helpful, particularly for smaller users.
- If you use a laptop, work with it on a table, never on your lap.
- Make sure you have enough workspace to take whatever documents or other equipment you need. Try different arrangements of keyboard, screen, mouse and documents to find the best arrangement for you. A document holder may help you avoid awkward neck and eye movements. Position the mouse within easy reach, so it can be used with the wrist straight. Sit upright and close to the desk, so you don't have to work with your mouse arm stretched. Move the keyboard out of the way if it is not being used.
- Arrange your desk and VDU to avoid glare, or bright reflections on the screen. This will be easiest if neither you nor the screen is directly facing windows or bright lights. Adjust curtains or blinds to prevent unwanted light. Adjust the brightness and contrast controls on the screen to suit lighting conditions in the room.
- In setting up software, choose options giving text that is large enough to read easily on your screen, when you are sitting in a normal, comfortable working position. Select colours that are easy on the eye (avoid red text on a blue background, or vice-versa). Individual characters on the screen should be sharply focused and should not flicker or move. If they do, the VDU may need servicing or adjustment.
- Do not sit in the same position for long periods. Make sure you change your posture as often as practicable. Some movement is desirable, but avoid

repeated stretching to reach things you need (if this happens a lot, rearrange your workstation).

· Try to break up periods of computer use with other work: phone calls, writing/reading work, talking with colleagues. Even coffee breaks! Some work – e.g. checking for spelling errors – is better done with a printed off draft rather than on screen. Aim for at least a five-minute break every hour and do not spend a whole day on computer-based activities. If you work on a computer at home, remember to fit in breaks there as well. Surfing the net or playing computer games do not count as a break.

## ▷ ACTIVITY 4

Look at the 'before' and 'after' drawings below (which are reproduced from a publication of the Health and Safety Executive A Pain in your Workplace: Ergonomic Problems and Solutions.)  Identify the improvements that have been made.

This activity covers performance criterion A in Element 22.1.

[Answer on p. 90]

### 5.7 Hazards you can deal with yourself – machinery and electrical equipment

People using particular pieces of equipment regularly should be given appropriate training, as well as access to full instruction manuals for reference purposes. You must observe the manufacturer's instructions in operating any machinery. This applies to office items such as photocopiers and computers.

Ensure that all guards and safety devices are in place when the equipment is in use. Do not be tempted to remove guards in order to improve speed or performance. If a machine becomes jammed be sure to follow instructions, switching the machine off if necessary. Beware when applying oils, powders or other chemicals to equipment. Many such additives are toxic.

Basic tasks involving electricity should be done with great care. Potential hazards can be minimised by:
· not overloading electrical circuits
· keeping liquids out of contact with electrical circuits
· taking plugs from sockets correctly. (You should first turn off the switch, then grasp the plug to remove it; do **not** just pull on the cord.)

All equipment should be properly maintained and tested at recommended intervals.

### 5.8 Hazards you can deal with yourself – work related stress

It is easier to define and protect the physical well-being of employees than their mental well-being. Health and Safety legislation and ergonomics all try to make sure that work can be carried out for the duration of a person's career, without damage to health or efficiency. Unfortunately, work related stress can have a negative impact on an individual's performance and can lead to job dissatisfaction, accidents, high labour turnover and absenteeism. Stress arises from an imbalance between the demands made upon individuals and their capacity to cope with such demands.

Alleviation of stress can be achieved by:
· attempting to control the situation e.g. by avoiding unrealistic deadlines
· discussing problems with others
· planning carefully the time available for doing jobs
· obtaining sufficient exercise and relaxation.

---

### ▷ ACTIVITY 5

What action would you take in each of the following cases?
· You notice two boxes of stationery placed in front of a fire exit.
· You notice that the casing of an electric socket is coming away from the wall.
· You are last to leave the office one evening and you notice that the photocopier has been left on.
· You realise that a heavy file you use in work is awkwardly positioned on a high shelf just above and behind your shoulder.
· In a recent office reorganisation you find that your desk has ended up squarely in front of a fire extinguisher.
· A filing cabinet, which is used regularly by all staff in your office, is placed where you can conveniently reach files without leaving your seat. Other staff must reach awkwardly around the edge of your desk to access the cabinet.

This activity covers performance criteria C and D in Element 22.1.

[Answer on p. 91]

---

## 6 Health and safety policy

### 6.1 Starting a new job.... what to find out

When you start a new job you will be given lots of information about the organisation, the buildings, your work routine and people you will work with. Information about how health and safety works in your organisation should be given to you on your first day at work. This includes:

· the company health and safety policy
· the person who is responsible for health and safety
· the person who is the first aider
· the written health and safety rules
· what to do in case of fire
· who your supervisor is.

Ask about any signs that you see and do not understand.

Your supervisor will need to know if you have any disabilities such as asthma, epilepsy or colour-blindness.

Remember that Health and Safety rules will change, you will need to keep your knowledge up to date.

## 6.2  Health and Safety management

The proper and effective management of health and safety can reduce the risk of accidents occupational ill health and the associated costs that go with them.

Good health and safety management at work will involve the following:
· **Planning** – setting out a programme to tackle the identified hazards.
· **Organising** – who will deal with each identified area and in what timescale.
· **Controlling** - deciding what control measures would be appropriate and suitable.
· **Monitoring** – checking that those controls are operating effectively.
· **Reviewing** – setting a date for future reviews of control measures and systems.

By incorporating the above into a written 'health & safety policy' organisations can comply with the prime duty contained in the 1974 Act.

Each business operator should appoint a **'competent person'** to assist in complying with health and safety legal requirements. They should have sufficient training, expertise and knowledge to carry out their functions and may be appointed from within the business itself.

## 6.3  What you should do in the event of serious accident or illness

> · Stay calm.
> · Act quickly.
> · Call for assistance.

Staff at your organisation will be trained in first aid and names should be displayed on notice boards. Contact one of them and/or telephone 999 and obtain the required service. Report the accident briefly and accurately, stating the exact location. Make sure someone meets the ambulance at the main entrance to the building. Be aware of the following basic first aid actions:

- **Do not move the casualty** unless in imminent danger. Stay with him/her if possible. Take care not to endanger yourself.
- In the case of an **electric shock**, do not touch the casualty unless confident that the current is switched off.
- If **vomiting**, turn the casualty on his/her side to allow draining.
- Stem any **bleeding** by applying pressure to wound and elevating the affected area.
- **Reassure the casualty** that help is on the way.

### 6.4 Reporting of accidents

Accidents could be described as 'incidents at work, or as a result of a work activity, which cause injury'. They are caused by many different things, from 'not looking where you are going' to bricks falling on someone's head. Almost all accidents are caused by unsafe acts or unsafe conditions, often both. Most can be avoided.

> The following are some of the most common causes of accidents at work:
> - obstructions – objects left on the floor
> - falling objects
> - lifting heavy objects
> - wet and slippery floors
> - machines – unsafe or unguarded
> - electricity – leads and plugs
> - slipping and tripping.

When an accident occurs at work it must always be reported. Even accidents that seem at the time insignificant might become a problem later on. The information enables the Health and Safety Executive (HSE) and local authorities (referred to as 'the enforcing authorities') to identify where and how risks arise and to investigate serious accidents.

RIDDOR stands for the Reporting of Injuries, Diseases and Dangerous Occurrences Regulations 1995. It places a legal duty on employers, the self-employed and those in control of premises to report some work-related accidents, diseases and dangerous occurrences to the relevant enforcing authority for their work activity. The regulations also include, under the definition of accidents, any acts of violence that occur towards a person at work and also acts of suicide committed on railway or tramway systems.

If any of the following occur, and arise 'out of or in connection with a work activity', they must be reported to the Incident Contact Centre at Caerphilly Business Park, Caerphilly CF83 3GG by the quickest practicable means:
- the death of any person as a result of an accident, whether or not they are at work
- someone who is at work suffers a major injury as a result of an accident (major injuries are listed in Schedule 1 to the Regulations)
- someone who is not at work (e.g. a member of the public/guest/customer) suffers an injury as a result of an accident and is taken from the scene to a hospital

· one of a list of specified dangerous occurrences takes place. (Dangerous occurrences are events that do not necessarily result in a reportable injury, but have the potential to cause significant harm.)

Any telephone or e-mail notification should be followed up in writing within ten days of the accident occurring. The statutory form for accident reporting is an F2508.

The following incidents, again in connection with a work activity, should only be notified in writing within ten days – also on an F2508 form:

· someone at work is unable to do the full range of their normal duties for more than three consecutive days as a result of an injury caused by an accident at work
· a person at work suffers one of a number of specified diseases, provided that a doctor diagnoses the disease and the person's job involves a specified work activity.

A copy of the F2508 form is shown below:

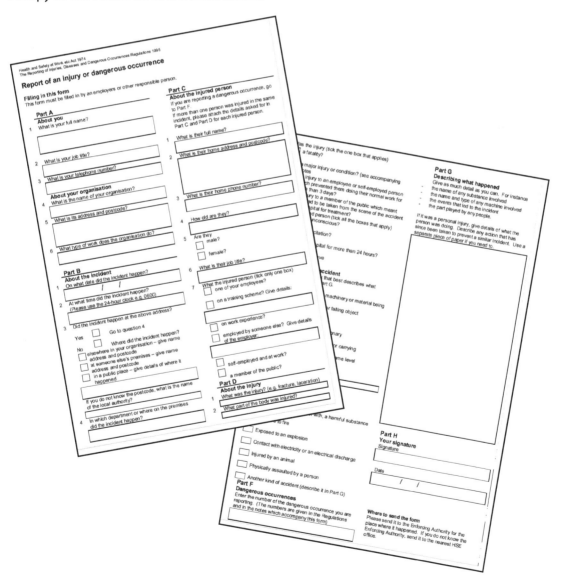

### 6.5 Illness

Simple illness is not normally a great problem in the workplace. Unlike with accidents, employees are not likely to be suddenly afflicted with a serious illness. Of course, this can occasionally happen (e.g. food poisoning from a meal eaten the previous night), but the remedy is usually simple, and in more extreme cases will be dealt with simply by getting the employee to hospital as quickly as possible. From the health and safety perspective, therefore, the main concern under this head is the possibility of communicable disease. Clearly employees suffering from a contagious or infectious illness should be encouraged to stay at home and seek suitable treatment from their doctor, rather than reporting in to work and possibly spreading the illness.

> ☐ **DEFINITION**    ☐ ☐ ☐ ☐
>
> **Communicable disease** – contagious or infectious illness.

Your organisation will have procedures for reporting illness. This normally includes requiring employees or their representative phoning the manager of their department as early as possible on the first day of the illness. It is obviously helpful to indicate how long the illness is likely to last if possible. They will also have procedures in respect of providing medical certificates and/or self-certification.

Some more serious complaints are referred to as **reportable diseases** because there is a duty on the employer to report them to the relevant authority (on form F2508A). These complaints include some poisonings, some skin diseases (such as skin cancer), lung disease (such as pneumoconiosis, common in miners), occupational asthma, asbestosis and certain infections (such as hepatitis and tuberculosis).

### 6.6 Accident book

An accident book should be provided on your premises (a simple exercise book labelled 'Accident Book' will suffice) and staff should be aware of where the book is normally kept. The book should be used to record any relevant details of accidents affecting employees, visitors or members of the public which either occur on your premises or as a result of the work activities associated with your business – whether the accident is a notifiable one or not. For example, a driver engaged on company business might cause damage to property as a result of careless driving.

It will give details of:
· the injured person (name, address, age, department, etc)
· the injury sustained
· details of the accident or injury (what happened, date, time and location)
· first aid or medical treatment received
· name (and if necessary, address) of witness(es).

It is recommended that the accident book be reviewed periodically to ensure that reportable accidents are not missed, and to identify possible trends in accident occurrences. It is also recommended that 'near miss' incidents are recorded and reviewed, as these indicate where accidents are likely and, if acted upon, can prevent injuries.

Where you have any doubt as to whether or not to report an accident or incident, you should contact your local enforcing authority for clarification. A record of any reportable injury, disease or dangerous occurrence must be kept for three years after the date on which it happened.

There is no special format for an accident book. The one shown below may be laid out differently from the one you have seen at work. Yours may be arranged in columns over two pages of a book or it may consist of loose-leaf sheets.

In any case, you must familiarise yourself with the format in use in your organisation.

---

## ACCIDENT REPORT FORM

Date and time of accident _____.

Location of accident _____

Names of any injured parties _____

_____

Method and date of reporting to enforcing authority

_____

Details of accident (include names of any witnesses), to be completed by injured party or a witness

_____

_____

_____

Completed by _____

Signature _____

FIRST AID TREATMENT (to be completed by first aid officer)

ACTION TAKEN TO PREVENT RECURRENCE (to be completed by safety officer)

---

### 6.7 The person(s) responsible for health, safety and security in your workplace

The Health and Safety at Work Act introduced Safety Representatives to achieve maximum employee involvement in safety matters. Certain functions of the safety representation have been identified; these are
·   to investigate potential hazards
·   to investigate complaints
·   to make representations to the employer
·   to carry out inspections
·   to represent the employees
·   to receive information from inspectors.

A safety representative must be permitted to take time off with pay for the purposes of performing these functions.

### 6.8  Safe working practices

In terms of an office this can be divided into:
·   **good housekeeping** – tidiness and cleanliness of working areas and safe storage of dangerous or inflammable substances e.g. thinners
·   **equipment** – no electrical hazards through trailing leads or broken sockets. Any equipment that can give out dangerous fumes should be kept in a well-ventilated preferably separate room
·   **office technology** – VDUs to be installed where there is plenty of light to eliminate glare. Workstations large enough for equipment and papers
·   **furniture** – safety stools provided for reaching items stored on high shelves, adjustable chairs to reduce backache
·   **accommodation** – no overcrowding; temperature not too hot – above 16°C (61°F); good ventilation and blinds for windows in direct sunlight; good lighting; safe floor surfaces and adequate toilet facilities
·   **noise** – kept to reasonable limits
·   **safe work habits** – no running down corridors; not carrying heavy objects or so many items that vision is obscured
·   **provision of information** – all employees need to know the correct proce-dure in case of fire; where fire extinguishers are situated; who the first-aiders and safety representatives are and how to report an accident.

It is important that each employee has a thorough knowledge of the employer's health and safety procedures.

KAPLAN PUBLISHING

## 7 Test your knowledge

1 Under the Health and Safety at Work, etc Act 1974, what are the employee's duties?

2 What does RIDDOR stand for?

3 Give an example of a reportable disease.

4 List some of the details that should be recorded in the organisation's accident book.

5 What are the main types of fire equipment and facilities maintained by employers?

6 When using an extinguisher what does the phrase 'P.A.S.S.' stand for?

7 Outline the steps for a risk assessment.

8 What is repetitive strain injury?

[Answers on p. 91]

## 8 Summary

This chapter has examined safety issues within the workplace and considered methods of minimising risks. Now that you have studied this chapter you should be familiar with the legal framework within which employers operate in regard to health and safety matters. You should also be equipped to deal with existing or potential hazards by either removing the risk, managing it or reporting it to the relevant authority.

### Answers to chapter activities & 'test your knowledge' questions

| ACTIVITY 1 |
| --- |
| Attention to the manufacturer's instructions makes the answer clear. Case (a) is a class B fire and should be tackled with the carbon dioxide extinguisher. Case (b) can be tackled by the gas cartridge type of extinguisher. |

## △ ACTIVITY 3    △ △ △ △

(a) Under the COSHH2 regulations Jonty Sheds Ltd should conduct a full Health and Safety assessment of the potential risks posed by the substance. Where possible the risks should be eliminated possibly by using a substitute product. Where this is not possible the risks should be minimised by:

· reducing exposure time

· providing protective equipment, for example, rubber gloves or face masks to minimise inhalation

· considering non-manual ways to remove the wood from the preservative

· providing training to operatives to minimise contact time with the substance.

(b) Under the Health and Safety at Work Act 1974 employees have a duty to protect themselves and their colleagues from threats to their health and safety. Operatives should consider the method of handling the substance and suggest ways of improving safety, for example, avoiding spillages or contact with skin. In addition, under the legislation if two or more employees request a safety committee then the employer is obliged to set one up. Operatives at Jonty Sheds Ltd could request a Safety Committee be set up and appoint a Safety Representative from amongst themselves to protect their interests. The Safety Representative would be obliged to keep themselves informed on the issue and particularly on any research proving or disproving the claim that the substance was carcinogenic.

## △ ACTIVITY 4    △ △ △ △

Improvements include:

· lowering the height of the chair. This means that the employee no longer has to bend her neck to see the screen, or bend her wrists to use the keyboard

· new seat design enables the employee to use the backrest for support

· use of document holder reduces the need for neck movements

· re-arrangement of desktop provides space for the employee to rest her hands between typing.

## △ ACTIVITY 5  △ △ △ △

· Obstruction of a fire exit is an obvious hazard and it makes sense to remove the boxes. If the area is often used as a 'dumping place' it might be wise to bring it to the attention of a responsible official, who can issue an appropriate notice.

· Don't meddle with electrical wiring – you are more likely to cause a hazard than to remove one! Report it promptly to a responsible official.

· You should turn the photocopier off. This is only partly to economise on power costs; the more important reason is to avoid the machine over-heating and causing a fire risk.

· You could easily incur a muscle strain in reaching for the file. Re-organise your workspace so as to place the file in a more accessible position.

· Access to fire extinguishers should of course be unobstructed and you should either move your desk or move the fire extinguisher. It sounds as if the fire officer was not consulted about the office re-organisation, and this may be the time to do so.

· The cabinet is easily accessible for yourself but not for others. It should be re-positioned so that everyone has comfortable access to it.

### Test your knowledge  △ △ △

1 Under the Health and Safety at Work etc Act 1974, employees and the self-employed have to take reasonable care to avoid injury to themselves and others and to co-operate with anyone carrying out duties under the Act (including the employer). They must make sure they know what the health and safety rules of the employer are, keep these rules, correctly use work items provided by the employer including personal protective equipment in accordance with training or instructions and never interfere with or misuse anything provided for their health, safety or welfare.

2 RIDDOR stands for the Reporting of Injuries, Diseases and Dangerous Occurrences Regulations, 1995. The reporting of some accidents, diseases and dangerous occurrences, etc at work is a legal requirement that is laid down by RIDDOR.

3 A reportable disease may be a skin disease (such as skin cancer), lung disease (such as pneumoconiosis, common in miners), occupational asthma, asbestosis and certain infections (such as hepatitis and tuberculosis).

4 In the case of a person at work, the details that should be recorded in the accident book include the full name and address of the injured person, their occupation and details of the injury. You also need to record the date and time of the accident and the place where it occurred and a brief description of the circumstances of the accident e.g. the cause, any witnesses and details of any action taken (including first aid) and any remedial works done to prevent recurrence.

5   The equipment and facilities include fire doors, fire notices, fire alarms and fire extinguishers.

6   When using an extinguisher remember the phrase, 'P.A.S.S.'
·   Pull out the pin.
·   Aim the extinguisher nozzle at the base of the flames.
·   Squeeze the trigger while holding the extinguisher upright.
·   Sweep the extinguisher from side to side, covering the area of the fire with the extinguishing agent.

7   Risk assessment is actually the identification of hazards in the workplace and the quantifying of the risk that such hazards might cause harm. This means looking for hazards, deciding who might be harmed, and how, evaluating the risks arising and deciding if existing precautions are adequate, recording your findings, reviewing your assessment periodically and revising as necessary

8   Repetitive Strain Injury is a condition that arises when you work for long periods at a VDU. Common complaints include backache, eye strain and muscular problems

KAPLAN PUBLISHING

# SECURITY OF THE WORKPLACE

**INTRODUCTION**

In this chapter we examine the security aspects of the workplace - the building where you work and the people and physical things in it - looking at the key steps involved in ensuring physical security against theft and other damage. Organisational assets should be protected by means of physical security measures, back-up arrangements, and appropriate insurance.

**KNOWLEDGE & UNDERSTANDING**

- The importance of security in your workplace (Item 1)
- The basic requirements of the health and safety and other legislations and regulations that apply to your workplace (Item 2)
- The person(s) responsible for security in your workplace (Item 3)
- The common security hazards that affect people working in an administrative role and how to identify these (Item 6)

**CONTENTS**

1. The importance of security
2. Security risks
3. Security of premises
4. Security of property

**PERFORMANCE CRITERIA**

- Make sure you read, comply with and have up-to-date information on the security requirements and procedures for your workplace (Item A in Element 22.1)
- Make sure that the procedures are being followed and report any that are not to the relevant person (Item B in Element 22.1)
- Identify and correct any hazards that you can deal with safely and competently and within the limits of your authority (Item C in Element 22.1)
- Promptly and accurately report any hazards that you are not allowed to deal with to the relevant person and warn other people who may be affected (Item D in Element 22.1)
- Follow your organisation's emergency procedures promptly, calmly and efficiently (Item E in Element 22.1)
- Identify and recommend opportunities for improving security to the responsible person (Item F in Element 22.1)
- Complete any health and safety records legibly and accurately (Item G in Element 22.1)

## 1    The importance of security

### 1.1  Security awareness

---
**□ DEFINITION**         □ □ □ □

**Security** - described in terms of the measures taken to protect against theft, unauthorised access, and espionage, it is a process, not a product.
Security is a combination of delaying unauthorised access and raising the alarm promptly when a breach of security has been identified.

---

You cannot buy security and install it. It is a collection of different measures, tailored to your own organisation's needs, methods and ways of working. You may ask why security is important; after all, most people are relatively honest. Unfortunately, there are always people who steal and cheat; large-scale theft is possibly more prevalent than ever before. The amount of violence used in pursuit of theft is also on the increase.

In the workplace, millions of pounds are lost every year through thefts of money, stock, equipment, vehicles and information, as well as by shoplifting, fraud and forgery, and bad housekeeping (e.g. failure to keep proper records of stock movements). If not checked, thefts and frauds lead to lower profits, possibly higher prices, higher costs for insurance and certainly less overall prosperity in the organisation.

### 1.2  Elements of business security

Business security includes the following:

(i)  **Security measures**  like fences, locks, security patrols, CCTV and alarms – which aim to make entry or assault difficult for criminals, and thus deter them, and which also facilitate detection. It should be stressed that no individual measure will prevent crime. Each security measure is part of a system, which will have an impact by either deterring, preventing or minimising the loss. Security is a combination of delay and then of alarm.

(ii)  **Personnel with a commitment to the well-being of the company and its property** – so that each individual has a sense of responsibility. Security and prevention require discipline. The best and most comprehensive burglar alarm is only effective if it is switched on. Failure to switch on the alarm system could result in the denial of a claim for loss or damage.

(iii) **Management initiatives to ensure the effective use and maintenance of physical measures,** – to create a security-conscious ethos which involves every single member of staff, and to establish correct procedures covering all aspects of security including:

- visitors
- cash handling
- protection of valuables and equipment
- safeguarding of personal property
- lost property
- key control.

A good working relationship within the organisation, and well understood procedures are highly effective in reducing losses at little or no cost.

### 1.3 The security requirements and procedures for your workplace

One of the criteria for this unit is to carry out organisational security procedures correctly. Security of the assets of an organisation can be encouraged through security policy and procedures and also by careful training and treatment of staff, and efficient working procedures.

All organisations are going to have different security requirements, so you should check the procedures manual that applies to your department/building and find out what your responsibilities are.

---

Your organisation's procedures may cover any or all of the following matters, and perhaps more besides.

- Identifying staff members and other regular visitors to the premises. This may involve identity badges or passes, and/or possibly the use of an entry keypad. For some organisations it might simply be signing in and out.
- Identifying other people with a legitimate reason for visiting the premises. It is common to ask the person being visited, or his/her secretary to go to reception and accompany the visitor through the building.
- Locking up – windows, filing cabinets, etc. Often the primary responsibility lies with the person in whose work area these are located. Of course, security staff may notice an open window, but this should be a last resort, not a first line of defence.
- Safeguarding the assets – you might be responsible for locking away calculators or other small pieces of equipment.
- Protecting documents and information - locking away files and ledgers.
- Computer security – logging on and logging off procedures, use of passwords, etc.
- Emergency procedures in the event of security being breached. These should include the names and telephone numbers of people who need to be informed of the breach.

---

Procedures may not always be written down and easily accessible, but employees will be expected to know what to do in certain circumstances. If you are unsure of the procedure to follow where security is involved, it will only show how competent you are if you ask for some clarification from your supervisor or manager.

### 1.4 Personnel

Some of the best methods of safeguarding the organisation's possessions revolve around the staff. Efficient managers will do their utmost to make all employees mindful of the importance of security. Involving staff in decisions that affect them and are related to their jobs, treating people as more than numbers and setting a good example all help towards the creation of a loyal workforce.

Careful recruitment, staff training and the operation of incentive schemes relating to security in supervision and constant alertness all lead towards better security. From an individual's point of view, it is often easier for an employee to know when colleagues are a potential security risk: for example, if they are unhappy and wanting to leave the company, especially when their feelings are strongly negative and they feel they have an axe to grind.

### 1.5  The relevant information on security in your workplace

Your employer should train you so that you know what to do, how to follow safe working procedures, and how to operate security equipment. As with health and safety incidents, you must report incidents to your supervisor, manager or nominated security contact. You must know who to alert and follow procedures for entering any accident or incident in the accident book.
Be prepared - know what to do if there is a robbery.  Where it is seen to be appropriate for your physical protection, your employer might have installed security devices (such as CCTV and panic buttons) and you should be shown how to operate them. In armed robberies you should do what the robber tells you, not resist, avoid sudden movements, and not raise the alarm until it is safe to do so. There will be procedures in place to deal with most events and these should make it clear to staff that they should not risk their safety to protect property.

You must not put yourself at unnecessary risk e.g. when banking cash and cheques you should not go to the bank on foot or by public transport, you should not go alone, and you should have had proper training. You should also avoid working alone at high-risk times, such as late at night.

### 1.6  Emergency procedures

In the event of a breach of security, you will need to know the names and telephone numbers of the security officers or specified person and the information they will need to be given. This might include location of intruders, how many were/are involved, time of entry and missing or damaged items. You may have to enter the incident in the accident book.

For criminal activity (disturbance, bomb threat, arson and armed robbery) if you are nearby, you need to get a good description of the person or persons committing the crime. Note all the usual characteristics – height, weight, sex, colour, approximate age and clothes. If a car is involved, note the number, make, model, colour, etc.

If your organisation is vulnerable to armed robbery, the employer will have installed security devices and you should have been trained in how to operate them. In armed robberies you should do what the robber tells you, avoid sudden movements, and not raise the alarm until it is safe to do so. Under no circumstance should you risk your safety to protect property.

Because of the increased threat of terrorist activity, it is important that organisations develop written procedures for dealing with the threat of terrorism, for example, bomb threats. It is also essential that front line staff receive training, and are vigilant, when dealing with members of the public.

---

### ▷ ACTIVITY 1

An engineer is working on your office photocopier and nobody seems to know why or who called him in. After about ten minutes he comes to you – as the most senior person in the office today – and tells you that he will have to take the machine away to repair it. He makes a phone call and another man, who was waiting in a van outside, comes in to help him take the machine away.

One of the criteria for this unit is to make sure that procedures are being followed and report any that are not to the relevant person. Explain what procedures you would follow before allowing the machine to be taken away.

[Answer on p. 107]

---

## 2 Security risks

### 2.1 Identifying risks

There are some people and many types of belongings that may be at risk. The people include key personnel who could be held to ransom, employees with custody of assets and security staff in the front line.

> Belongings include:
>
> · ownership documents e.g. share certificates and deeds
> · cash and cheques
> · stock
> · equipment
> · vehicles
> · files and documents
> · keys or passes to gain access to buildings.

Organisations may identify security risks in a number of ways, for example if there is a facility manager they may assess the risks associated with the incidents by working with the police and or an outside security consultancy company:

> The types of risk that might be identified include:
>
> · bomb threat
> · persons breaking into the building or gaining entry unlawfully and stealing cash, cheques, stocks, equipment, documents or confidential information
> · employees stealing from organisation – fraud
> · arson
> · theft from car park
> · computer hacking
> · industrial espionage.

Once the risks are assessed the outside advisers will suggest possible actions to overcome the risks identified.

---

### ▷ ACTIVITY 2

(i)  In the organisation you work for, or in any organisation with which you are familiar, what are the assets (tangible or intangible) that may be exposed to security risk?

(ii) What types of risk might apply in each case? (Ignore fire risk, which has been covered already.)

[Answer on p. 107]

---

### 2.2 Risks to physical assets

We have already outlined the risks that affect such things as stocks, cash etc. Note that the purpose of this course is not to turn you into a security expert but rather to make you aware of the sort of things that can go wrong and we shall expand on some of these now.

**(a) Risks caused by poor systems**

Some risks are caused by a poor system. For example if you are the accountant or one of the accountants you may be able to identify weaknesses in the systems that could lead someone less honest than yourself to remove cash or stocks without the company's permission. Perhaps stock requisition forms are never completed properly or are not authorised correctly. Perhaps the quantity requisitioned is left blank for someone else to fill in. Are the petty cash vouchers properly completed and authorised? We are not suggesting that you become obsessed with the systems or point an accusing finger at possible weaknesses that may be under the control of a colleague, but you should tactfully point out weaknesses where possible.

**(b) Risks caused by poor physical security**

Some risks are caused by poor physical security. The stores may allow anyone to wander in and collect material without authorisation. The stores may be the only route to another part of the building making it impossible to control access. Many thefts and burglaries, often accompanied by damage to property and equipment, are not well-planned crimes. Simple security precautions could prevent them. For example, windows and doors left open or unlocked, and ladders left lying about, all help the illegal entry of intruders. By being alert to these risks, you could prevent a breach of security in your company.

Other obvious risks include:
- poor door or window locks
- the receptionist regularly taking lunch at the same time and no one else being available to control access to the building
- the fire door at the rear of the building being propped open to allow cool air into the building in the summer.

All very obvious but police records show that many domestic and car thefts take place because the doors were not locked or even closed. This unit does not therefore ask you to plan how to defeat the master criminal who is plotting the perfect theft; rather, it is more about stopping the casual thief who simply wanders in and picks something up.

(c) **Risks caused by talking**

Do you tell people about your office; when staff arrive and take lunch; when deliveries are made; how the security man always pops out at 12.00 precisely for a cigarette because he is not allowed to smoke in the stores? All very dangerous if you do. Do people ask you about such things?

(d) **Inefficiency**

Not all the losses in companies are caused by criminal activities, or covered in general procedures. In many instances, losses can be attributed to bad practices, carelessness and general inefficiency. Examples include the following:
- staff may be able to help themselves to stock without permission
- clerical errors, such as failing to check goods properly when they are delivered, can lead to payment for goods not received
- stock requisition forms may not be filled in correctly – the quantity required may be left blank for someone else to complete and they may not be authorised properly
- careless treatment of stock and equipment could lead to items being written off before they should have been
- the system for obtaining petty cash may be too lax
- staff may talk carelessly or gossip about sensitive work-related matters with or within the hearing of people who are not authorised
- treating customers badly can lead to incalculable losses in future, and possibly present, business: consumers who are badly treated tell others.

### 2.3  Risks to information

As we have already noted, information can be damaged, lost or stolen the same as equipment and other assets can.

An organisation can lose valuable information in a number of different ways.
- The most common threat and most difficult to discover is 'by word of mouth' by disaffected or dishonest staff – often by an employee who is about to leave and join a competitor. Temporary staff may also be suspected.

· By direct over-viewing or overhearing of information by outsiders. Cleaners are the most serious threat, since they usually have unlimited access to all departments while otherwise unattended. They are often issued with master keys, which they use themselves or may lend to others if dishonest. They can thus make copies of confidential data in relative safety. Being relatively low-paid, they are open to bribery.

· By collecting the contents of wastepaper baskets, possibly from waste bins put out for refuse collection. Shredders that only cut into strips (rather than cross-cut into confetti) are a target for information-seekers, since presumably shredded information is likely to be valuable and it is not difficult, with some patience, to reconstitute strip-shredded paper.

Risks to information also cover risks to the organisation's computer system. Computers are used by most organisations to store information of all kinds, ranging from details about employees to financial accounts. If such information is lost or destroyed, the consequences might be disastrous.

The biggest problems associated with computer systems are the risks associated with corruption and destruction of software and information. This includes viruses, magnetic sources and extreme heat as well as the risks from hacking.

---

### ▷ ACTIVITY 3

What kinds of security procedures, systems and devices can you think of to reduce the security risks discussed above?
This activity covers performance criterion F in Element 22.1.

[Answer on p. 107]

---

### 2.4 Hazards you can put right yourself

Your organisation will have procedures to reduce or eliminate the security risks identified above. As an employee, there are some obvious security problems that you can deal with yourself e.g. locking filing cabinets, closing windows, avoiding careless talk, shutting down computers, changing passwords regularly and reporting suspicious actions or intruders.

However, you should not attempt to confront a colleague that you suspect of stealing, take it upon yourself to cross-question an unfamiliar visitor or approach vandals destroying a car in the car park.

## 3 Security of premises

### 3.1 Access to buildings

Sound physical security is the minimum requirement for any business premises, regardless of whether other categories of security are also in use.

Physical equipment includes locks, safes, shutters, grilles and fences and a host of specialised items such as armoured glass. In the main, physical security measures work to physically harden a building against unlawful entry or attack, making an intruder's task difficult, time-consuming and noisy. Its efficiency is, therefore, related to the intruder's skill and determination, which will generally increase in line with the possible benefits of crime. Broadly speaking, the more valuable, transportable or readily disposable a building's contents, the more effort will be made by criminals and the more extensive its physical protection needs to be.

For a larger budget, electronic security provides a variety of comprehensive security systems to suit every business. Electronic security includes intruder alarms, access control systems and closed-circuit television (CCTV). These systems support physical protection by impeding unauthorised movement and enabling the detection of intruders.

Another option is to use manned security, and if permanent staff are too expensive, a more affordable option is to use security patrols on an occasional basis to disrupt patterns of criminal behaviour before they become established. Patrols have proved to be extremely effective against vandalism. Cost-sharing arrangements can often be arranged with other local businesses.

Depending on the size of the organisation, there are a number of access controls that could be used. Sophisticated control systems provide for control by card access at a single door, or a network of doors, parking places, lifts and turnstiles. Less sophisticated systems include burglar alarms, some of which may be connected to the local police station.

### 3.2 Visitors

Many large companies have a gatehouse where security staff check visitors as they enter the premises and issue a special visitors' badge or card. These identity cards may be colour coded, or have a built in control, to only allow access to distinct areas of the building. The visitor will be asked to sign in, using a visitors' book, stating their name, company and other relevant details of their visit. Often the car registration number of the visitor is included if the car is parked in a company car park. Highly security-conscious companies may insist that any large bags are left in the gatehouse

and collected on departure. They may also insist on escorting visitors from one department to another.

It is important that, as an employee, you are aware of the security procedures for dealing with visitors to your company. Any breaches of this security, which you can identify, should be reported to the appropriate person immediately, even if it is only a case of someone being over-polite and keeping a door open so that a visitor can pass through without using a pass.

### 3.3 Bomb threat

There are two types of telephone bomb threats:

(1) threats that actual devices have been planted – the aim is to save life, thus giving the warning

(2) threats where no device has been planted, designed to disrupt.

Malicious pranksters, whose threats are empty, make the overwhelming number of telephoned bomb threat calls. But making such calls is a crime, and they should always be reported to the police. The calls constitute a threat to lives and must always be treated seriously and handled urgently.

Anyone may be a recipient of a bomb threat call. Handling them is not simple. It is difficult to remain calm and react effectively.
The golden rules are:

· keep calm
· try to obtain as much information as possible
· report to your security officer and the police.

The Metropolitan Police have issued a guide for small businesses, which includes an action checklist for anyone receiving a bomb threat over the telephone. If you can't find any written procedures for this type of situation, you should ask your local Crime Prevention Officer to obtain a copy for your company.

Points to note are as follows:

(a) try to keep the caller on the line, but try not to cut off the conversation or ask the caller to hold

(b) do not ring off or become flustered or excited because you will need to report the details

(c) ask if there is a code to verify that this is not a hoax call

(d) take the message about where the bomb has been planted and the time it is to go off

(e) ask what the device looks like

(f) ask why the caller is doing this

(g) ask the caller's name

(h) make a note of all the caller's characteristics: for example, male or female, alone or with others, approximate age, accent, whether intoxicated, laughing or serious, inconsistent or rational, and whether it sounds like the message is being read or is spontaneous

(i) pay attention to background noises (e.g. interruptions from someone else, music, children, machinery, road noises).

After the call, you must collect the notes you made during the conversation and inform your immediate superior and, of course, the police. Even bogus calls must be taken seriously.

---

### ▷ ACTIVITY 4                                                          ▷ ▷ ▷ ▷

Outline a three-step procedure for identifying unauthorised personnel at work.

[Answer on p. 108]

---

### 3.4 Arson

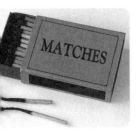

Arson is an ever-present threat to offices, storage premises and factories. Much of the arson is associated with vandalism and burglaries and the security measures will be a combination of those for burglary and fire hazards. Extra precautions will include:

·   gaps under doors should be as small as possible
·   letter boxes should have metal containers fitted on the inside
·   stored material of any kind should not be stacked adjacent to fences or walls where it could be set alight from outside, etc.

The person responsible for fire safety will also be responsible for protection from arson attack. This will be the person you will contact if you need to report any suspicious activities or to suggest any improvements to existing security arrangements.

**Rubbish** – can provide a ready source of ammunition for arson attacks. Even if the fire is not malicious, careless litter and rubbish can easily cause accidental fires. Your rubbish can also provide a thief with valuable information – not just information that is subject to Data Protection or even confidential client information, but the waste boxes will inform a burglar that you have new computers and printers. Lockable bins or skips placed away from the building would mean that if the bins were set on fire, the damage would be minimal.

Occasionally, employees or ex-employees commit arson attacks in the workplace. Employers and other workers should be aware of this potential threat and be alert for early signs, such as a series of unexplained small fires.

## 4    Security of property

### 4.1 Stock

An organisation can suffer stock losses because of:
(a)   the dishonesty of its staff and customers (e.g. at the checkout points)
(b)   shoplifting
(c)   burglary and fraud
(d)   poor management (e.g. failure to keep proper records of goods and raw materials received).

Many of these losses, referred to as leakages, are caused by poor practices being used when goods and raw materials are received. Saying 'Thank you' and asking the driver to put the package out of the way is not good enough when a delivery is made to the organisation. It can lead to the company paying for goods that have never been received.

### 4.2 Goods-in procedures

To check the stock losses, the organisation should have a set of goods in procedures to follow. The types of check that might be included are as follows:

(a)   all goods must be delivered to the company's delivery area between certain times (e.g. 10 am-1 pm, 2 pm-5 pm)
(b)   a note of damaged or opened parcels must be made on the delivery sheet
(c)   goods must be checked against the advice note when they are delivered
(d)   where stock is valuable, it should be locked in secured rooms
(e)   goods should never be left outside store rooms
(f)   waste should be cleared regularly.

### 4.3  Receiving parcels

Companies differ in their policy about whether parcels and packages should be delivered unopened or opened by the mail room staff. If you receive a parcel, you will be expected to sign for it. Unopened parcels should be signed for with an additional note to say 'contents not checked'. Parcels that are already opened should be checked carefully and a note made of any discrepancies. If possible, a damaged parcel should be refused on delivery and returned to the sender. The alternative is to sign for it as 'damaged on delivery'.

### 4.4  Suspicious packages

Certain organisations face the problem of receiving suspicious packages in the mail (e.g. suspected letter bombs). If you work for an organisation, which considers itself vulnerable, there is probably a screening device which scans all mail before it is opened. The machine will discriminate between potentially harmful contents and routine items such as paper clips and staples. The Post Office routinely scans mail.

Even companies that are not involved in sensitive areas of work should be aware of the threat of a letter bomb or package arriving through the mail. You should check whether the company that you work for has information, leaflets or posters to remind staff of the problem and the correct procedure to follow. Because a letter bomb or package is designed to kill or maim when opened, everyone should be alert to the possibility that a letter or package is an explosive device.

There are a number of indications that should rouse your suspicions:
(a)   a smell of almonds or marzipan
(b)   grease marks on the wrapping
(c)   visible wiring or tin foil seen through the outer wrapper
(d)   excessive wrapping
(e)   heavy for its size
(f)   too many stamps for the weight of the package
(g)   delivery by hand from an unknown source
(h)   posted or delivered from an unexpected source
(i)   poor handwriting, typing or spelling.

If you are suspicious, you should inform your supervisor immediately. If this is not possible because you are on your own, you should treat the package with caution; isolate it in a locked room, preferably on a table and away from the windows. Leave the room or building and telephone the police.

## 4.5 Equipment

Good equipment is both costly and vital to the efficient working of the organisation. Within the office environment, great care must be taken with the maintenance, operation and custody of equipment.

At the end of the day's work, small valuable pieces of equipment, such as calculators, should be securely stored away. Filing cabinets and desk drawers must be locked when work is finished. The keys must be removed and held by a responsible employee; keys must not be hidden in the office. Where it is possible, offices should also be locked when they are empty.

## 4.6 Suspicious behaviour

Access to offices is far too easy. People posing as cleaners, decorators, delivery or repair personnel, window cleaners, and gas, electricity and telephone officials carry out thefts. If you see anyone who appears to be acting suspiciously, or whose presence in the office you cannot account for, politely ask the nature of their business and whether or not you can help. If you are still not satisfied, you should report the matter at once to one of your superiors.

## 4.7 Cheques

Your organisation will hold a supply of cheques, which it issues to suppliers and to its staff. The cheques will probably be kept in a fireproof safe, with a lock or unique security number, which can only be opened by the cashier or assistant cashier. Whilst the arrangements will differ from organisation to organisation, there will always be safeguards for protecting the cheques.

## 4.8 Petty cash

Petty cash is the term given to the money, often kept in a tin, to cover small day-to-day items of expenditure in an office, which would not be paid for by cheque (e.g. tea, coffee or magazines for the reception area). The amount kept is generally sufficient to cover expenditure for a week or a month, depending on the company policy. To make sure that only correct amounts for authorised payments are paid out, petty cash vouchers are used to record the money spent. These vouchers are numbered and issued in numerical order.

Strict control must be kept over the petty cash tin itself and the money paid out to prevent loss of money through mistakes, pilferage or deliberate fraud. If it is part of your duties to look after petty cash, there are a number of rules, which should be adhered to:

(a) the petty cash tin should be locked when not in use and kept in a secure place; although its whereabouts are often common knowledge within an office, you should not discuss where it is kept with anyone else

(b) unused vouchers should be kept safely, preferably within the tin

(c) completed vouchers should be filed and kept in a secure position

(d) any lost or missing vouchers should be reported immediately

(e) payments must not be made without an accompanying voucher and requests for 'advances' from petty cash by any colleague should be denied and reported to your superior.

Although you may not have access either to the cheques or to the petty cash, you should be aware of the security procedures within your department, and if you suspect that there are security risks you should report them promptly to the appropriate person.

---

## ▷ ACTIVITY 5

There may be a number of indications, or warning signs, which suggest that an employee's behaviour should be investigated more closely. For the sake of the organisation's security, what should you look out for?
This activity covers performance criterion D in Element 22.1.

[Answer on p. 108]

---

## 5 Test your knowledge

1 Why is it important to have personnel with a commitment to the well being of the company?

2 What four types of risk may pose a threat to physical assets?

3 List some typical organisation's security procedures.

4 Apart from the risk to information when using computers, outline three other ways an organisation can lose valuable information.

5 Give two examples of how you could lead another employee into a breach of security.

[Answers on p. 109]

## 6 Summary

This chapter has highlighted a range of security risks that may threaten the workplace and indicated how breaches to security may be identified. Having studied the chapter you should be familiar with the types of security risks that you may encounter and the organisational procedures that may be adopted to counter threats to security. You should now feel confident to rectify security risks within your authority or to make a timely report to the relevant person about security risks you have identified.

KAPLAN PUBLISHING

## Answers to chapter activities & 'test your knowledge' questions

△ **ACTIVITY 1**   △ △ △ △

You will obviously be very suspicious. Photocopiers do not often have to go away to be repaired.

Normally, an organisation's procedures would require you to ask to see the men's identification and establish the facts before allowing any assets to be taken out of the building.

The next step would be to find out which company normally services the equipment and, if it is the same company that the men claim to work for, telephone them and ask whether these men are employees and are responding to a call placed by someone in the organisation. They should be able to give you the name of the person reporting the fault in your organisation and you can then contact that person and explain the situation so that he or she can take responsibility for dealing with the situation.

Alternatively, if the men do not work for the company that they claim to work for or you cannot contact their company offices, your organisation's procedures would probably require you to telephone the security department or to report the matter to the police.

△ **ACTIVITY 2**   △ △ △ △

- Cash and/or cheques – subject to loss, theft by internal staff, theft by external parties.
- Stocks – subject to theft or damage (e.g. by excessive dampness).
- Vehicles – subject to theft, damage by careless driving.
- Equipment such as computers – subject to theft, damage arising from inappropriate ambient conditions, or disk corruption.
- Information on computers disks or on files – subject to theft or unauthorised amendment.
- Trade secrets – subject to deliberate theft, or to the risk of careless talk.
- Staff members – subject to attack by intruders, and to emergencies affecting the building (e.g. bomb scares).

△ **ACTIVITY 3**   △ △ △ △

This will obviously vary in detail from one organisation to another, but some of the elements below will be present in almost every organisation.
- Locks – on doors, cash tills, windows and filing cabinets.
- Fortified doors and windows.
- Combination locks on doors – the employee taps in a number through an electronic keypad to gain access.
- Contact details of the person responsible for security should be circulated to everyone.
- Other admission and exit controls, such as voice recognition, plastic entrance cards.
- Surveillance cameras.

· Passwords on computers.
· Security guards in reception, during and after office hours.
· Security badges with photos.
· Alarm systems – on doors, windows, motor vehicles etc.
· Procedures for accessing confidential documents.
· Protective clothing – e.g. helmets for security guards carrying cash.
· Reception staff vet all visitors to ensure they are expected.

## △ ACTIVITY 4    △ △ △ △

A three-step procedure for identifying unauthorised personnel at work would include:
1   showing an entry pass to the security guard at reception
2   wearing an identity badge at all times
3   signing in and out of the building.

## △ ACTIVITY 5    △ △ △ △

Some of the warning signs would come under the heading of unduly lavish lifestyle. These could include:
· new-found wealth with no boasting of a win on the pools, enabling the purchase of a house or new car
· spending patterns which are higher than usual e.g. entertainment, gambling or a Caribbean cruise.

Other signs that may arouse suspicion include:
· working after hours even when it is not necessary
· new 'friends' in a rival business organisation
· lack of respect for the company with expressions of disaffection or insubordination

KAPLAN PUBLISHING

**Test your knowledge** △ △ △

1 Some of the best methods of safeguarding the organisation's possessions revolve around the staff. Efficient managers will do their utmost to make all employees mindful of the importance of security. Involving staff in decisions that affect them and are related to their jobs, treating people as more than numbers and setting a good example all help towards the creation of a loyal workforce.

2 Four types of risk are those caused by poor systems, by poor physical security, by talking and by inefficiency.

3 Your organisation's procedures may cover any or all of the following matters, and perhaps more besides:
   · identifying staff members and other visitors to the premises
   · locking up – windows, filing cabinets, etc
   · safeguarding the assets
   · protecting documents and information
   · computer security – logging on and logging off procedures, use of passwords, etc.

4 Three other ways an organisation can lose valuable information are:
   · 'by word of mouth' by disaffected or dishonest staff
   · by direct over-viewing or overhearing of information by outsiders
   · by collecting the contents of wastepaper baskets, possibly from waste bins put out for refuse collection.

5 You could lead another employee into a breach of security by persuading the security guard to allow you to enter the building without an entry pass, by lending your keys to a colleague for unspecified purposes or by asking a friend to sign you in knowing you are going to be late for work.

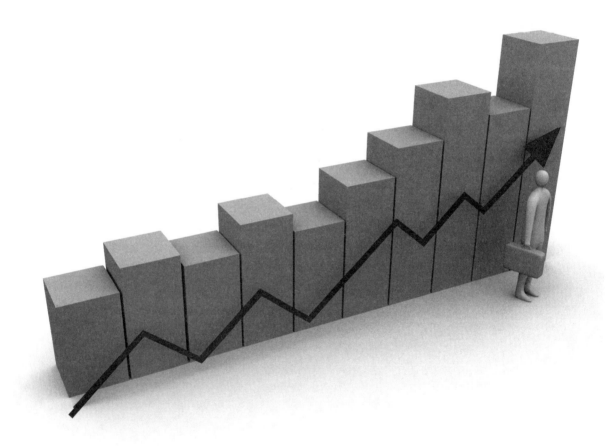

KAPLAN PUBLISHING

# WORKING PRODUCTIVELY

**INTRODUCTION**

In this chapter we will discuss the role of the employee in making sure that the working environment – the immediate work area and the 'office as a whole' – is both effective and efficient. The two key factors in this are firstly, being organised and secondly, being aware of the needs of other employees and the organisation.

**KNOWLEDGE & UNDERSTANDING**

· How the conditions under which you work can affect your effectiveness and efficiency and the effectiveness and efficiency of those around you (Item 13)

· How to organise your own work area so that you and others can work efficiently (Item 14)

· Your organisation's requirements on how you organise your working area (Item 15)

· The importance of organising your work area so that it makes a positive impression on other people and examples of how to do so (Item 16)

· The importance of working in a way that shows respect for other people and examples of how to do this (Item 17)

· Conditions you can put right yourself and conditions you would have to report (Item 18)

· Manufacturer's instructions and your organisation's procedures for the equipment you use as part of your job (Item 19)

**CONTENTS**

1 Evaluating efficiency and effectiveness
2 Organising your work area
3 Using and maintaining equipment
4 Working with others

**PERFORMANCE CRITERIA**

· Organise the work area you are responsible for, so that you and others can work efficiently (Item A in Element 22.2)
· Organise the work area you are responsible for, so that it meets your organisation's requirements and presents a positive image of yourself and your team (Item B in Element 22.2)
· Identify conditions around you that interfere with effective working (Item C in Element 22.2)
· Put right any conditions that you can deal with safely, competently, within the limits of your authority and with the agreement of other relevant people (Item D in Element 22.2)
· Promptly and accurately report any other conditions to the relevant person (Item E in Element 22.2)
· Use and maintain equipment in accordance with manufacturer's instructions and your organisation's procedures. (Item F in Element 22.2)

# 1    Evaluating efficiency and effectiveness

## 1.1  Influences on work methods

The type of accounting work that you do is governed by the task, the requirements of the law and organisational policy, by formal instructions and the customs developed by the work group.

· The task covers - what needs to be done, how it should be done and the order in which it must be done to do the job.
· The requirements of the law and regulations ensure that the tasks are completed in accordance with the rights of individuals and society - with safety and fairness in mind.

· Organisational policies are the way the company interprets the task, the law and its own goals and objectives.
· Formal instructions are given by people in authority. Your manager or supervisor will tell you what needs to be done and how you should do it.
· The customs or informal ground rules are developed by the work group and tend to be 'the way things are done around here'.

## 1.2  Job description

Certain tasks must be done so that the department and the organisation can meet their objectives. These tasks must be allocated to specific job positions or individuals for effective planning and control.

---

**□ DEFINITION**                                          □□□□

A **Job Description** is a broad statement of the purpose and scope of the job. It specifies the tasks, details responsibilities, sets authority limits, distinguishes accountability and outlines the organisational relationships that the job entails.

---

The statement will include the following points:

- **Identification of the job** – this includes the job title, the department/organisation structure and the number of people doing the job.

- **Purpose of the job** – identifying its objectives in relationship to overall objectives, e.g. to provide clerical support to all activities in the sales department.

- **Position in the organisation** – indicating the relationships with other jobs and the chains of responsibility. For this purpose, many firms include a small organisation chart.

- **Duties** – the principal duties to be performed, with emphasis on key tasks, and limits to the job-holder's authority. Usually under this heading is included an indication of how the job differs from others in the organisation. A further breakdown of principal duties is made identifying specific tasks in terms of what precisely is done and in what manner, and with some explanation, both in terms of quantity and quality.

- **Responsibilities** – a statement outlining the responsibilities for the resources e.g. staff, money and machinery.

- **Physical conditions** – including details of noisy, dirty, dangerous conditions or pleasant office conditions and also hours of work, overtime, unsocial hours, etc.

- **Social conditions** – the type of group the employee will be concerned with.

- **Grade and salary/wage range and fringe benefits** – details of the rates for the grade, increments, piece-work, bonuses and commission, plus fringe benefits such as luncheon vouchers, pension schemes, company car, etc.

- **Promotion prospects** - to whom the job reports and at what level, with possible indications about future succession, prospects of promotion or transfer.

- **Key difficulties** – no job description is complete without a full identification of the key difficulties likely to be encountered by the job-holder.

### 1.3 Goals and objectives

The work that you do will be organised so it can be done effectively and efficiently. The manager or supervisor will structure the work within the department or section to enable smooth flow and co-ordination, and establish relationships between positions in terms of authority and responsibility. You will know who to report to and who gives the instructions and you will also know if you are responsible for helping anyone else with their work.

Knowing who you report to and what your job entails is one thing but if you have no idea (or only a vague idea) of what you are supposed to accomplish in a day or week or year, there is no way of telling whether you have done it or not. This is why you need goals and objectives.

It is quite difficult to distinguish between goals and objectives. However, where a distinction is drawn, then goals are defined as long-term statements of ambition. Objectives will normally be the term used to refer to short-term means employed to attain the longer-term goals or ends. For example, a long-term personal goal might be for you 'to be promoted to supervisor of your section by the end of next year'. To achieve this goal one of the objectives might be to achieve competence in Units 22 and 23 and pass the devolved assessment by September.

---

### ☐ DEFINITION   ☐☐☐■

**Goals** are defined as long-term statements of ambition. Objectives will normally be the term used to refer to short-term means employed to attain the longer-term goals or ends.

---

Objectives can be assessed against the following criteria (for which the mnemonic is **SMART**).

·   **Specific** – all objectives should be clearly expressed.
·   **Measurable** – there must be some quantifiable yardstick of attainment.
·   **Achievable** – an objective should not appear impossible.
·   **Result-oriented** – objectives should focus on key tasks or performance areas.
·   **Time-bounded** – there should be a deadline.

Goals and objectives influence motivation in two ways. First, they provide a target to aim at, something to aspire to. Their existence generates motivation in a person to work towards their achievement. Second, they provide a standard of performance. A person is doing well if they have achieved a goal or an objective or are on the way to achieving it. On the other hand failure to achieve a goal or at least to make some progress toward it is evidence of unsatisfactory performance.

KAPLAN PUBLISHING

Although it sounds silly, try setting yourself a goal of always answering the phone before the third ring. By the end of the first day, you will have impressed many of the people you have spoken to by the prompt service and you will also have the personal satisfaction of having achieved something you set out to do.

## ▷ ACTIVITY 1  ▷ ▷ ▷ ▷

By knowing exactly what their personal objectives are, employees can do which three of the following?
(a) Plan and direct their effort towards the objectives
(b) Estimate how much time off they can have
(c) Monitor their performance against objectives and adjust (or learn) if required
(d) Experience the motivation of a challenge
(e) Organise colleagues who are willing to help

[Answer on p. 129]

### 1.4 Efficiency and effectiveness

Establishing your goals and objectives is just a start. You also need to measure success in achieving those goals.

Performance is measured in terms of effectiveness and efficiency. It is important to be clear what is meant by these two concepts that are often confused.

## ☐ DEFINITION  ☐☐☐☐

**Effectiveness** is 'doing the right things' and is a measure of the match or mismatch between what you produce (your actual output) and what you should be producing (defined in terms of your organisational goals). It means setting the right goals and objectives and then making sure they are accomplished. Being effective means getting the result that you want.

**Efficiency** is 'doing things right' and is a measure of the resources used in producing your actual output. Efficiency means getting the most from your resources.

Efficient is not the same as effective. It means getting the result that you want with the minimum waste of effort and resources. This is, of course, an important objective in any organisation. But note that an efficient working environment will not always be effective. For example, a line manager may be ruthlessly efficient in saving time and money, but the workforce may be demotivated and levels of performance will fall off. The working environment will become less effective.

The ideal working environment is one that balances effectiveness and efficiency. The job is done well with the minimum wastage of effort and resources.

### 1.5  Working conditions

Managers are ultimately concerned with ensuring that employees meet the targets set for them i.e. a certain quantity of work over a period of time and a certain quality within that quantity.

However, the productivity will be affected by the conditions under which people work. To increase productivity there are:

·   ways of introducing economies at work, thus keeping costs down

·   measures that reduce fatigue and tiredness - particular attention should be paid to the physical conditions such as heating, lighting, ventilation and noise in order to ensure the best possible environment conducive to the most efficient performance of duties

·   measures designed to reduce noise or minimise movement e.g. layout of office

·   ways of increasing job security – if people feel secure then they are likely to be happy and achieve their work goals more effectively and more often. They will be able to respond fully to challenges and to actively seek advancement without worrying about job security. This in turn will lead to greater job satisfaction and more contentment on the part of individuals

·   methods of improving job satisfaction – these are normally achieved by using skills and knowledge in response to challenges and the individual recognising the importance of self-development and initiative. However, there does appear to be a positive correlation between working conditions and satisfaction at work. Factors such as temperature, humidity, ventilation, noise, hours of work, cleanliness and adequate tools and equipment have their effect on job satisfaction. The reasons for this are straightforward. Good working conditions lead to greater physical comfort, they enable the job to be done more effectively and safely and, finally, good conditions such as a shorter working week or flexitime will facilitate the pursuit of off-the-job activities like hobbies or pastimes.

### 1.6  Workplace regulations

The Workplace (Health, Safety & Welfare) Regulations 1992 require the provision of a safe and healthy workplace in terms of lighting, heating, washing facilities, sanitary conveniences, and traffic routes. They lay down minimum standards that are necessary to promote efficiency and effectiveness amongst employees. The provisions include:

·   **Ventilation** – should remove and dilute warm, humid air and provide air movement, which gives a sense of freshness without causing a draught. Fresh, clean air should be drawn from a source outside the workplace and be circulated through the workrooms. In a stuffy, 'heavy' atmosphere the level of carbon dioxide in the room increases and this reduces brain activity, thus reducing output.

·   **Temperatures** – if it is cold people are more concerned with trying to keep warm than with work efficiency. If it is too warm people become lethargic. Comfort depends on air temperature, radiant heat, air movement and humidity. Where the activity is mainly sedentary, for example offices, the temperature should normally be at least 16°C. If work involves physical effort it should be at least 13°C.

· **Lighting** – should be sufficient to enable people to work and move about safely. Good daylight is the best type of lighting. If necessary, local lighting should be provided at individual workstations, and at places of particular risk such as crossing points on traffic routes. Lighting and light fittings should not create any hazard.

· **Cleanliness and waste materials** – apart from preventing potential health problems, a clean office helps to create an atmosphere conducive to work. Every workplace and the furniture, furnishings and fittings should be kept clean. Waste should be stored in suitable receptacles.

· **Room dimensions and space** – workrooms should have enough free space to allow people to move about with ease. Each person should have at least 11 cubic metres of space - ignoring parts of the room above 3.1 metres above the floor. This might sound a lot of space but what it actually means is that your desk and chair, plus the passageway around it to allow you to get in and out safely must be at least 1.88m square (~ 6ft square) assuming the ceiling is about 10ft high.

· **Workstations and seating** – should be suitable for the people using them and for the work. People should be able to leave workstations swiftly in an emergency. If work can or must be done sitting, seats that are suitable for the people using them and for the work done there should be provided. Seating should give adequate support for the lower back, and footrests should be provided for workers who cannot place their feet flat on the floor.

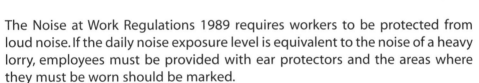

· **Drinking water** – an adequate supply, with an upward drinking jet or suitable cups should be provided.

The Noise at Work Regulations 1989 requires workers to be protected from loud noise. If the daily noise exposure level is equivalent to the noise of a heavy lorry, employees must be provided with ear protectors and the areas where they must be worn should be marked.

This is very unlikely in the office environment but it is still an important issue because employees are often distracted by noise with a resulting break in concentration. To overcome the problems in modern buildings special floor and wall materials are used which absorb sounds. Management should also pay attention to the positioning of noisy machines and equipment. Where this is not possible ways of reducing the level of noise should be found e.g. telephones with quiet tones.

### 1.7 Appraisal of the clerical work procedures

As in any office it is important that the systems in the accounts department are based on sound principles. The procedures followed should be recorded in a manual and should be subject to periodic reviews to establish whether improvements in methods of working could be introduced.

Before any necessary improvements can be formulated and implemented, a review of existing procedures must be undertaken. This may be divided into two parts:

(i) A general view of the office as a whole and the role it plays within the organisation. This will consider what actually happens and who does what within the office, the techniques and methods employed by staff in carrying out assigned responsibilities and the quality of performance.

(ii) A more detailed step-by-step view of the procedures themselves. Of each operation, and the procedure as a whole, the following questions could be asked:

· Is this operation essential?
· Is the information used?
· What is the information used for?
· Is the information already provided elsewhere?
· Can the method of working be simplified?
· Would computerisation be appropriate?
· Are there any bottlenecks?
· Is work fairly divided between staff?
· Are the correct grades of staff employed for each stage?
· Does the work flow correctly?
· Would a change in office layout be helpful?
· Are the correct instructions given to staff?

From such approaches great savings in clerical procedures costs have been achieved in many organisations.

### 1.8 Efficient work practices

The majority of organisations approach work planning methodically. Employees, however, often do not realise that if they do not plan their own individual and personal approach to work then the results desired by the organisation will not be achieved despite the efforts of the organisation.

A well-organised employee should try to ensure that as a general guideline the following factors are considered:

· **Neatness and tidiness** – keeping desk, shelves, cabinets, etc tidy not only has the advantage of pleasing appearance but also, provided items are tidied in order, aids retrieval and efficiency.

· **Order** – there are distinct advantages to be gained from ensuring that tasks are tackled in some semblance of order, be it chronological or priority. Once a task has been commenced it should be completed as far as is practically possible. Moving from one task to another impairs efficiency. It is improved if work is grouped into batches of the same type and carried out at the same time.

· **The establishment of routine** – the following items typify the approach to be adopted:

(i) Important and difficult tasks should always be attempted when the employee is fresh, normally during the morning.

(ii) Tasks, requests and instructions should be written down; memory often proves defective.

(iii) The adage 'never put off until tomorrow what can be done today' should be put into action.

(iv) Often there are tasks which need to be done daily. These tasks should indeed be carried out each day, preferably at the same time.

(v) The regular routine, once established, should be written down. This will enable the employee to use it as both a reminder and a checklist. Additionally, if the employee is absent or leaves the organisation the written routine will enable a substitute or replacement to function more effectively.

Although emphasis has been placed above on the employee working methodically it must be remembered that the method employed by the organisation in devising, implementing and operating administrative systems and procedures is of equal importance.

The importance of writing down your work schedule cannot be stressed enough.

## 2  Organising your work area

### 2.1  Working environment

In your office, furniture and equipment should be arranged to give the best possible use of the space allocated. The emphasis should be on a simple flow of work with documents going forward in a straight line through the office. Gangways should be free from obstruction and allow easy evacuation in case of emergencies.  With careful planning an office layout should help to increase the efficiency of work, should be economic in the use of floor space and yet give an attractive appearance and provide a comfortable environment to maintain staff morale.

It is your responsibility to identify conditions in the working environment that interfere with effective working, for example where your workplace is too cramped or badly laid out, too hot or too cold, too stuffy or too draughty, too bright or too dim or too noisy

Problems like this can reduce both your effectiveness (getting things done) and your efficiency (getting things done with the minimum of wastage). For example:

· an office with poor heating will reduce your ability to work; some tasks may not get done and other tasks will take much longer, costing the organisation more
· poor air quality may result in you becoming ill: again some tasks may not get done and the organisation is likely to have the extra cost of sick pay.

Sometimes you can do something about problems like these, and should take action. Other times you will have to refer the problem to someone else to sort it out.

### ▷ ACTIVITY 2                    ▷ ▷ ▷ ▷

You are an accounts assistant at an insurance company, Freedom plc, based in Feltham. When you started work in the office you got on well with your colleagues, but you noticed that the working environment was not as ideal as your previous office at Jugglers Limited where you trained in accounts work.

You have noted a number of problems and wonder how you should deal with them. Should you take action yourself or should you refer the matters to Chris Triggs, the line manager?

The problems are as follows:

1. Your desk is awkwardly situated by the photocopier. People using the machine disturb you, and you do not like the fumes the machine gives off. You notice that there is a space for a desk nearer to the workstations, which deal with the sales and purchases processing.

2. The office is very warm to work in, particularly in the afternoon when the computers have been running for a while. The heating comes from an air conditioning system that has a thermostatic switch on the office wall. You often feel very sleepy after lunch and sometimes go home with a headache. You talk to your colleagues about this and they agree with you - the office needs to be cooler and fresher, and then you will all work better.

3. The office has a big window, which has the sun shining through it for much of the day. There are blinds, but they are stuck in the open position, and you, along with many others, find the light so dazzling that you cannot see your VDU very well.

4. You sometimes suffer from pains and discomfort in the neck, shoulders or arms when you get home from work at night.

This activity covers performance criterion D and E in Element 22.2.

[Answer on p. 129]

## 2.2 Efficient work area

Your work area is not just the desk or workstation, it is the area that surrounds it, involving desk, chair and any furniture and filing cabinets in the vicinity.

The state of the work area is your responsibility as the user.

The way in which it is (or is not) organised says a great deal about you. A tidy desk normally means a tidy mind, just as an untidy work area often indicates a person who finds organisation rather a struggle.

An organised work area has a number of characteristics:

· it is tidy - keeping desk, shelves, cabinets, etc. tidy not only has the advantage of pleasing appearance but also, provided items are tidied in order, aids retrieval and efficiency

· it is clean

· you know where everything is and can find it quickly

· everything is within easy reach

· the VDU is correctly set up and the chair is correctly adjusted for you.

The test of a well-organised work area is whether your colleagues can also find what they want. Suppose you are an accounts assistant who deals with sales orders. You are out at lunch and an important customer telephones and asks if a recently issued sales order can be checked as an incorrect catalogue code may have been quoted on the document. Can the sales order be found? Is it in an organised filing system or pending tray, or is it buried under a pile of unsorted papers? Worse still, is it there at all?

It is not difficult to see from this that if a work area is organised properly, it will be:
· effective because tasks can be completed and the job done
· efficient because time (and therefore money) will not be wasted.

## 2.3 The importance of efficiency

Examples of efficiency in the working environment are:
· having resources that you need within easy reach and not in a filing cabinet at the other end of the office
· carrying out tasks in the time allotted – other people may be waiting for you to finish checking documents so that they can carry out a task
· not wasting resources such as photocopy paper
· taking care of resources so that they will last, e.g. storing computer disks correctly.

Efficiency is important not only because cutting down on wastage means greater profit for the organisation, but also because it has a direct influence on the effectiveness of other members of a workplace team.

## 2.4 The organisation's guidelines for the work area

Employees sometimes like to personalise their working environment to establish their identity in the workplace and provide a psychological sense of security. Examples of this include plants, photographs of friends and family, postcards received at work and small posters saying things like 'you don't have to be mad to work here, but it helps'

Your work area will tell you a lot about yourself. The organisation you work for will, however, have guidelines that will regulate the extent to which you can put up posters, postcards and other items. It is unlikely that these guidelines will be written down, but they will normally be based on a test of what is 'reasonable' and be enforced either by a line manager or by the comments of colleagues objecting to what they think is unreasonable!

What is reasonable depends on the nature of the workplace. If you work in a closed office that is rarely visited by outsiders, you are likely to have the freedom to personalise your work area, as long as what is displayed is not offensive to colleagues or to management.

If your office is open plan and open to the public gaze, the organisation is likely to require that personal items should be unobtrusive. A bank customer services desk, for example will be kept very tidy and have welcoming features, such as flowers.

The posters on the wall are not likely to be the employees' personal choice but advertise the products of the organisation.

This gives a very positive image to the public of the financial services team that operates in the office.

## 3   Using and maintaining equipment

### 3.1  Equipment in daily use

The office normally has a wide variety of complex equipment, which is in daily use. You, as an accounts assistant, for example may have to use computer hardware – processing units, backup devices and printers, a fax machine, a photocopier, a scanner, a credit card terminal and a shredder.

We have noted in an earlier chapter that both the employer and the employee have duties of care under Health and Safety regulations when using this type of equipment. In this chapter we look specifically at the guidance that exists for the operation and maintenance of equipment in the workplace. This guidance can be found in the instructions provided with the equipment – this may take the form of a manual, a sheet, or online assistance and the separate guidelines issued by the employer.

The important point here is that these guidelines and instructions must be followed:
· when setting the equipment up and before operating the equipment
· when something goes wrong
· when maintenance is needed.

You must never adopt your own remedy!

### 3.2  Using equipment safely

Only use machines that you know how to operate and are authorised to do so. Never attempt to operate an unfamiliar machine without reading the machine instructions or receiving directions from a qualified employee. In addition, follow these guidelines to ensure machine safety:
· Secure machines that tend to move during operation.
· Do not place machines near the edge of a table or desk.
· Ensure that machines with moving parts are guarded to prevent accidents. Do not remove these guards.
· Unplug defective machines and have them repaired immediately.
· Turn off and unplug equipment before making any adjustments.
· Transfer pointed objects to others with the point away from them.
· Do not use any machine that smokes, sparks, shocks, or appears defective in any way.
· Close hand-operated paper cutters after each use and activate the guard.

· Take care when working with copy machines. If you have to open the machine for maintenance, repair, or troubleshooting, remember that some parts may be hot. Always follow the manufacturer's instructions for troubleshooting.

· Unplug paper shredders before conducting maintenance, repair, or troubleshooting.

· Open only one file drawer at any one time. Two open drawers may offset the balance of the cabinet.

· Fill file cabinets from the bottom up. Top-heavy cabinets may tip over.

### 3.3 Dealing with the photocopier

Your office probably has a photocopier that is used fairly heavily for copying commercial documents such as purchase orders and invoices, and also the routine office paperwork. Most offices have a maintenance contract with a company, which provides toner, annual maintenance and a call out service in case of major breakdowns. There will be most likely a printed sheet of internal regulations governing the use of the photocopier by employees.
An example is shown below:

---

### PHOTOCOPIER USE

- No unauthorised copying.

- No copying of copyright material (with © symbol) without reference to line manager.

- Be sure to turn **OFF** the power switch, but leave on at mains:

  - when you leave your office at night

  - if a power failure occurs.

- Be sure to turn **OFF** the power switch immediately and call for service:

  - if an unusual noise is heard from the copier

  - if the outside of the copier becomes unusually hot

  - if any part of the copier is damaged, or if it has been dropped

  - if the copier has been exposed to rain or liquid.

- Renew paper in cassette tray if paper out light is on.

- Toner to be replaced by senior assistants only.

- If you cannot clear a paper jam, please refer to senior assistant.

- Refer major faults to line manager.

- If the maintenance light or call light is on, refer to line manager.

---

The manufacturer's instructions for the photocopier will be set out in a booklet, but you will mostly rely on the common instructions that are printed on the top panel of the photocopier.

Some examples of these are shown below:

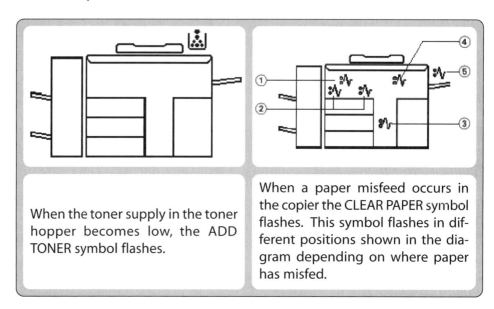

When the toner supply in the toner hopper becomes low, the ADD TONER symbol flashes.

When a paper misfeed occurs in the copier the CLEAR PAPER symbol flashes. This symbol flashes in different positions shown in the diagram depending on where paper has misfed.

### 3.4 The printer
The regulations for using the printer in your office will be very similar to those of the photocopier.

---

**PRINTER USE**

- Be sure to turn **OFF** the power switch, but leave on at mains:
  - when you leave your office at night
  - if a power failure occurs.
- Be sure to turn **OFF** the power switch immediately and call for service:
  - if an unusual noise is heard from the printer
  - if the outside of the printer becomes unusually hot
  - if any part of the printer is damaged, or if it has been dropped
  - if the printer has been exposed to rain or liquid.
- Load paper in tray if LOAD PAPER message is displayed.
- Toner to be replaced by senior assistants only.
- If you cannot clear a paper jam, refer to senior assistant.
- Refer major faults to line manager.

---

The manufacturer's instructions for the printer are also set out in a booklet, but several diagrams on how to un-jam the printer are probably stuck to the desk that the printer is on.

An example is shown below:

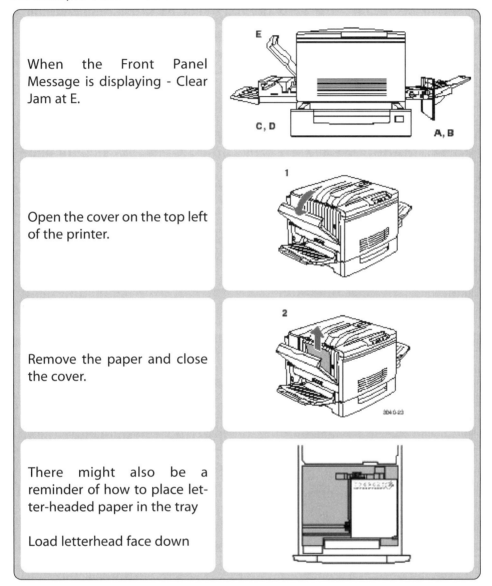

| | |
|---|---|
| When the Front Panel Message is displaying - Clear Jam at E. | |
| Open the cover on the top left of the printer. | |
| Remove the paper and close the cover. | |
| There might also be a reminder of how to place letter-headed paper in the tray<br><br>Load letterhead face down | |

## 4 Working with others

### 4.1 Role and responsibilities

An important skill in working with others is being able to identify what behaviour is expected of you in your position and also to know what roles other people have and your relation to them. It is often easier to work with people when you know what is expected of you and how you fit into the organisation. In this way it is more likely that you and the people you work with will have the same expectations and for example make the same assumptions about who is responsible for what at work.

If you know where you stand, it will help you avoid inappropriate behaviour e.g. in your dress code and insubordination when discussing matters irrelevant to the situation.

In most organisations this role and the responsibilities involved in the role will be determined by the job description. You should try to ensure that you have a detailed job description. Only then can you fully appreciate your own role and responsibilities.

### 4.2 Co-ordination

Because of the nature of the work you do (working in a department, section or team), your role and responsibilities should not be considered in isolation. You will have joint objectives and goals that require you to pool your resources, information and efforts and you will almost certainly have to co-ordinate your objectives and goals with those of other individuals and sections. The efforts of individuals at work represent part of a co-ordinated effort designed to meet overall organisational goals e.g. to increase profits by 5% or to reduce operating costs by 10% over the next twelve months.

To function productively and maintain smooth operations, management must co-ordinate the organisation's activity - which involves a range of people, tasks, technologies and resources - so that they are in the right place at the right time and working in the right way. They should ensure that instructions are clear and effective and performance is monitored and controlled

Co-ordination and team working is important, especially when some activities of the organisation are dependent on the successful and timely completion of other activities. You must be aware of the plans and deadlines of your colleagues and know how your work integrates with other people's work.
Poor co-ordination can lead to:
· workflow problems with alternating overloads and waiting periods as work arrives unplanned or later than planned from other sections or departments
· disagreements between departments over who is to blame for the problems
· complaints from clients and other external parties indicating that products and/or services are not being delivered on time or different departments are giving out different information.

Two of the most effective tools of co-ordination are communication and co-operation and both are partly **your** responsibility.

· **Communication** means sharing task-related information so that the inter-relationships of different activities and plans is understood and any variation from the plan, or difficulty meeting the deadline, are notified to other people who are likely to be affected by it.
· **Co-operation** means controlling conflict by taking other people's needs into consideration and not competing or hoarding valuable information.

KAPLAN PUBLISHING

### 4.3 Constructive working relationships

To establish constructive working relationships with other individuals the following points must be taken into consideration:

· Not all employees will have the same aptitudes, learning or experience as you. This does not mean they are better or worse than you at their job but these elements should be taken into consideration when dealing with that individual.

· Some employees will be highly motivated while others will be hardly motivated at all. In the work environment it is likely that you will deal with individuals with a wide range of motivation levels. Again this aspect must be taken into consideration when dealing with an individual.

· The employees that you have to work with will have a wide range of personalities. Some of these personalities will be akin to your own, but others will not. Wherever possible you should attempt to ignore any personality conflicts that might occur.

There are a variety of ways of establishing constructive working relationships, for example:

· build up trust - never let people down, violate confidentiality or break promises
· try to help colleagues whenever possible
· provide information requested by the deadline specified
· bring any potential issue/problem to the attention of your manager/supervisor at the earliest possible opportunity
· do not take part in arguments
· refrain from 'office gossip'
· try to find a compromise where you cannot do everything required of you or cannot meet a deadline.

In general you should consider not only your own position but also that of the person you are dealing with. A good rule is to treat others in the way in which you would yourself expect to be treated.

This means having a polite attitude, tact and sensitivity that applies in all situations.

## ○ EXAMPLES                                          ○○○○

Some examples of appropriate and inappropriate actions and styles of approach in different situations are given below.

· Care should be taken in the form of address of individuals. Obviously it is more than likely that you will address your colleagues by their first names. However unless it is company policy that all members of staff are addressed by their first names it is probably more appropriate to, at least initially, address a more senior person by their title i.e. Mr, Mrs etc and their surname. This may well lead to an immediate invitation to call the manager by their forename, but it is better to err on the side of politeness than on the side of over-familiarity.

· However you may communicate with friends in general, try to avoid any familiar expressions or friendly endearments such as 'darling' or 'dear'. In business such phrases can sound either over-familiar, and un-businesslike, or simply patronising.

· Respect. This applies to both your superiors and your colleagues and subordinates. It will often be the case that you do not like a manager, or even consider that manager to be no good at his or her job. However they are in a position of authority because the organisation believes that they do a good job. You should always bear this in mind and respect them for it. In a similar way colleagues and subordinates also deserve your respect and politeness. Simply because you have authority over another person's work does not give you the right to treat them with any less respect.

· Most individuals have good and bad days. Whatever your personal situation at a particular time, even if you are angry, frustrated or bored, do not let this show in your communication with others. Certainly explain any anger, frustration or boredom to the appropriate person but no benefit will be achieved by losing one's temper or appearing to be whining or whinging.

· Respect the fact that you may work with people from a variety of different social, ethnic and religious backgrounds. You may not fully understand an individual's cultural background but you should be prepared to accept it even if you do not fully comprehend.

## 5   Test your knowledge

1   What will a job description include?

2   Objectives can be assessed using the mnemonic SMART. What do these letters stand for?

3   Distinguish between efficiency and effectiveness.

4   The Workplace (Health, Safety & Welfare) Regulations 1992 lays down minimum standards in which areas?

5   What are the characteristics of an organised work area?

6   Poor co-ordination can lead to workflow problems with alternating overloads and waiting periods as work arrives unplanned or later than planned from other sections or departments. What sort of knock-on effect does this have?

7   List the ways to establish constructive working relationships.

[Answers on p. 131]

## 6 Summary

Working productively means working efficiently and effectively. It is important for you to organise your workspace so that you and all employees who use that work area can accomplish this.

Employees naturally like to bring personal items into the workplace. If you choose to do so, you should take notice of the organisation's guidelines and also your colleagues' views on what is acceptable. The aim should be to give a positive image both to colleagues and to outsiders who are visiting.

You should be able to identify problems with the working environment - such as noise, heat and lighting conditions - which might interfere with effective and efficient working. You should also be able to decide whether to deal with the problem yourself, or in consultation with colleagues, or whether to refer them to your manager or supervisor.

Equipment in the work area will normally be provided with the manufacturer's instructions for the use and maintenance of that equipment. The organisation may also provide written guidelines for the use of the equipment. It is the responsibility of every employee to be aware of the instructions and guidelines and to take notice of them when using the equipment and encountering problems.

### Answers to chapter activities & 'test your knowledge' questions

| △ ACTIVITY 1 △△△△ |
| --- |
| By knowing exactly what their personal objectives are, employees can do the following:<br><br>(a)  Plan and direct their effort towards the objectives.<br>(b)  Monitor their performance against objectives and adjust (or learn) if required.<br>(c)  Experience the motivation of a challenge. |

| △ ACTIVITY 2 △△△△ |
| --- |
| ·  Your desk is awkwardly situated by the photocopier. You work inefficiently because you are some distance from the accounts workstations. Your position also affects your effectiveness because of the fumes from the machine. You obviously cannot drag the desk across the office, nor is office layout something that you can make a decision about. So you will have to refer the problem to Chris Triggs, your line manager. If there is space in the part of the office you have identified, Chris can arrange to have the desk moved, but not before careful measurements have been made and the matter referred to the office staff.<br>·  Temperature and air quality in an office are critical factors for effective working. If the working environment is too hot, as could be the case here, people become drowsy and headachy; if the office is too cold, people are |

uncomfortable and distracted from their work. A further aspect of the problem is that some people like higher temperatures than others. The situation in this office, as in many other offices, is that the temperature rises in the afternoon. The solution is for you to discuss the matter with your colleagues, in one of your regular team meetings. If there is a majority in favour of turning the heating down – which can easily be done using the thermostatic control on the wall – you could do this at the appropriate time of day. You would, of course, have to consult first with Chris, your line manager, but he is unlikely to object.

· Dazzling sunshine can be very pleasant when you are out for lunch, but can reduce effectiveness and efficiency in a workplace. You and your colleagues find that not being able to see a VDU properly can result in eye-strain. The solution here is simple. You show some initiative and one lunchtime spend half-an-hour untangling the cords which operate the blinds. They can now be opened and closed normally, to the benefit of everyone. This is not a problem that you need to refer to a line manager or even to all your colleagues – you just take a decision and get on with it.

· A number of things can cause pains or discomfort in the neck, shoulders or arms. For example, sitting in the same position for a long time and/or rapid or repetitive movements of the head, body or arms.  If your job involves working at a computer then you should be aware of how you can adjust your chair and VDU to allow you to be more comfortable. You should try to:

· Leave plenty of space to move your legs under the desk.
· Make sure your chair armrests do not collide with the desk or prevent you sitting as close as you want to your workstation.
· Keep forearms approximately horizontal. The right kind of armrests should help you achieve this.
· Avoid undue extension and bending of wrists.
· Set computer screen height to prevent awkward neck positions. Looking straight at the screen is much better than peering up, down or sideways at it for hours on end.
· Use the keyboard in the flat position; your forearms should be level with the work surface and your wrists should rest on the work surface
· Use a footrest when the desk and chair heights are set up right but you cannot rest your feet flat on the floor

**Test your knowledge** △ △ △

1 A job description is a broad statement of the purpose and scope of the job. It specifies the tasks, details responsibilities, sets authority limits, distinguishes accountability and outlines the organisational relationships that the job entails.

2 Objectives can be assessed against the following criteria (for which the mnemonic is SMART): specific, measurable, achievable, result-oriented, time-bounded.

3 **Effectiveness** is 'doing the right things' and is a measure of the match or mismatch between what you produce (your actual output) and what you should be producing (defined in terms of your organisational goals). It means setting the right goals and objectives and then making sure they are accomplished. **Efficiency** is 'doing things right' and is a measure of the resources used in producing your actual output. Efficiency means getting the most from your resources.

4 The regulations require the provision of a safe and healthy workplace in terms of lighting, heating, washing facilities, sanitary conveniences and traffic routes. They lay down minimum standards that are necessary to promote efficiency and effectiveness amongst employees.

5 An organised work area has a number of characteristics: it is tidy; it is clean; you know where everything is and can find it quickly; everything is within easy reach; the VDU is correctly set up; and the chair is correctly adjusted for you.

6 The knock-on effects could include disagreements between departments over who is to blame for the problems and complaints from clients and other external parties indicating that products and/or services are not being delivered on time or different departments are giving out different information.

7 To establish constructive working relationships you should try to build up trust by never letting people down, violating confidentiality or breaking promises. You should try to help colleagues whenever possible, provide information requested by the deadline specified (finding a compromise where you cannot do everything required of you or cannot meet a deadline), bring any potential issue/problem to the attention of your manager/supervisor at the earliest possible opportunity, avoid arguments and refrain from 'office gossip'.

# PLANNING AND ORGANISING WORK

## INTRODUCTION

Planning at the organisational level is the process of deciding what should be done, who should do it and when and how it should be done. At the individual level it involves scheduling routine tasks so that they will be completed in time and working into the routine any urgent tasks that interrupt the usual level of working. Work planning means establishing priorities and allocating and scheduling tasks using planning aids such as lists, action plans, timetables, diaries and charts.

## KNOWLEDGE & UNDERSTANDING

· Sources of legal requirements: companies acts (Item 2)
· Employee responsibilities in complying with the relevant legislation (Item 4)
· Work methods and practices in your organisation (Item 5)
· The scope and limit of your own authority for taking corrective action (Item 14)
· Target setting, prioritising and organising work (Item 16)
· Work planning and scheduling techniques and aids (Item 17)
· Time management (Item 18)
· Team working (Item 19)
· Showing commitment and motivation towards your work (Item 22)
· Deadlines and timescales (Item 23)
· Dealing with changed priorities and unforeseen situations (Item 24)
· The organisational and departmental structure (Item 28)
· Own work role and responsibilities (Item 29)
· Colleagues work roles and responsibilities (Item 30)
· Reporting procedures (Item 31)

## CONTENTS

1 Organisational objectives
2 Organisation structure
3 Work planning
4 Planning methods
5 Time management
6 Difficulties in meeting deadlines

**PERFORMANCE CRITERIA**
· Identify and prioritise tasks according to organisational procedures and regulatory requirements (Item A in Element 23.1)
· Recognise changes in priorities and adapt resources allocations and work plans accordingly (Item B in Element 23.1)
· Use appropriate planning aids to plan and monitor work progress (Item C in Element 23.1)
· Identify, negotiate and co-ordinate relevant assistance to meet specific demands and deadlines (Item D in Element 23.1)
· Report anticipated difficulties in meeting deadlines to the appropriate person (Item E in Element 23.1)
· Check that work methods and activities conform to legal and regulatory requirements and organisational procedures (Item F in Element 23.1)

# 1 Organisational objectives

## 1.1 Introduction

An organisation will establish goals, objectives and strategies and then determine the policies and procedures necessary to achieve its stated aims. Its effectiveness is generally determined by how well the objectives are being achieved.

Once the objectives are set management will structure the tasks that need to be performed, and decide which department and which individuals will complete which task and when.

## 1.2 Work methods and practices

The work methods and practices are influenced by:
· the job that needs to be done – its purpose, manner, order and deadline
· the law – making sure the job is done in a safe and secure manner in accordance with the regulations and codes of practice
· the culture of the organisation – the 'way we do things round here' based on the organisation and work group's values.

The work methods chosen should bring together the above to ensure jobs gets done in the right order and in the best way possible in accordance with legal requirements and the organisation's procedures. There should be no duplication or part cover of the work and efforts should be harnessed to a common goal.

## 1.3 Performance and motivation

Recognising appropriate direction techniques requires identification and selection of the most efficient means of stimulating outstanding performance.

The work methods and practices chosen by the organisation will not work to get the job done unless the person chosen to do the job is sufficiently able and motivated.

One of the models of motivation shows what job performance depends on:

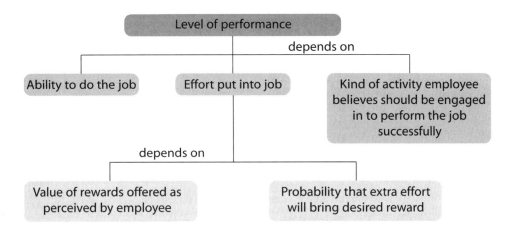

This model shows that in any given situation the greater the number and variety of rewards available to an employee, the greater is the probability that extra effort will be put into attaining the targets set, in the hope of gaining the rewards desired.

## 1.4 Legal, regulatory and organisational requirements

Laws or agreements of confidentiality will cover some information from within your organisation. For example, you may be required by contract not to disclose financial information. Many of the activities and procedures in the finance section of an organisation will be aimed at producing returns and forms to conform to the legal and regulatory requirements associated with payroll, VAT and tax returns.

The legal and regulatory requirements that you must consider are those under the Data Protection Act and the Companies Act.

**The Data Protection Act** – is all about protecting data concerning individuals where this data is processed automatically i.e., by computer. This is important from your work point of view in that personal details of employees are confidential under the Act and you might have access to these if you are dealing with payroll details. Because computers can bring together vast amounts of information, process it rapidly and transfer it instantly anywhere in the world, there is an inherent danger that information could be corrupted, used out of context or lost in the system, with the result that individuals would suffer.

**The Companies Act** – provides a statutory framework for the preparation of the accounts of limited companies. It outlines formats, fundamental accounting principles, valuation rules and possible exemptions for small and medium-sized companies.

The most important deadlines for a company are those where penalties arise if returns and payments are not made in time. Many of the activities and procedures in the finance section of an organisation will be aimed at producing returns and forms to conform to the legal and regulatory requirements associated with payroll, VAT and tax returns.

Some examples of penalties include:
· £100 fine if you do not file your income tax return by 31 January.
· Failing to register at the correct time – there are significant penalties for being late in notifying the HM Revenue and Customs of a requirement to be VAT registered.
· Failing to submit returns on time.
· Incorrect returns – errors discovered by the HM Revenue and Customs may carry a 15% misdeclaration penalty. Failure to submit an EU sales statement may give rise to penalties.
· Record-keeping – you need to record all your business transactions, and keep documents including bank statements, bills, receipts and cheque stubs to back them up. You also need to separate your business transactions from your personal finances.

Rather like keeping records for HM Revenue and Customs, you need to be meticulous about VAT. For VAT purposes, you must keep a record of all the supplies you make and receive, and a summary of VAT for each tax period covered by your tax returns. Records must be up to date and easy to find, and if you register for VAT you must keep your records for six years.

## 2 Organisation structure

### 2.1 Structural relationships

There are different ways of looking at this topic. We can start with the structural types of roles and relationships that show how power, authority and influence are built into the organisation. Working relationships can also be considered in terms of their contractual, ethical and legal effect. Overlaid on the structural factors, there are interpersonal relationships, which include team working, inter-departmental relations and networking.

The formal structure, communications and procedures of the organisation are based on authority, responsibility and functional relationships. You need to know what areas you have authority over and how far that authority extends – who you report to and who reports to you. The basic relationship in an organisation is that between superior and subordinate. The superior has authority i.e. the right or power to make decisions or give instructions or orders to the subordinate.

There are also the peer relationships – people you work with and who share similar goals to you. Your plans and schedules need to dovetail with those of other individuals and teams with whom your work is linked.

In most organisations this role and the responsibilities involved in the role will be determined by the job description. Every employee should have a detailed job description. Only then can one fully appreciate one's own role and responsibilities.

As well as being aware of your role and responsibilities, in some organisations there is a process of management by objectives (MBO) in which your supervisor or manager will agree specific, measurable goals with you on a regular basis. He or she will also agree on working methods and schedules as well as agree the resources to complete the job. You are then responsible for attaining these goals within a certain time. After this time has elapsed you should meet up with your superior again to discuss results and establish new objectives.

## 2.2 Authority and responsibility

Organisation structure is the division of work among members of the organisation and the co-ordination of their activities so they are directed towards the goals and objectives of the organisation. It means grouping people into departments or sections, defining tasks and responsibilities, work roles and relationships and channels of communication and allocating authority and responsibility.

---

### □ DEFINITION □□□□

**Authority** can be defined as the right that an individual has to require certain actions of others i.e. it is the right to use power.

**Responsibility** is the duty of an official to carry out his or her assigned task or to get others to do it.

**Delegation** is the act by which a person transfers part of their authority to a subordinate person.

---

This creates a hierarchy or chain of command where authority flows downwards from the top management to each level of the organisation. This chain is illustrated below with the arrows down showing the delegation:

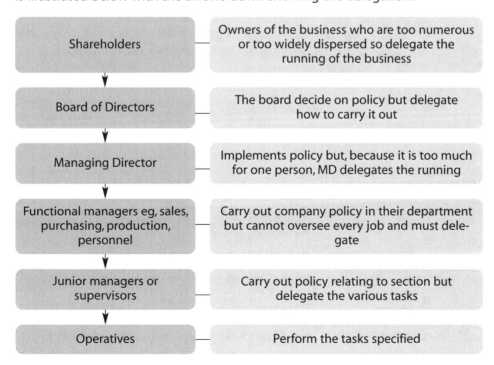

| | |
|---|---|
| Shareholders | Owners of the business who are too numerous or too widely dispersed so delegate the running of the business |
| Board of Directors | The board decide on policy but delegate how to carry it out |
| Managing Director | Implements policy but, because it is too much for one person, MD delegates the running |
| Functional managers eg, sales, purchasing, production, personnel | Carry out company policy in their department but cannot oversee every job and must delegate |
| Junior managers or supervisors | Carry out policy relating to section but delegate the various tasks |
| Operatives | Perform the tasks specified |

The chain of delegation gives employees the means to resolve or refer any problems or queries regarding work activities to the appropriate person.

### 2.3 Organisational and departmental structure

An organisation must be set up in a formal manner to give it some authority or some standing. This means that those within the organisation must be organised so that they know what to do and whom to ask for advice.

· An organisation chart describes in diagrammatic form the structure of the organisation. It illustrates who communicates with whom, how the control system works, who is in control, who has authority and above all, who is responsible. It shows:
  – direction of responsibility (the chart indicates the direct relationship between a group and its immediate supervisor and subordinates)
  – relationships between various sections within a department.

It can outline areas of responsibility for each department and line manager and be extended down to individual employees if necessary.

There are a number of ways to show the grouping of people in the organisation. The functional structure (see below) shows responsibility allocated to specialised functions:

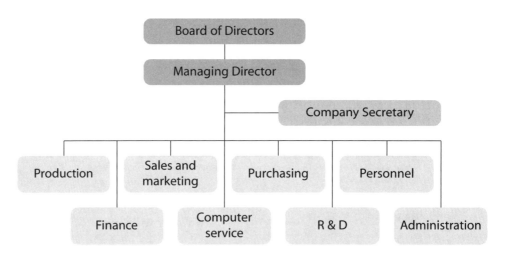

The organisation chart of the finance department might be shown as:

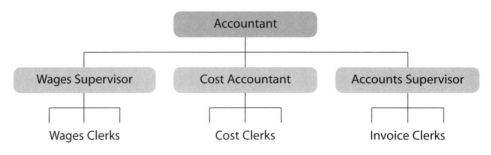

## 2.4    Teams and teamwork

The basic work unit of organisations has traditionally been the functional department, such as accounting or sales. In more recent times, organisations have adopted smaller, more flexible and responsible units – set up as matrix structures, which tend to favour team working.. This allows work to be shared among a number of individuals so that it gets done more efficiently and effectively than by individuals working alone. Teams are particularly effective for increasing communication, generating new ideas and evaluating ideas from different viewpoints.

A team may be set up as a separate unit on a more or less permanent basis, with responsibilities for a certain product or stage of a process; alternatively, it may be on a temporary basis for the attainment of the task or project and after it is completed, the team is disbanded or members are re-assigned to a new task.

Multi-skilled teams bring together individuals who can perform any of the group's tasks. These can be shared out in a flexible way according to availability and inclination.

Multi-disciplinary teams bring together individuals with different specialisms so that their skills, knowledge and experience can be pooled or exchanged.

## 2.5  Work roles and responsibilities

You will notice that there are three basic relationships between roles at work:
1    the **subordinate** role – in which you work for and report to others
2    the **peer** role – where you work with others to achieve certain goals, and
3    the **authority** role – where other people work for and report to you.

In most organisations this role and the responsibilities involved in the role will be determined by the job description.

Every employee should have a job description that specifies the tasks; details responsibilities; sets authority limits; distinguishes accountability; and outlines the organisational relationships that the job entails. There are various methods of classification but most include all of the following points:
·    **Identification of the job** – this includes the job title, the department/organisation structure and the number of people doing the job.
·    **Purpose of the job** – identifying its objectives in relationship to overall objectives, e.g. to manage the manufacturing unit of the department making garden gnomes and plant pots.
·    **Position in the organisation** indicating the relationships with other jobs and the chains of responsibility. For this purpose, many firms refer to existing organisation charts.
·    **Duties** – the principal duties to be performed, with emphasis on key tasks, and limits to the job-holder's authority. Usually under this heading is included an indication of how the job differs from others in the organisation. A further breakdown of principal duties is made identifying specific tasks in terms of

what precisely is done and in what manner, and with some explanation, both in terms of quantity and quality. When listing all the tasks involved it is preferable to use an active verb to precede each duty e.g. types letters to clients; lists totals of debtors.

- **Responsibilities** – a statement outlining the responsibilities for the resources e.g. staff, money and machinery.
- **Physical conditions** – including details of noisy, dirty, dangerous conditions or pleasant office conditions, and also hours of work, overtime, unsocial hours etc.
- **Social conditions** – the type of group the employee will be concerned with.
- **Grade and salary/wage range and fringe benefits** – details of the rates for the grade, increments, piece-work, bonuses and commission, plus fringe benefits such as luncheon vouchers, pension schemes, company car, etc.
- **Promotion prospects** – to whom the job reports and at what level, with possible indications about future succession, prospects of promotion or transfer.
- **Key difficulties** – no job description is complete without a full identification of the key difficulties likely to be encountered by the job-holder.

You should try to ensure that you have a detailed job description. Only then can you fully appreciate your own role and responsibilities.

For example you are a sales ledger clerk with certain responsibilities for a number of customer accounts. You have made an appointment with the sales ledger manager to discuss the credit limits of seven of your current customers. During the course of the meeting with your manager he makes it quite clear that the subject of credit limits is the sole responsibility of another member of the staff. They are quite clearly outside of your own responsibilities.

The result of not knowing your own role and responsibilities has meant wasted time for both yourself and your manager.

### 2.6  Colleagues' work roles and responsibilities

If you wish to discuss a work related matter then an initial problem is who is the appropriate or relevant member of staff to discuss this matter with. This will usually depend on the roles and responsibilities of other members of staff, which you may not know in detail. However the options are usually as follows:

- **Line managers** – these are managers who manage various areas or departments of a business, for example the production manager, sales manager, marketing manager, finance manager etc. If the matter to be discussed appears to be important or personal then the appropriate line manager will probably be the person to approach.
- **Immediate colleagues** – if the matter to be discussed is regarding, perhaps, advice as to how to approach a routine task then a colleague with more

experience than yourself might be the appropriate person. It is worth bearing in mind that a great deal can be learnt from colleagues with greater experience than oneself.

· **Other members of staff with related work activities** – in many instances knowledge and understanding of a particular matter will be shared by a number of members of staff throughout the organisation, even though they are in different departments or activity areas. These could be the appropriate people to discuss matters with in certain circumstances.

In practice, it may be difficult to know exactly who is the appropriate member of staff for a particular piece of information or message. It is unlikely that each individual fully understands the role and responsibilities of all other individuals in the organisation.

You should be aware of the line and staff relations in your organisational structure. Draw an organisation chart of your company, putting names and a brief job description beside the line managers, immediate colleagues and other members of staff with related work activities.

| Knowing who does what and where, enables you to: |
| --- |
| · communicate more freely and efficiently |
| · seek and exchange information, advice and support |
| · negotiate the assistance of others |
| · transfer telephone calls to the right person |
| · deliver mail accurately |
| · handle any enquiries effectively. |

## 3 Work planning

### 3.1 Planning and organising

All levels of management are involved in planning. At the top level decisions are made on what to do and as you come down the hierarchy the plan is fleshed out to incorporate how it is to be done and when it is going to be done.

Organising is the next stage after planning. It means working out the actual jobs needed to be done to fulfil the plans agreed upon, grouping activities into a pattern or structure and giving specific jobs to people in the organisation to achieve the plans agreed upon and setting deadlines for their completion.

At the individual level work planning involves scheduling and timetabling routine tasks so that they will be completed at the right time and handling high priority tasks and deadlines, which interrupt the usual level of working.

The basic steps and objectives in work planning include the following:

the establishment and effective treatment of priorities (considering tasks in order of importance for the objective concerned)

scheduling or timetabling tasks, and allocating them to different individuals within appropriate timescales (e.g. continuous routine work and arrangements for priority work with short-term deadlines), to achieve work deadlines and attain goals

co-ordinating individual tasks within the duties of single employees or within the activities of groups of individuals

establishing checks and controls to ensure that priority deadlines are being met and work is not 'falling behind', and routine tasks are achieving their objectives

agreeing the mechanism and means to re-schedule ordinary work to facilitate and accommodate new, additional or emergency work by drawing up 'contingency plans' for unscheduled events. Because nothing goes exactly according to plan, one feature of good planning is to make arrangements for what should be done if there were a major upset, e.g. if the company's computer were to break down, or if the major supplier of key raw materials were to go bust. The major problems for which contingency plans might be made are events that, although unlikely, stand a slim chance of actually happening.

The tasks you do at work will fall into four categories:

1   daily e.g. routine tasks such as recording sales invoices in sales day book or recording cash received
2   weekly e.g. preparing journal entries to post totals from books of prime entry to nominal ledger
3   monthly e.g. bank reconciliation or sales ledger reconciliation
4   one-off e.g. information for a report.

Most employees in an organisation will spend the majority of their time working on the routine tasks that are part of their job and responsibilities. However at times unexpected and non-routine tasks may arise. These must also be dealt with without affecting the routine responsibilities. The performance criterion states that you should:

·   identify and prioritise tasks according to organisational procedures and regulatory requirements
·   recognise changes in priorities and adapt resources allocations and work plans accordingly
·   check that work methods and activities conform to legal and regulatory requirements and organisational procedures.

### 3.2 Agreeing timescales

The planning of work involves the allocation of time to the requirements of work to be done. This must be applied to the organisation as a whole, to individual departments and sections, and to single employees. Planning must be geared to periods of time, and the degree of flexibility built into planning will vary according to the length of time being planned for. The principles of planning will revolve around:

(a)   determining the length of time covered by the plans

(b)   planning by departments and groups of individuals

(c)   planning by individuals.

There are three time ranges, which are normally involved in planning work:

(a)   long-term

(b)   medium-term

(c)   short-term.

These three terms are really only expressions of convenience. Time is relative. For example, a length of five years might be considered long-term within an organisation producing footwear but short-term in, say, the aviation industry. It may well be that three years is short-term to an organisation but to a department within that organisation it may be medium-term whilst to an individual employee it may be long-term. It is important that, whatever the relevant time span may be to a group or individual, work is allocated accordingly.

### 3.3 Identifying priorities

Much office work is of a routine nature although there are exceptions. Priorities must be established with regard to the cyclical nature of routine work and unexpected demands.

The cyclical nature of routine work often means that certain tasks have to be completed by a certain time. In such cases other work may have to be left in order to ensure that the task with the approaching deadline date is given priority. Such tasks might include:

·   the preparation of payroll sheets for a weekly computer run

·   the despatch of monthly statements to account customers

·   the checking of stock levels at predetermined intervals and appropriate action such as re-ordering.

Unexpected demands are often made at departmental, sectional or individual level. If management requires urgent or additional work to be carried out then, obviously, some other tasks will have to be postponed.

Given that routine tasks may be anticipated and that unexpected demands cannot, this area of priority identification can be divided into routine tasks, which can be accommodated within normal sensible planning and 'emergency-type' tasks that must be performed at short notice.

Routine work usually includes a number of tasks that, as a matter of course, fall into a natural order in which they should be performed. This 'natural order of events' approach can usually be incorporated into the normal routine of the office and/or the individual to such an extent that often it is not apparent that there has ever been a problem with the identification of priority tasks.

Where tasks/events of an 'emergency-type' nature arise the main problem facing an individual will be that of deciding which of the routine tasks should be postponed. However, the postponement of one routine task will automatically delay successive tasks.

### 3.4 Guidelines for determining priorities

In determining priorities, the following should be noted.
- Wherever it is possible for a priority to be anticipated, such as in the case of the 'natural order of events' described above, then associated difficulties will usually be overcome by sensible, logical planning.
- If an 'emergency type' task occurs, then normal routine work will automatically take second place. It is here that decisions must be taken to decide which routine tasks should be postponed. Also, plans should be formulated and implemented to ensure that the routine work postponed is carried out as soon as possible, resulting in minimum disruption to the normal routine.

Often there may arise situations where one priority comes into conflict with another. Here the task deemed more important by a responsible individual should take preference.

Unfortunately, individuals within one department or section often become blind to the needs of other departments or sections. A task that is classed as low priority within one department or section may be of the utmost priority to another. Thus in arriving at any decision the individual making that decision must ensure that the effect on each department is included in the decision-making process.

A responsible individual should determine priorities. Often, especially in the matter of routine cycles, the individual responsible for that work will be qualified to determine any priority. However, the greater the effect and the wider the span of influence of priority determination, the more responsible the individual should be.

When an unexpected task is given to you then you must have the flexibility to be able to reschedule your routine work in order to complete this task.

### 3.5 Setting priorities

Activities need to be sequenced and scheduled. There may be conflict between the two planning tasks since the best sequence of activities to put the plan into place might not be consistent with the schedule of when particular activities need to be completed. The sequence of activities may be determined by the following:
- An activity must precede another when it is a pre-requisite for later activities. Assembly of a car cannot precede the manufacture or purchase of its components.

- The sequence of activities may be dictated by the ease with which they can be done. New products or services are often introduced into the most receptive parts of the market first.
- An activity may be considered more important than others, e.g. in the building industry priority will be given to outdoor work when the weather is favourable to minimise the risk of delays later.

The organisation's operations require proper scheduling of resources to run efficiently and avoid periods of over and under utilisation. Some activities must occur at precisely the right time, e.g. specific day and time slot for advertising a new product. The scheduling of tasks can also affect customer service in terms of delivery.

### 3.6  Prioritisation of routine tasks

Routine tasks may be tasks that are performed a number of times each day, tasks performed once or twice each day, tasks necessary each week, or at the end of each month perhaps.
Examples of routine tasks might include the following:
- sending out of invoices to customers each day
- opening the post at the beginning of the day and again after the second post has arrived
- filing all copy invoices at the end of the week
- preparing a list of outstanding customer balances at the end of each month.

Priorities are tasks listed in order of importance. Each day employees will need to prioritise the tasks that they are required to do during that day.

The first job of the day might be to open the post, as the post may contain urgent items to be dealt with by yourself or other members of the department. This will therefore be a high priority job and should not be left until the middle of the morning.

If your job includes responsibility for sending out invoices to customers then it will be a fairly high priority that these invoices are sent out on the same day as the sale or customer order. The task of filing copies of the invoices is less urgent. It may be possible to leave this until later in the day, or even later in the week.

Another skill you can use to analyse jobs is sequencing. When you put things in sequence, you arrange steps in the order that you do them. When you work out the sequence to carry out the tasks, you are judging two things:
- How urgent is the task?
- How important is the task?

These are not the same thing. Urgent tasks need to be completed within a particular time limit. Important jobs may affect a lot of people or cost a lot of money. They may also have major implications if they are not done, or if they are done badly. If you are going abroad on holiday, it is important that you have a passport. If your holiday isn't for six months, it isn't urgent. It becomes urgent if you leave it too late.

### 3.7 Prioritisation of unexpected tasks

Unexpected or non-routine tasks will normally occur for one of two reasons.

1   The unexpected tasks may be due to additional activity in the organisation, such as a new product launch or takeover of another company.
2   Unexpected tasks can also occur due to some 'emergency' within the organisation such as a fellow member of staff being off work sick or an error being found which must be dealt with immediately.

They should be fairly easy to identify, as they will normally involve instruction from a more senior member of staff. For example if a member of your department is off sick, and is unlikely to return for the rest of the week, it is likely that the manager or supervisor will re-schedule that person's tasks to be dealt with by the other members of the department.

However some unexpected tasks might not be so clearly signalled. For example suppose that you answer the telephone for a colleague during his lunch break. The call is from a customer with an urgent request for information then this customer query may be an unexpected task that you will need to deal with.

If an unexpected task is identified then this must also be prioritised and fitted in with the routine tasks of the individual's job. Unexpected tasks will not always be necessarily urgent, although many will be. When an unexpected task is identified the individual should ensure that he or she fully understands the following points:
·   the precise nature of the task
·   the resources or information required to carry out the task
·   the time required to obtain those resources or information
·   the time that the task is expected to take (remember that as an unexpected task it is unlikely that the individual will have performed this task before)
·   the time allowed for this task and deadline set for it
·   the importance of the task
·   the priority it should be allocated in respect of the work being carried out.

Only when aware of all of these points is it possible to correctly prioritise the task and schedule it together with their remaining routine tasks.

For example suppose that you are required to produce a report for a board meeting on Wednesday 12 March. Today is Monday 3 March. In order to produce the report you will require a number of files from the central filing system which are likely to take two days to be accessed and delivered. The manager of the department who has commissioned this report estimates that there will be approximately one full day's work obtaining the relevant information from the files and another half day in actually preparing the report itself. Owing to backlogs in the typing department your manager suggests that the report is with the typist by next Monday morning, 10 March, at the latest in order that it can be typed, proof read and any adjustments made in time for the board meeting on Wednesday 12 March.

In this instance the only task that you will need to perform immediately, a high priority today, is to inform central filing of the files that are required for the report. As the files will not reach you until Wednesday then there can be nothing else done for this task until that day. You must then ensure that during Wednesday, Thursday and Friday approximately a day and a half is set aside to prepare and write the report. You must also ensure that when the report is returned from typing at the beginning of the following week the proof reading is again given a high priority.

As a further example suppose that a colleague in your department has called in sick with flu this Monday morning. Your manager estimates that your colleague will not return to work this week and therefore all of his responsibilities must be dealt with by the other members of the department for the entire week. One of your colleague's responsibilities, which your manager has allocated to you, is to deal with customer complaints. It is the organisation's procedure to ensure that all complaints are dealt with, even if this is simply an acknowledging letter, on the same day as the complaint is received. Therefore, in order to comply with organisational procedures, you will need to give priority to any complaints received in the post each morning and any telephone complaints received during each day. Again you must also ensure that your own priority routine tasks, such as sending out invoices on the day of the order, are completed at the appropriate time.

---

▷ **ACTIVITY 1**

List all of your routine daily tasks.

Make a separate list of all non-routine tasks that may arise, and state why they arise. (By their nature non-routine tasks are unexpected and you may need to invent possible non-routine tasks!)

This activity covers performance criterion A in Element 23.1.

[Answer on p. 159]

---

### 3.8 Prioritisation using the Time Management Grid

Prioritisation is a difficult skill that many employees simply never learn to do – they never learn to distinguish between important and urgent. Something may be important (e.g. a report to management) but may not be urgent, it may not be required until next month. Something else may be **urgent** (requisition of copier paper which has run out) but it is not important!

What often tends to happen is that we do the easy or quick jobs first regardless of their urgency or importance. The trouble is that a lot of quick and easy jobs often take up an inordinate amount of time and have a habit of multiplying. Meanwhile important jobs that require a little more thought and effort are only forced upon us as they grow in urgency and deadlines approach. The longer an important job is kept waiting in the in-tray the more difficult it seems to grow in our minds! A further problem is that an important job done under time pressure is often not done as well as it could have been done given plenty of time. How often have we all wished we had started a difficult job much sooner!

Sometimes it helps to use the idea of importance and urgency to work out the order in which to do tasks. This diagram can help you to sort your tasks and plan when to do them.

|  | **Urgent** | **Not Urgent** |
|---|---|---|
| **Important** | Must be done soon<br>Do you need help? | Plan a time for it to be done |
| **Unimportant** | Can someone else do it?<br>If not, do it quickly | Does it need doing?<br>Can someone else do it? |

### □ DEFINITION

The **Time Management Grid** is a system of ranking jobs according to their urgency and their importance (with 1 being low and 10 being high). A grid is then drawn with important 1 to 10 on the y axis and urgent 1 to 10 on the x axis. The x and y axis intersect each other at 5. This creates four areas in the grid: Urgent and important; urgent but not important; important but not urgent; and finally, neither important nor urgent. From a list of jobs each one is given a ranking for urgency and importance, which can then be 'plotted' on the grid. This gives a graphical representation of how jobs should be prioritised.

The solution to the following activity demonstrates how a Time Management Grid should be drawn

### ▷ ACTIVITY 2

Write down a list of at least 8 to 10 jobs that you must do. Try to categorise them as important or urgent and rank them on a scale of 1 to 10 (with 10 being least important or urgent). Now look at the grid given in the answer, which shows how prioritisation can be illustrated graphically.

This activity covers performance criterion A in Element 23.

[Answer on p. 159]

### 3.9  Change in priorities

The paragraphs so far have discussed the fact that if unexpected tasks are identified then the priorities of an individual may change. One of the performance criterion for this chapter states that 'where priorities change, work plans are changed accordingly'. If the priorities for a particular day change then it is highly likely that the work schedule must also be changed or adapted. For example suppose that an individual's schedule for a day showed the following tasks:

· open the post and deal with any urgent matters
· send out invoices for that day's orders
· fill out time sheet due in three day's time
· prepare notes for meeting with manager in one week's time.

When opening the post an urgent matter is discovered that is likely to take up to three hours of your time. Your manager is insistent that this matter must be dealt with today.  In this case, unless you are to work for two or three extra hours in the day, the daily schedule will need adapting.  The routine tasks that must be carried out each day must still also be done.  Therefore the sending out of sales invoices must also take place in the day.  However the filling out of the time sheet has three days of slack built into it and the preparation of notes for a meeting has a week of slack.  Therefore these items can be viewed as far less urgent and may well be postponed to a later day.

When re-scheduling work for a day students should always ensure that items that must be done that day are covered.  Only items with a degree of slack built into them i.e. items due at some point in the future can be postponed. When adapting or altering work schedules students should always bear in mind any effect that this will have on other members of staff and their own priorities and work schedules.

## 4    Planning methods

### 4.1  Introduction

Different organisations, groups and individuals have individual characteristics, tastes, styles, preferences and objectives. These particular objectives may well be attained via different methods and systems of scheduling work.
As a method of planning group work, it is vital that these efforts are co-ordinated – not only with each other but with all actions taken. The method used can be a means of communication and support within the group, assuring all members of the group progress towards their goal.

The following planning methods and systems are probably the most common:
(a)   checklists
(b)   bar charts
(c)   bring-forward, bring-up and follow-up systems
(d)   activity scheduling and time scheduling
(e)   action sheets
(f)   other systems, including planning charts and boards, and diaries.

Each of these methods and systems will be discussed individually below. However, any combination may be in use at any one time within an organisation or by an individual employee.  It is vital therefore that these efforts are co-ordinated, not only with each other but with all actions taken.

### 4.2  Checklists

Checklists are often used on an individual basis and are perhaps the simplest system, being essentially a list of items or activities. The preparation of a typical checklist would involve the following:
(a)   the formulation of a list of activities and tasks to be performed within a given period
(b)   the identification of urgent or priority tasks

(c)    the maintenance of a continuous checklist with the addition of extra activities and tasks as and when required.

This system is obviously limited in its application because of its simplicity. It is suited to fairly mundane or routine tasks, but it is these tasks, which are often the very essence of the attainment of objectives.

Typical uses of checklists would include the following:
(a)    purchasing requirements
(b)    points to cover at an interview
(c)    points to cover at a meeting (e.g. an agenda)
(d)    organising a conference or meeting.

Below is a checklist to show when certain returns associated with PAYE are due.

**STATUTORY RETURNS SCHEDULE**

| Returns | Description | Date Due | Forward To |
|---------|-------------|----------|------------|
| P60 | This is a total of the employee's year-end earnings including tax and NI. | 05.2006 | Employee |
| P9D | Must be completed for all employees earning less than ?8,500 (including reimbursed expenses and the taxable values of benefits) and for Directors for whom forms P11D are not required. | 07. 2006 | Employee and HM Revenue and Customs |
| P14 | Summary of deductions such as tax, NI, SSP, SMP. | 05.2006 | HM Revenue and Customs |
| P35 | Statement of tax, NI, SSP and SMP for each employee together with an overall summary of the NI monthly or quarterly payments made by the employer in respect of that tax year. | 05.2006 | HM Revenue and Customs |
| P38S | Relates to students who work for an employer during their holidays. | 05.2006 | HM Revenue and Customs |
| WTC | Year-end summary of Working Tax Credits paid to employees throughout the year. | 05.2006 | HM Revenue and Customs |
| DPTC | Year-end summary of Disabled Person's Tax Credit paid to employees throughout the year. | 05.2006 | HM Revenue and Customs |

### 4.3  Bar charts

A bar chart has two main purposes:
(a)    to show the time necessary for an activity
(b)    to display the time relationship between one activity and another.

Bar charts are particularly useful for checking the time schedules for a number of activities that are interdependent. A bar chart for the building of a house extension might be shown over a period of six months and an example is given below.

| Task | March | April | May | June | July | August |
|------|-------|-------|-----|------|------|--------|
| Dig foundations | ▬▬▬ | | | | | |
| Walls/floors | | ▬▬▬ | | | | |
| Windows | | | ▬▬▬ | | | |
| Door frames | | | | ▬▬▬ | | |
| Roof | | | | ▬▬▬ | | |
| Electric wiring | | | | ▬▬▬ | | |
| Plumbing | | | ▬▬▬ | | | |
| Glazing | | | | | ▬▬▬ | |
| Plastering | | | | | | ▬▬▬ |

This illustrates the importance of bar charts in showing:
(a)   overall progress to date, thus assisting in monitoring
(b)   the progress attained at an individual stage of a multi-stage process.


### 4.4  Bring-forward, bring-up and follow-up systems

These systems are more sophisticated than checklists and bar charts. They are particularly useful for coping with documentation and are utilised in many offices. The systems involve the filing of details of work to be done and the dates on which this work is to be done. A routine is established with a view to allocating necessary tasks to the precise day.

The systems all operate around the following principles:

a note is made of anything to be done in the future, showing details of the appropriate action or format (e.g. make a telephone call or write a letter)

↓

the note is filed away in a concertina folder with separate files for each day

↓

each appropriate file is checked at the start of each day and the action required that day noted

↓

the action is carried out.

### 4.5 Activity scheduling

> **☐ DEFINITION**
>
> **Activity scheduling** is concerned with the determination of priority and the establishment of the order in which tasks are to be tackled. The establishment of an order of priority is not as easy in practice as it may appear in theory.

Some tasks must be completed before others may be commenced, some may need to be carried out at the same time as others and some may need to be completed at the same time as others but factors such as finance or manpower may prevent this. A typical problem that is particularly suited to activity scheduling is the arrangement of an interview where, say, three panel members are required and six candidates have been short-listed for interview. Obviously, mutually convenient dates must be found when all nine parties are available and the room, which is to be used for the interview, must be free for use on these days.

Activity scheduling involves the identification of key factors and their assembly on a checklist. In the example given above, the two key factors are room availability and people availability. It may be used for any task, which involves a number of actions that must necessarily be undertaken in some sequence.

### 4.6 Time scheduling

> **☐ DEFINITION**
>
> **Time scheduling** is an extension of activity scheduling by indicating the required time for each task. It follows the preparation of an activity schedule and involves the determination of time required for each activity.

Given that within an activity schedule some tasks will be performed simultaneously, it should be noted that the time period in which the series of activities will be completed may not equate to the total of the individual activity times.

Effectively a time schedule determines the order in which activities are scheduled on a checklist, the time required for each activity also being shown alongside each item. Tasks that can be done in parallel are noted. The total of the individual activity times, with allowances for simultaneous activities, will produce the time allowed for one complete group of activities.

Time scheduling is thus particularly useful in the process of planning, especially as it enables the initial deadlines to be set.

### 4.7 Action sheets

This system is a natural progression from activity and time scheduling. Action sheets summarise the time that the stages of the individual task should take, and contain estimates of the start and finish dates of each stage.

The example below depicts an action sheet for a wedding.

| Activity number | Detail | Number of weeks in advance | Certification of completion *(initials or signature)* |
|---|---|---|---|
| 1 | Book church | 26 | |
| 2 | Book reception hall | 26 | |
| 3 | Send out invitations | 12 | |
| 4 | Receive replies | 4 | |
| 5 | Order food/refreshments | 3 | |
| 6 | Check arrangements | 2 | |
| 7 | The wedding day | – | |

Action sheets are widely used and are often utilised in conjunction with bar charts.

## 4.8 Planning charts and boards

These usually show information in summary form and any required item of information may be seen at a glance. They are often used to show details of future events that affect departments (e.g. to plan staff holidays).

## 4.9 Diaries

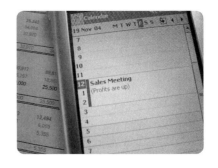

Diaries are an obvious and consequently often over-looked aid to planning. They can range from simple hand-written diaries showing an individual's appointments, meetings etc through to sophisticated computerised diaries either as part of the organisation's computer network or alternatively in some form of electronic personal organiser. Diaries can also usefully be used, not just to show appointments etc, but also to highlight matters that should be followed up or chased up on a particular date. For example suppose that you have been involved in a number of telephone discussions with a potential customer. The potential customer has indicated that he will have decided whether or not to go ahead with an order by Thursday of this week at the latest. You may wish to make a note in your diary for Wednesday to give the potential customer a telephone call in order to determine whether there is any additional information that you can provide.

Diaries are especially suited to individual employees but only if the employee ensures that all relevant details of any appointments are entered as a matter of course. This matter of full details is important because the failure to note down full and appropriate information regarding a particular appointment could have serious repercussions for the organisation, particularly if an appointment has to be rescheduled or handled by someone else. It is sensible to have a routine for making appointments and indeed to create a 'checklist for appointments'.

---

### ▷ ACTIVITY 3 ▷ ▷ ▷ ▷

Kate has recently joined a busy administration department in a manufacturing organisation. She is slightly shocked that the organisation seems to lack formal procedures. She feels that her job is one of 'fire-fighting'. Once one crisis is over another one arrives. She feels there is never a spare moment in the day from 9am when she arrives to 5.30pm when she goes home. She is constantly responding to so called 'urgent' requests from other people to: "just do this for me Kate please, it won't take a moment", or "this job's top priority – can you rush it through please?" Every job seems to be 'top priority'!

How will this 'Crisis Management' method of working impact on Kate? What are the consequences for her work? What time management techniques could Kate use to help organise and prioritise her workload?

This activity covers performance criteria C, D and E in Element 23.1.

[Answer on p. 160]

---

## 5 Time management

### 5.1 Timetabling tasks

Work planning ensures that commitments to others are met within agreed timescales and necessitates planning and organising on the part of the organisation and the employee.

Your time needs to be properly managed if you are to work efficiently and effectively. The first way to start to organise your time is to plan your use of time.

---

### ○ EXAMPLE ○ ○ ○ ○

Here is Joe's diary for the coming week:

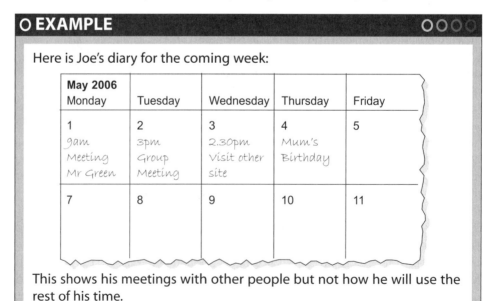

| May 2006 Monday | Tuesday | Wednesday | Thursday | Friday |
|---|---|---|---|---|
| 1 <br> 9am <br> Meeting <br> Mr Green | 2 <br> 3pm <br> Group <br> Meeting | 3 <br> 2.30pm <br> Visit other <br> site | 4 <br> Mum's <br> Birthday | 5 |
| 7 | 8 | 9 | 10 | 11 |

This shows his meetings with other people but not how he will use the rest of his time.

---

KAPLAN PUBLISHING

Here is a more useful version of his diary for the same week:

| May 2006 | | | | | |
|---|---|---|---|---|---|
| | Monday | Tuesday | Wednesday | Thursday | Friday |
| 9am | Meeting Mr Green | Record Cash | Record Cash | Record Cash | Record Cash |
| 10am | | | | | |
| 11am | Record Cash | Update cash book | Bank reconciliation | Finish bank reconciliation | Prepare cash flash figure |
| 12pm | | | | | |
| 1pm | Lunch | Lunch | Lunch | Buy card | Lunch |
| 2pm | Record cash continued | Prepare for meeting | Site Visit | Prepare info for report | Prepare journals |
| 3pm | Speak to Pat about new system? | Group meeting | | | Count petty cash |
| 4pm | | | | | |
| 5pm | Home early | | | | Request cash |

Notice how all the major tasks have been timetabled. Joe has estimated the amount of time to complete each task and blocked out that time. This ensures that Joe has sufficient time to complete tasks before the necessary **deadline**.

## ACTIVITY 4

Do you allow your days to be filled with routine tasks? If so you may be neglecting longer term goals because of this. Draw three columns and in each write down one objectives or target you would like to achieve in the next 12 months. Under each objective you need to plan how it will be achieved. Set any interim targets or shorter-term deadlines that you will need to meet and what action or resources you need to succeed. (If you find setting objectives for the next 12 months too long a time-frame then try setting them on a quarterly basis).

This activity covers performance criterion B in Element 23.1.

[Answer on p. 160]

### 5.2 Timing of tasks

Whatever function you perform at work, you will always have tasks, which fall into four categories:

| Category | Examples |
| --- | --- |
| 1. Daily | Recording cash received<br>Recording sales invoices in sales day book<br>Recording purchase invoices in purchase day book |
| 2. Weekly | Preparing journal entries to post totals from books of prime entry to nominal ledger |
| 3. Monthly | Sales ledger reconciliation<br>Purchase ledger reconciliation<br>Bank reconciliation |
| 4. One-off | Information for reports |

Joe also keeps a list of quick tasks to do at appropriate times. As he does them, he crosses them off his list.

### 5.3 Review of work plans

Each evening before he goes home, Joe reviews his work schedule and updates it for:
(a)   things to carry over
(b)   any other changes (e.g. meeting times changed).

Even if you do not have the opportunity to schedule your work, try scheduling your studies and your free time! You should find you get more out of your time.

## 6    Difficulties in meeting deadlines

### 6.1 Introduction

The syllabus area here is that you 'report anticipated difficulties in meeting deadlines to the appropriate person'. There will always be occasions, when for one reason or another the deadline or target cannot be met. Often individuals are vague regarding the information they require, which may mean wrong or incomplete information is provided. It may be that the deadline cannot be met because of problems encountered by the supplier of information. Perhaps if a student is required to provide some information, he/she might be unable to gather the information by the deadline either because of lack of sufficient working hours, or owing to personal circumstances such as doctor's/dentist's appointments.

Alternatively the problems with meeting the deadline may be due to a third party. Perhaps the information required has to be acquired from a third party. If this third party does not provide the information by the deadline you have set, then you are obviously unable to pass this information on by your deadline.

Identified below are typical examples of problems that may be encountered.

(a)   Files, books, etc may be borrowed and not returned.

(b)   Reference journals may not be kept up to date.

(c)   Access to information may be denied due to security/confidentiality considerations.

(d)   Computer systems may 'crash'.

(e)   International time differences may mean that offices are not open when required.

(f)   Files, books or journals may be incorrectly filed.

(g)   Wrong or insufficient information is provided.

(h)   Delays may occur because information has been archived.

Whatever the reason for not achieving the target or deadline it is vital that students understand the importance of reporting and explaining this fact.

## 6.2  Difficulties are promptly reported

It is tempting in any situation to put off dealing with any problems. In a business context if it appears likely that a deadline is not to be met then it is tempting to put off telling the appropriate person about this in the hope that the information can eventually be reported by the required deadline.

This really is the wrong attitude. As far as your manager or colleague, who has requested the information, is concerned it is far better that he or she knows of any possible delays at the earliest opportunity. It is therefore far better to report any possibility of non-achievement of a target at an early stage than to leave such news until the last minute. This gives the manager a chance to revise his or her plans accordingly.

The rule is therefore that if you become aware of the possibility of not being able to meet a deadline for the supply of information then this should be reported immediately. If the circumstances are eventually favourable and the information is reported by the deadline this will be an added bonus. However if the anticipated circumstances exist and the information is not available then at least the manager concerned has been able to work around the problem.

## 6.3  Explanation of delays

If you are unable to perform a duty by a specified deadline then not only must this fact be reported but it must be reported in an appropriate manner. Not only must politeness be considered but also businesslike behaviour.

Even if you believe that the deadline that has been set is impossible to meet, there will be nothing to be gained from an aggressive or impolite attitude towards the person requiring the information. There will be instances when deadlines are set that are earlier than is absolutely required, and provided that you give your explanation of not being able to meet that deadline in a reasonable manner then it is likely that the deadline will be extended.

In other circumstances the deadline will be vital. Again any aggressive approach by the student concerned will only heighten the displeasure of the manager at the deadline not being met. The best way to deal with any situation where a target or deadline is not achieved is to explain politely and rationally why this has not been achieved. This may be, as mentioned earlier, due to personal circumstances or due to delays from third parties.

## 7  Test your knowledge

1  What is the penalty for not filing your income tax return by 31 January?

2  As a process of management, what does MBO stand for?

3  What are three basic relationships between roles at work?

4  Organising is the next stage after planning. What is involved in this stage?

5  Give an example of a daily, weekly and monthly task.

6  How does an urgent task differ from an important task?

7  What do the four areas of the Time Management Grid represent?

8  Name five aids or tools to work planning.

9  Give six examples that could cause a delay in meeting a deadline.

[Answers on p. 161]

## 8  Summary

This chapter should help you to focus on the way you manage your own workload. How you plan, prioritise and organise both routine and non-routine work is of critical importance to how efficient and effective you will be. Now that you have read the chapter you should be aware of the importance of anticipating problems before they arise and asking for assistance where necessary. Identifying any weaknesses in your own skills, level of experience, or ability to meet deadlines is critical to working effectively as a member of a team.

## Answers to chapter activities & 'test your knowledge' questions

### △ ACTIVITY 1                                                    △ △ △ △

Possible routine tasks for someone working in, for example, purchase ledger, could include:

· opening and distributing the post
· taking telephone calls from suppliers
· processing supplier invoices
· posting supplier invoices to purchase ledger
· filing all invoices received
· maintaining up to date records of the outstanding creditor position and when payments are due.

Possible non-routine tasks could include:
· provide up to date aged creditor analysis to new investor
· raise sales invoices when colleague off sick.

### △ ACTIVITY 2                                                    △ △ △ △

| | Job | Importance ranking | Urgency ranking |
|---|---|---|---|
| 1 | Bank cheques | 9 | 9 |
| 2 | Order stationery | 2 | 5 |
| 3 | Make dental appointment | 1 | 1 |
| 4 | Send out customer invoices | 5 | 8 |
| 5 | File supplier invoices | 3 | 2 |
| 6 | Open post | 5 | 8 |
| 7 | Make coffee | 1 | 1 |
| 8 | Holiday application form | 1 | 2 |
| 9 | Report to Director due next week | 10 | 4 |
| 10 | Memo to manager re broken window catch | 3 | 7 |
| 11 | Deal with irate window cleaner | 2 | 10 |

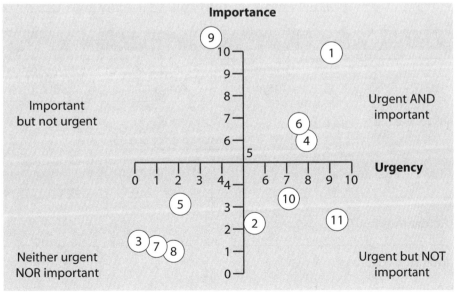

## △ ACTIVITY 3                                △ △ △ △

Kate appears to have always respond to others demands upon her time and has little control over planning her own time or work. The likely impact of this method of working on Kate is that it will be stressful and unsatisfying. The consequences for her work are that it is likely to deteriorate in quality and important deadlines may be missed as others encroach upon her time.

It is important that Kate learns strict time management techniques such as daily lists and action plans. She needs to prioritise her tasks perhaps in negotiation with those supplying her with the tasks. To do this she need to communicate very firmly and clearly with those supplying her with work. Next time someone asks her to do something that is supposed to be 'top priority' she must ascertain exactly when the work is required by and firmly negotiate a reasonable deadline. In this way colleagues may learn to respect that she is a busy person who has other demands upon her time than simply responding to their demands.

What people tend to notice is that they regularly do the urgent but not important jobs before the important but not urgent jobs. This is quite wrong. Prioritisation is all about ensuring important jobs are done first. Therefore the jobs that fall into the top part of the graph - the important jobs, are those that should be focussed on. In this case, job number 9 the report to a director due next week is the job that should be focused on, bearing in mind any other deadlines that must be met. Of course other people's needs (such as the irate window cleaner) will get in the way of achieving this aim but as a general rule you should focus on the important jobs first, such as the report to the director and banking cheques, slotting in any urgent jobs as best you can. Yet how often do you get to the office, make a coffee, fill in your holiday application form and order some new stationery all because you think they are quick, simple jobs that will only take a minute!

Whilst it would not be practical to draw a Time Management Grid every day to help prioritise tasks, it gives useful practice in learning how to prioritise tasks, especially when under time pressure or during busy periods of the year.

## △ ACTIVITY 4                                △ △ △ △

|  | Objective / target 1 | Objective / target 2 | Objective / target 3 |
|---|---|---|---|
| Overall goal: |  |  |  |
| How? |  |  |  |
| Action required? |  |  |  |
| Interim targets? |  |  |  |

| | Objective / target 1 | Objective / target 2 | Objective / target 3 |
|---|---|---|---|
| 3 months? | | | |
| 6 months? | | | |
| 12 months? | | | |
| Resources required? | | | |

## Test your knowledge △ △ △

1  There is £100 fine if you do not file your income tax return by 31 January.

2  MBO stands for Management By Objectives.

3  The three basic relationships between roles at work are the subordinate role - in which you work for and report to others; the peer role – where you work with others to achieve certain goals; and the authority role – where other people work for and report to you.

4  Organising means working out the actual jobs needed to be done to fulfil the plans agreed upon, grouping activities into a pattern or structure and giving specific jobs to people in the organisation to achieve the plans agreed upon and setting deadlines for their completion.

5  Daily tasks include routine tasks such as recording sales invoices in the sales day book or recording cash received. Weekly tasks include preparing journal entries to post totals from books of prime entry to nominal ledger and monthly tasks include bank reconciliation or sales ledger reconciliation.

6  Urgent tasks need to be completed within a particular time limit. Important jobs may affect a lot of people or cost a lot of money. They may also have major implications if they are not done, or if they are done badly.

7  The Time Management Grid has four areas: urgent and important; urgent but not important; important but not urgent; and finally, neither important nor urgent.

8  Planning methods and systems include checklists, bar charts, bring-forward, bring-up and follow-up systems, activity scheduling and time scheduling, action sheets, planning charts and boards, and diaries.

9   Examples that could cause a delay in meeting a deadline include being given wrong or insufficient information, files or books that may have been borrowed and not returned or may be incorrectly filed or archived, reference journals not kept up to date, access to information denied due to security/ confidentiality considerations, computer systems that may 'crash', and international time differences resulting in offices not being open when required.

# WORKING RELATIONSHIPS

**INTRODUCTION**

The efficient running of organisations requires that all the members of the organisation work together towards the achievement of the organisation's objectives. This working together requires the adequate understanding of what others are doing. It requires a high level of co-ordination and control, and fundamentally it requires communication, which is efficient and effective.

**CONTENTS**

1 Co-ordination
2 Communication
3 Methods of communication
4 Confidential information
5 Interpersonal skills
6 Teams
7 Handling disagreements and conflicts

**KNOWLEDGE & UNDERSTANDING**

· Relevant legislation: copyright, data protection, equal opportunities (Item 1)
· Sources of legal requirement: data protection, companies acts (Item 2)
· Work methods and practices in your organisation (Item 5)
· Handling confidential information (Item 6)
· Establishing constructive relationships (Item 7)
· Why it is important to integrate your work with other people's work (Item 8)
· Maintaining good working relationships, even when disagreeing with others (Item 13)
· The scope and limit of your own authority for taking corrective actions (Item 14)
· Use of different styles of approach in different circumstances (Item 15)
· Seeking and exchanging information, advice and support (Item 20)
· Handling disagreements and conflicts (Item 21)
· Showing commitment and motivation towards your work (Item 22)
· Informing and consulting with others about work methods (Item 25)
· Negotiating the assistance of others (Item 26)
· Co-ordinating resources and tasks (Item 27)
· Reporting procedures (Item 31)
· Procedures to deal with conflict and poor working relationships (Item 32)
· Where to access information that will help you learn, including formal training (Item 33)
· The people who may help you plan and implement learning you may require (Item 34)

**PERFORMANCE CRITERIA**

· Identify and prioritise tasks according to organisational procedures and regulatory requirements (Item A in Element 23.1)
· Communicate with other people clearly and effectively, using your organisation's procedures (Item A in Element 23.2)
· Discuss and agree realistic objectives, resources, working methods and schedules and in a way that promotes good working relationships (Item B in Element 23.2)
· Meet commitments to colleagues within agreed timescales (Item C in Element 23.2)
· Offer assistance and support where colleagues cannot meet deadlines, within your own work constraints and other commitments (Item D in Element 23.2)
· Find workable solutions for any conflicts and dissatisfaction, which reduce personal and team effectiveness (Item E in Element 23.2)
· Follow organisational procedures if there are difficulties in working relationships that are beyond your authority or ability to resolve, and promptly refer them to the appropriate person (Item F in Element 23.2)
· Treat others courteously and work in a way that shows respect for other people (Item G in Element 23.2)
· Ensure data protection requirements are followed strictly and also maintain confidentiality of information relating to colleagues. (Item H in Element 23.2)

# 1    Co-ordination

## 1.1  Co-ordination and communication

As we have already noted, an appropriate organisation structure will ensure that all sections of the business are pursuing common objectives and clearly defined job descriptions will improve appreciation of the interrelatedness of tasks and should prevent overlapping or areas of responsibility being missed. Standard instructions and procedures are a way of reducing the risk of conflicting practices within the company.

However, your role and responsibilities are an integral part of the organisation's structure and cannot be treated in isolation from other people. Your colleagues will have joint objectives and goals, which will necessitate pooling resources, information and efforts.

Any business activity is in part about ensuring the co-ordination of organisational and individual endeavour, and of co-ordinating the work of individuals and teams. Some activities will be dependent on the successful and timely completion of other activities so you need to be aware of your own requirements as well as the plans and deadlines of others in the organisation.

Poor co-ordination is often at the heart of complaints from customers or colleagues eg, two departments giving different information. It can cause workflow problems if work arrives unplanned or later than planned from another unit. This can cause conflict between departments with one blaming the other for the problem instead of both working together and co-operating to perform effectively and efficiently.

KAPLAN PUBLISHING

In any organisation, the communication of information is necessary to achieve co-ordination.

## 1.2 Social skills

You will see that social skills are important to the organisation, as well as to the individuals employed and this is what we mean by working relations. There will be jobs where co-operation with colleagues is highly essential. It would, of course, be no good to have a large number of employees who all argue and disagree with each other. Apart from the disruption caused to each other, the organisation would also suffer since the amount of work carried out would probably be very small and perhaps even counter-productive.

What is meant by social skills? It means the ways in which we discuss work-related matters with others, or obtain information from them. You will be aware of the situation when you want to take some annual leave and need to ask your supervisor whether you can have the time off when you require it. The supervisor may tell you right away, ask you to put it in writing or need to ask the boss later. What is important is the way you 'get on' with your supervisor and perhaps the way in which they recognise you. If the approach is right, then you might be told right away there are no problems, even though there may be some particular way in which you should go about it. Your social skills or the way you put the question over is important, not only to you – especially if you want time off – but to the organisation because it is in this way that a certain amount of confidence builds up between you and the supervisor.

It is not unknown to find a clash of personality between individuals in a line organisation, and it is up to the senior officer in the organisation to take the appropriate action. Whilst there can be no hard and fast rules on what should be done, the interests of the organisation must take priority, although there may be certain circumstances where the individual's interests should be taken into consideration.

When dealing with other people in your organisation you should be as courteous and polite as when dealing with external customers.

## 1.3 Contractual and legal relationships

Employment is a legal relationship with your employer. There are underlying duties of to your employer under your contract of employment, including:

· **Duty of care** – there is implied into every contract of employment a duty that the employee performs his/her contract with proper care.
· **Duty of co-operation** – even where the employer promulgates a rulebook containing instructions for the execution of the work, the employee is under an obligation not to construe the rules in a way designed to defeat the efficiency of the employer's business.

· **Duty of obedience** – in the absence of express provisions an employee is required to carry out all reasonable and lawful orders of the employer. Some orders clearly do not require obedience e.g. falsify sales records on employer's instructions; drive an unroadworthy vehicle, which may lead to his prosecution under the Road Traffic Acts.

· **Loyal service** – this duty is to use all reasonable steps to advance his employer's business within the sphere of his employment and not to do anything which might injure the employer's business.

### 1.4 Equal Opportunities Legislation

'Equal opportunities' is a term describing the belief that there should be an equal chance for all workers to apply to be selected for jobs, to be trained and promoted in employment and have that employment terminated fairly. There are two main reasons for adopting equal opportunities policies:

(i)     it is morally wrong to treat parts of the population as inferior or inadequate

(ii)    organisations do not benefit from excluding any potential source of talent.

The legislation on equal opportunities is made up of several Acts:

· **The Sex Discrimination Act of 1975** renders it unlawful to make any form of discrimination in employment affairs because of marital status or sex.

· **The Race Relations Act of 1976** ensures that there should be no discrimination on the grounds of colour, nationality, ethnic origin or race

· The Equal Pay Act 1970 is concerned with equality of pay and related matters. The Act aims to ensure that where men and women are employed in 'like work' or 'work of equal value' or 'rated as equivalent', they will receive the same basic pay.

· **The Disability Discrimination Act 1995** provides for disabled people not to be discriminated against in a variety of circumstances including employment.

· **The Rehabilitation of Offenders Act 1974** provides that a conviction, other than one involving imprisonment for more than 30 months, may become erased if the offender commits no further serious offences during the rehabilitation period.

Discrimination may operate in all kinds of areas including sex, sexuality and marital status, race and colour, religion, politics, disability and conviction of a criminal offence. Forward-looking organisations will have a positive attitude to equal opportunities and operate non-discriminating procedures in all aspects of personnel management, including recruitment and selection, advertisements, access to training and promotion, disciplinary procedures, redundancy and dismissal.

As an employee you also have responsibilities under the equal opportunities legislation not to discriminate or show prejudice against people on the grounds of sex, race or disability.

## 1.5  Carrying out instructions

An employee who will not carry out instructions will not be welcomed by most firms. The instructions are given so that the work to be performed can be understood and will fit into the total workload of the department. Failure to carry out instructions may:

(a)  delay a piece of work needed urgently by a customer

(b)  completely wreck the rest of the work performed by everyone else

(c)  endanger lives or health of other employees or customers (e.g. by operating a machine without following instructions or smoking in 'non-smoking' areas).

Employees should expect their employers to give proper instructions at the right time, in the right manner and in the right place. Failure to do so can mean that the employees might lose pay bonuses because they are unable to complete the work within a prescribed time. It can also lead to poor morale due to workers arguing about what should be done, rather than being fully aware of their commitments.

In addition, instructions to protect employees' physical well-being which are not given properly, or not given at all, can result in disability or even death.

## 1.6  Asking for clarification when necessary

It is possible for instructions genuinely to be misunderstood or for completely wrong instructions to be given. If this happens to you at any time, you should ask for clarification of the instructions. Simply to carry on with the job when the instructions are genuinely not clear, or where they are obviously wrong, can cause all sorts of problems. Your employer or supervisor would therefore expect you to question the instructions in such cases.

Of course it is possible to be obstinate and obstructive by deliberately trying to misinterpret instructions. You must be careful to ensure that your manager or supervisor understands your proper concern at the lack of clear instructions and does not mistakenly assume that you are being unnecessarily awkward.

If you are ever unclear about instructions that you have been given you should always check them with the appropriate person.

## 1.7  Asking for assistance

If an individual feels that they are not up to the demands of a particular job or that a deadline cannot be met then this is likely to be due to either a lack of time, or a lack of skills or a lack of experience. A lack of time is almost impossible to deal with unless large amounts of overtime are to be worked. Lack of skills or experience however can be overcome if assistance is sought.

**Skills** – if the inability to perform a particular task is due a lack of skills or necessary knowledge for that task then there should be no embarrassment about admitting this fact.  For example suppose that you have never before performed a bank reconciliation and a stand-in supervisor in the department has suddenly asked you to prepare the monthly bank reconciliation by the end of tomorrow. Obviously this task is impossible for you. There is no point in attempting it alone as this will simply be an unproductive use of the organisation's time. However it is likely that colleagues in your department, or indeed the supervisor, may be able to instruct you in exactly how to perform a bank reconciliation. Therefore the only practical option for you is to seek assistance.

**Lack of experience** – it is often the case that an individual is probably capable of performing a task but does not have the confidence to go ahead with the task because of a lack of experience. Perhaps it is the first time that that individual has been required to perform a particular task. In such instances both informal and formal support can be sought. Colleagues may well be able to encourage an individual to feel confident of performing the task. However if the situation is such that an individual truly believes himself or herself to be incapable of performing the task then it is probably most appropriate to discuss this matter with the supervisor or manager.

### 1.8  Informal and formal assistance

Many people find it much easier to approach a colleague to ask for help – informal assistance – with a problem than to approach a more senior member of staff. This might well be appropriate if it is within the organisation's policies, the colleague is fully skilled in the area concerned and the colleague has the time, ability and inclination to help. In many cases this will be the most satisfactory way of dealing with a problem.

Formal assistance means approaching the supervisor or manager of the department to ask for help in dealing with a lack of skills. Once it has been realised that no training has been given in that particular area then the individual will not be allocated that task again until they are trained.

## 2    Communication

### 2.1  Introduction

In the last chapter, we noted that the organisation chart defines the lines of essential communication and provides a means of transmitting messages to people in a manner that stimulates response.

Element 23.2 is concerned with provision of information to others and communication in general. Communication is the basis of our relationships with other people. It is the means whereby people in an organisation exchange information regarding the operations of the enterprise. It is the interchange of ideas, facts and emotions by two or more persons. To be effective, the manager needs information to carry out management functions and activities. All organisations have formal, acknowledged, and often specified communication channels. There will be lists of people who are to attend briefings or meetings, and distribution lists for minutes of meetings or memos. There will be procedures for telling people of decisions or changes, and for circulating information received from outside the organisation.

Communication takes place between various employees of a business and the outside world, in such forms as:

(a)   reports and dividend payments to shareholders

(b)   invoices and correspondence to customers

(c)   orders, payments and queries to suppliers.

For the present purpose, our immediate concern is communication within a business, where the need arises because of:

·   day-to-day and periodic control needs

·   the incidence of unplanned change

·   the introduction of planned change

·   the usual interaction in the normal work situation.

## 2.2  Communication process

Communication is the process of passing information and understanding from one person to another. The communication process involves six basic elements: sender (encoder), message, channel, receiver (decoder), noise, and feedback. You can improve your communication skills by becoming aware of these elements and how they contribute to successful communication. Communication can break down at any one of these elements. The process of communication can be modelled as shown in the following diagram.

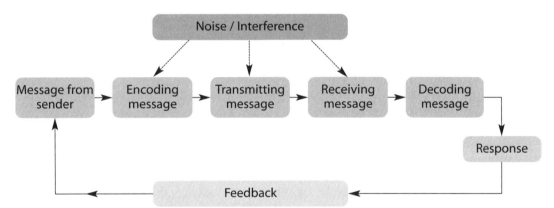

A sender will initiate the communication process. When the meaning has been decided, a channel for transmitting the messages to the receiver is selected and the message is put into words or images. When the receiver has heard the 'message' then they have to 'decode' it to make sure they understand what is being said.  For example, the sender may use 'jargon' which the receiver may not understand.

Sometimes the response may result in action taking the form of the receiver asking for clarification on respect of something they do not understand or asking for additional information

The final stage of the process is feedback, which can consist for example of the receiver indicating that they understood the message, or providing information.

Within the communication process it is also important to note the problem of 'noise': anything in the environment that hinders the transmission of the message is significant. Noise can arise from many sources, e.g. factors as diverse as loud machinery, status differentials between sender and receiver, distractions of pressure at work or emotional upsets. The effective communicator must ensure that noise does not interfere with successful transmission of the message.

### 2.3 Noise/interference

> ### ☐ DEFINITION
>
> **'Noise'** is full or partial loss of communication. It can arise at the collecting and measuring point, or there can be errors or omissions in transmission and/or misinterpretation or misunderstanding, or blatant disregard of communication.

The two principal types of noise are verbal and technical.

**Verbal noise** is the misunderstanding of words. Examples are:
(a) the misspelling or omission of an important word in a communication, so as to obscure or alter its meaning
(b) technical persons (such as accountants, who are some of the worst offenders) using jargon that is incomprehensible to non-technical persons
(c) the incorrect use of English, written in a style that is difficult to follow.

**Technical noise** is created by the information itself during communication. Examples are:
(a) in response to a request for a simple piece of information, a voluminous report may be prepared obscuring the vital information (accountants' monthly reports frequently have this failing)
(b) a message is left that is not sufficiently clear to convey its meaning when its intended recipient returns
(c) damage to an organisation's communications centre, such as its telephone exchange, prevents information from being transmitted clearly.

Failure to transmit information can have serious consequences on a company's operations. Some noise can be reduced, if not overcome, by using more than one channel of communication, so that if a message fails to get through by one channel, it may succeed by another. For example, a managing director may need the latest stock figures. To confirm the information from the accountant, the figures from sales and production may be analysed personally to find the relevant stock figures.

### 2.4 Formal communication channels

Formal communication channels are normally established as part of the organisation's structure. In a hierarchical structure the channels are largely vertical chains designed to allow effective communication between managers and subordinates. Organisational communication establishes a pattern of formal communication channels to carry information vertically and horizontally. (The organisational chart displays these channels.) The channel is the path a message follows from the sender to the receiver.

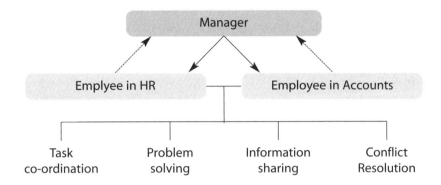

· Managers use downward channels as a basis for giving specific job instructions, policy decisions, guidance and resolution of queries. Such information can help clarify operational goals, provide a sense of direction and give subordinates data related to their performance. Downward communication also helps link levels of the hierarchy by providing a basis for co-ordinated activity.

· Employees use upward channels to send messages to managers. Upward communication provides management with feedback from employees on results achieved and problems encountered. It creates a channel from which management can gauge organisational climate and deal with problem areas, such as grievances or low productivity, before they become major issues.

· Horizontal channels are used when communicating across departmental lines, with suppliers, or with customers. Four of the most important reasons for lateral communication are:
  - **task co-ordination** – department heads may meet periodically to discuss how each department is contributing to organisational objectives
  - **problem-solving** – members of a department may meet to discuss how they will handle a threatened budget cut
  - **information sharing** – members of one department may meet with the members of another department to explain some new information or study
  - **conflict resolution** – members of one department may meet to discuss a problem, e.g. duplication of activities in the department and some other department.

## 2.5 Informal communication networks

In every organisation there are informal communication networks as well as the formal channels. This is often referred to as 'the grapevine', which has been defined as 'the network of social relations that arises spontaneously as people associate with one another. It is an expression of people's natural motivation to communicate'.

Grapevine activity is likely to flourish in many common situations, for example:

· where there is a lack of information about a situation and people try to fill in the gaps as best they can
· where there is insecurity in the situation
· where there is a personal interest in a situation e.g. when a supervisor disciplines a friend, people may well gossip about it
· where there is personal animosity in a situation and people seek to gain advantage by the spreading of rumours
· where there is new information that people wish to spread quickly.

Though the grapevine can pose a threat to management, it can also be useful as a means of making unofficial announcements, 'off-the-record' statements or intentional leaks of future plans.

### 2.6  Attributes of effective communication

The main attributes of effective communication are promptness and accuracy.

**Promptness** – if information is essential then it is likely to be urgent. It is therefore important that such information is passed on at the earliest possible opportunity.

In respect of messages, if at all possible you should try to identify how urgent the message is, for example, depending on the situation by asking the following questions:

'Jane Smith is in a meeting at the moment and will not be out until 3.00 pm. Would you like me to arrange for this message to be passed to her in the meeting?'

'Jack Little is in the building but I'm not sure where. Would you like me to arrange for him to be paged?'

'Peter Green is currently travelling to a meeting. Would you like his mobile telephone number?'

If the information is contained in a report or in some form of written document, then often couriers are used to ensure that they reach their destination that day or as early as possible the next.

**Accuracy** – accurate transmission of information is clearly vital. For example suppose that a client leaves a telephone message with you changing his meeting with your manager from 3.00pm until 4.15pm. If you tell your manager that the meeting is about 4.30pm this is likely to leave the client waiting for some considerable amount of time.

Always ensure you read back any messages taken to the person you are talking to. In this way telephone numbers etc can be checked.

KAPLAN PUBLISHING

## ▷ ACTIVITY 1 ▷ ▷ ▷ ▷

The following fax has just been received in the accounts department. It has been passed to you, the accounts clerk, as the most appropriate person available.

To:     J Patel, Quotations Manager

From:   Peter Allan, Sales Manager, East Sussex Materials Ltd

Further to our telephone conversation this morning I am prepared to drop the price of raw material XX5 to £2.42 per kg for the project that you explained to me this morning. I hope this is satisfactory.

Consider what the possible implications might be if you delay passing on this information to the quotations manager.

This activity covers performance criterion C in Element 23.2.

[Answer on p. 193]

### 2.7 Overcoming barriers to communication

A barrier to communication is anything that prevents, or may potentially prevent, communication from being effective.

Some general rules to ensure communication is effective are:

· avoid communication overload
· ensure the right information gets to the right person at the right time
· agree and confirm priorities and deadlines for receipt of information
· keep communication simple
· develop empathy with 'listeners'
· confirm, by repeating back, what has been said
· confirm that what information you have given has been understood.

## 3    Methods of communication

### 3.1 Oral communication – face-to-face and telephone

For the rapid interchange of information between people, the principal method of communication is the spoken word. Oral communication is preferable for emotive issues and persuasion since it has the advantage of immediate feedback. It is, however, time consuming and, unless recorded, there can be uncertainty about what was said.

**Telephone** – for many years the telephone has been most important both for internal and external communications. It is usually used when individuals are not on the same site, or when the conversation may be very short. The telephone can now be used for conference meetings, whereby everyone present at each end of the telephone can hear comments made by the other parties. This means people can convene meetings in two locations at the same time and carry out discussions.

**Face-to-face discussions** may be used where people need to exchange/ give/obtain information quickly, and or obtain documents. This form of communication is appropriate when working relationships need to be developed or negotiation/persuasion has to take place.

**Meetings** can be organised to include various departments, or may include outside representatives such as shareholders. They may include various levels of management and can be convened to provide information or discuss a specific topic e.g. year end accounts. In formal meetings minutes may be taken.

| Advantages of oral communication | Disadvantages of oral communication |
|---|---|
| there is the personal touch of seeing the face and/or hearing the voice | there is no permanent record, so disagreement can easily arise as to what was said |
| there is instant feedback with the opportunity to respond quickly to questions of misunderstanding and disagreement | vocabulary shrinkage occurs, in that we use only 66% of our full vocabulary when communicating orally – the full vocabulary is available to us only when writing |
| because of the strong personal aspect, it is a good persuasive medium encouraging people to take a certain course of action | we do not have the facility, as with writing, to go back, cancel out and replace an earlier sentence because we wish to amend its meaning. |
| the message can be unique to you as an individual - no-one else is likely to select your mix of words or emphasise the same key phrases. | |

### 3.2 Written communication – letters, memos and word-processed documents

Written methods of communication of all sorts – letters, memos, bulletins, files, circulars - are the norm in many companies. The dominant characteristic of many managers' working day is paperwork and meetings. They do have the advantage that being in permanent or hard copy form they are less open to misinterpretation. With meetings, for instance, formal minutes may be taken, circulated and agreed to as the definitive written evidence of the meeting. Written methods of communication can be very flexibly used. When trying to reach a number of workers in one place, notice-boards are often used, typically to announce meetings, job vacancies, health and safety notices, details of company social events and similar matters which are not of crucial significance

Most written communications will be word-processed documents nowadays with the exception of memos that are written by hand and placed in the internal mailing system. **Memos** can also be sent by electronic mail on the computer network. They are most useful where the same information has to be given to a number of people e.g. details of the date, time, location of a meeting.

**Letters** provide a written record and information of matters discussed. Used mainly for external communication.

**Notes** – you may need to write notes for a talk or a presentation. Other occasions when note taking is required might be in the preparation of a report or in connection with a meeting or a telephone call. Whatever the context, notes should suit their purpose and be neither too detailed that they resemble an essay nor too compressed that their meaning is lost.

Notes that are going to be used very soon after they have been written down can afford to be more condensed than notes, which will have to wait before they are written in a more acceptable form. Telephone messages tend to suffer from brevity and, with each hour that passes, recollection of the conversation will fade.

**Reports** may be for internal or external circulation and can take a variety of forms. Reports may contain data, graphs, complex facts and points for and against a variety of situations. This form of communication allows people to study the content in their own time. Some reports are required by law, while other reports may detail progress made in respect of a particular project.

**Word-processed documents** – word processing programs are now common in the workplace and used to produce a wide variety of written documents, often in a 'house style'. Standard letters and memos can be produced from template files set up on the computer. Mail-merge facilities enable a word-processed letter file to import names and addresses from a database and print out a batch for sending out.

Word-processed documents can have sophisticated page layouts and tables. They can import graphics and embody colour elements for illustrative purposes. They are also used in the form of transaction documents, such as payslips, invoices sent to customers, purchase orders sent to suppliers and works orders sent to the factory, day book listings or standard letters. Large numbers of these documents are produced, perhaps in electronic form and displayed on screens or perhaps as 'paperwork'.

**Bulletins and newsletters** usually provide details on major changes or events that will affect the organisation and may appear in the local or national press, for example a move to a new site or the creation of new jobs.

## 3.3  Visual communication

Visual methods are preferable where it is necessary for the eye to assist the ear; where the message can be made more vivid, or where distance, environmental or personal factors preclude the use of speech. Examples include films, videos, graphs, traffic signals and sign language.

Graphic displays of data can be an effective way of communicating. For example, sales data comparing this year with last year. Data can often appear more meaningful when presented in this way rather than just a list of figures.

Films and slides - allow information to be absorbed in an easily digestible way. Also, if entertaining and well put together, individuals are more likely to listen, concentrate and remember what is being said.

### 3.4 Electronic methods – fax, e-mail and video conferencing

More and more offices are increasingly reliant on a range of electronic communication equipment. Larger businesses link computers through the telephone network using modems leading to the use of electronic mail and computers 'speaking' to each other, some accessing databanks. Personal computers are being arranged in networks; fax machines, e-mail, value added networks (VANs) and dedicated satellite communication systems are becoming commonplace.

**Fax (facsimile)** – allows images of documents to be transmitted and then reproduced. It can handle photographs, hand-written notes, drawings, diagrams, charts, etc with no specialist skill to transmit. It is also easy to send the same document to many recipients. Developments include an interface between fax and the computer so that the latter is able to hold, store and process fax transmissions.

The system can 'read' the incoming fax material and relay it to the individual addressee (by displaying on the screen of the terminal).

The development of fax cards for fitting inside desktop and portable personal computers has eliminated much of the need for specialised fax machines. It is now possible to send and receive fax messages using a laptop PC and mobile telephone anywhere in the world.

**E-mail** – electronic mail is very popular as a form of communication that uses the Internet.

The following are hints on what to do and what not to do when using e-mail.
· E-mail is meant to be one of the quickest ways to communicate. It is much more efficient than a letter or even a phone call. Some people receive hundreds of e-mails a day, so keep e-mail short and to the point. But be aware – rushed messages can lead to bad grammar and miscommunication.
· You can send e-mail by following three simple steps:

KAPLAN PUBLISHING

1   Enter the recipient's e-mail address in the To field.

2   Type your message in the large text box. Avoid using a string of capital letters in your correspondence unless absolutely necessary. This is the online equivalent of SHOUTING!

3   Click on the Send button.

·   You can also use several options when addressing your message, such as:
1   Put additional or secondary recipients in the Cc (carbon copy) field.
2   When you are sending a message to many people, a long delivery list may appear at the top of the message. This can annoy readers. It also can make your message seem like junk mail. To hide the distribution list from all recipients, use the Bcc (blind carbon copy) field.
3   If you have created nicknames in the Address Book, you can just type the nickname in the appropriate field. In order to send your message to multiple recipients, separate each recipient by a comma. For example: nickname1, nickname2, recipient3@host.domain.

·   Although the **Subject** is an optional field, it is a good idea to enter one. Your recipients may receive many e-mail messages, perhaps even several from you alone. The subject helps distinguish between the different messages.

·   You can attach a file to your message by clicking **Attach**. The Attachment area will be opened in a new window. Click **Browse...** and search for the file or type the full path name of the file you wish to attach. Once found, press the **Upload file** button and the file name will appear in the Attachment List. In order to remove an already attached file, select the file from the Attachment List and press the **Remove** button. Finally, press the **OK** button to return to Compose window.

The file you attach can be of any type, for example: a sound file, an image or even a spreadsheet. Adding attachments to your message can be done at any time while composing the message. All files are scanned for viruses before they are attached to a message. If a file contains a virus that cannot be cleared by the virus scanning software, you will be unable to attach it to the message.

·   You can check the spelling of your message by choosing the language from the selection list and pressing the **Spell Checker** button. The Spelling area will be opened in a new window. The first word that was not found in the Spelling Dictionary will appear on the top of the page marked by red text. You will see a list of possible suggestions. Select the appropriate replacement from the list or write the replacement yourself in the Change to edit box. Than press the **Change** button to accept the change or the Ignore button to disregard it. This process will continue until the end of the message is reached.

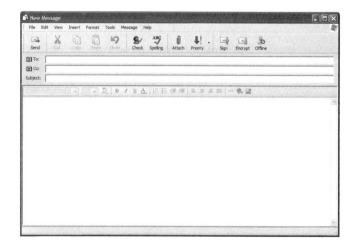

Pressing the Cancel button, before completion, will discontinue the spelling process.

· The sender of an e-mail message is not always apparent to the recipient simply by looking at the sender's address. It is good practice to sign your e-mail with your name and what company you are with, if applicable. You may want to include your e-mail address as well. Most e-mail services allow you to write a signature that will automatically be attached to each message you send.

**Video conferencing** is increasingly used as a medium whereby meetings are convened in two locations simultaneously.

# 4 Confidential information

## 4.1 Types of confidential information

You may handle information that is clearly confidential, such as payroll details. Some information may not appear to be confidential at first sight but could cause embarrassment or problems internally or externally if revealed, so it is best always to err on the side of discretion. For example:

(a) reports on purchases of new machinery whose introduction might lead to fewer jobs

(b) details of price rises not yet sent to customers

(c) news of changes in key personnel not yet communicated to customers and suppliers.

When dealing with customers and suppliers, you must also respect their own right to confidentiality. For instance, do not reveal details of a customer's account or type or level of purchases to another customer.

Remember that, if someone appears to be asking for confidential information or for information, which is none of their concern, it is always best to refer them to your supervisor.

In certain limited circumstances students may become aware of confidential information that needs to be passed to the appropriate staff member. This means that it should not be discussed in any circumstances other than with the person for whom the information was meant. The information should not therefore be discussed in passing with colleagues, managers or in social situations. Confidentiality should always be maintained where considered necessary. Your organisation's affairs and those of its clients are confidential and should not be disclosed to others unless the circumstances are appropriate.

If you are leaving a confidential message for someone who is not available it should be written down, and placed in a sealed envelope, marked 'Private and Confidential Addressee Only'.

Alternatively if you have to send a memo, letter or report, which contains confidential information, then you should ensure it is marked private and confidential and placed in a sealed envelope that is similarly marked.

### 4.2 Organisational procedures

It is each individual's responsibility to ensure that they are fully aware of the organisation's rules and procedures regarding confidential information. It is equally important that an individual follows them strictly.

For example if the organisation's policy is that documents marked as 'confidential' are kept under lock and key then it is important that such documents are stored in a locked storage cabinet or desk each night. This is reasonably easy to remember to do. It is perhaps harder to remember to keep the information locked away whenever the individual is not using it and is not in their office or at their workstation. Such information should not, under any circumstances, be left unattended on a desk.

When confidential information is considered, individuals should be aware that they are only likely to be able to access confidential information if they have been allocated a particular password. If an individual is given a password in order to access confidential information then under no circumstances should they tell anybody else what their password is.

Disclosure of information could damage the company if it fell foul of the data protection legislation and caused embarrassing publicity or helped a competitor by allowing sensitive information to be accessed by outsiders or non-related employees.

### 4.3 Handling confidential information

The increasing use of computers in all aspects of business has meant that increasingly large amounts of information about individuals are now kept by various organisations. For you to perform some of your tasks it may be necessary to obtain and keep confidential information. This is a great responsibility and should not be taken lightly.

There will be rules and procedures for compliance with the Data Protection Act and with the copyright laws, and to avoid any action that might reflect badly on the reputation of the company.

Under the terms of the Data Protection Act, the need for privacy is recognised by the requirements that all data should be held for clearly designated purposes. Accuracy and integrity must be maintained and data must be open to inspection. Only legitimate parties can access data and information must be secured against alteration, accidental loss or deliberate damage. Furthermore, the Act states that data must be obtained fairly, to precise specifications and must not be kept for longer than required.

Copyright law covers books of all kinds, sound recordings, film and broadcasts, computer programs, dramatic and musical works. Modern software packages are complex and costly to produce, but are often easy to copy and distribute. Manufacturers are increasingly bringing prosecutions to try to reduce the number of pirate copies of their software. There are steep penalties for companies prosecuted for software theft – unlimited damages, legal costs and the cost of legitimising the software.

However, not all information at work is covered by legislation. There will be times when you are told something and asked to 'keep it to yourself', either by a colleague, your supervisor or a visitor. Sometimes this will be in the context of a message you may have to pass on, but at other times it may be in the form of a confidence, which is entrusted to you. It is vital that you keep your word and do not pass it on to others at the earliest opportunity.

Working as part of a team will inevitably mean that you must pass information on to other members of the team. This must always be done accurately and promptly.

### 4.4 Copyright law

It is highly likely that when supplying information a student will use another individual's ideas or information. Is this a breach of copyright law?

Copyright law covers books of all kinds, sound recordings, films and broadcasts, computer programmes, dramatic and musical works, etc. Is it possible to legally photocopy or manually copy such information?

It is normally quite acceptable for an individual to copy a few pages of the work of another person. That other person may have signalled his copyright by the international symbol of ©; however, it is still quite acceptable to copy such works in small amounts either for personal or business usage.

Unless you intend to copy an entire book or reproduce a copyright article for the entire organisation, it is unlikely that any copyright law would be infringed.

## 5   Interpersonal skills

### 5.1 Definition

Interpersonal skills can sometimes be called interactive, face-to-face or social skills used in establishing and maintaining relationships between people. If you can answer yes to any of these questions, it indicates your power is based on interpersonal skills.

·   Do you have a sense of relationship – rapport – with other people?

- Are you an 'active listener? Do you make sure you have understood the other person's point of view? Do you make it clear to them that you understand and empathise?
- Do you avoid being either passive or aggressive in formal or informal discussions with others in the organisation?
- Can you persuade or influence another person?
- Are you aware that people admire you in some respects, and do others copy you?
- Do people want to be with you at informal meetings?

## 5.2 Steps to improve your people skills

Being able to manage your relationships at work, so that they have the effect you want, is a prerequisite of optimum performance. Key interpersonal skills are the building blocks of relationships:

1 **Self-management** – when we think of people skills, we usually think of them in relation to other people, rather than how we handle ourselves, and yet most of us realise that we are better or worse at relating to people depending on our 'mood' or attitude. The reason for the 'mood' is the way we are choosing to react to a particular situation; we can learn to choose consciously, and use a mood to our advantage in any situation. We all know the difference it makes to a working day when we wake up feeling good, rather than feeling that it is 'going to be one of those days'. Make a conscious effect to seek the benefits of each situation, to enjoy the process as well as the end results of work. What we tell ourselves is very powerful in affecting our state; we can talk ourselves 'up' or 'down'.

2 **Building rapport** – the word 'rapport' comes from the French word that means carrying something back; rapport is about actively making sure that we have some shared message that we both send and receive. We can build rapport by being aware of the non-verbal messages we communicate. If we make eye contact, use a friendly tone of voice, turn towards them, look relaxed and smile, we create the impression of being someone easy to deal with.

3 **Giving attention** – paying attention is not the same as listening, and if we want to develop good people skills, we need to learn to pay close attention to people. When someone is really paying attention we feel not just that they have listened, but that they have understood where we are coming from and what we really mean. To pay full attention requires:
   - listening with your ears – you pick up the words someone is saying
   - listening with the inner ear – we pick up the tone of voice, the meaning behind the words, the emphasis and hesitations
   - attending with your eyes – how the person's body language supports or negates what they are saying
   - attending with your guts – this is the intuitive level, we get a sense of something not being communicated
   - attending with your heart – we view the person sympathetically rather than judgmentally, and get a sense of what it is like from their point of view.

4    **Recognising and working with differences** – most of us have not been brought up to value other people for their difference, often we have to learnt to judge others because of it. By finding out how others are different from us, we gain very useful information to help us to deal with them more effectively. We can find out about other people's approaches or perspectives by asking 'what' and 'how' questions; e.g. How did you do that? What prompted you to handle it in that way? How is that important for you? If you were left to your own devices, how would you deal with this? Once you have found out what really matters to the other person, you can make your communication with them much more effective.

5    **Conveying your message clearly** – if we want to be sure our message is received correctly, it is important that we are sure what our message is! You may wish to tell people about new working practices, but additionally, your tone of voice, body language, choice of words will tell them what sort of person you are, what you feel about your overt message, how you operate in the world and what you think and feel about your listeners. Being clear in our own minds what our message is, and what we want the listener to do or feel as a result helps to ensure that the right message is conveyed.

6    **Using feedback** – this is a term that describes a loop of action and reaction. The most common feedback we receive is that which is given unconsciously, it is the immediate response or reaction to what we have done or said. If you are not sure of someone's reaction, asking them is the simplest way of finding out, but we need to guide the feedback, as most people are not good at giving useful information about their reactions and will tend to rationalise or justify their responses.

7    **Working in a team** – good team skills include respect for each other's viewpoints, sharing information, mutual support, and presenting a coherent front.

8    **Dealing with conflict** – when you strongly disagree with someone, it is hard to maintain a good working relationship, as we tend to equate the disagreement with the person. It is important in dealing with conflict to step back and assess the situation objectively. Identify the reason for the conflict (misunderstanding, different approaches, different interests?) and where possible find common ground. Changing the language of discussion can improve the situation; notice the difference in feeling these pairs of comments produce:

| You make me angry. | I am angry about X. |
| You're wrong. | I don't agree with what you are saying. |
| You don't understand. | I haven't made myself clear. |

KAPLAN PUBLISHING

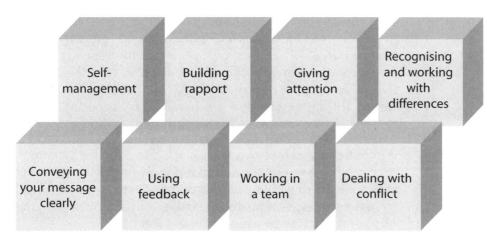

## 5.3 Responding to requests

To be able to communicate effectively you must have the ability to:
- pass on information accurately and without delay so that all concerned are aware of the situation and the correct action can be taken
- talk to a wide range of people with whom you have had little or no previous contact
- converse with your colleagues in a way which will promote and maintain a harmonious working atmosphere
- interpret non-verbal communication gestures and their meanings
- put people at their ease.

Even if you can schedule a lot of your own work, you will inevitably be asked to do things by your supervisor or other managers. In any job, you will have to do things you do not like. The important thing is to accept that everyone is in the same position and so you should try to carry out unwelcome tasks without complaining.

The way you act is very important. Do you appear disinterested when other people ask you to do something or do you appear attentive? Do you interrupt or do you let the other person finish first?

When dealing with colleagues, it is important to think about not only what you say but also the way you say it.

## 5.4 Asking for help

Sometimes you will need help from other people, but think carefully before asking. You may waste other people's time if you ask them for simple factual information that you could find elsewhere.

If you do need help, do not be embarrassed to admit that you do not know the answer.

When asking for help it is important that you listen to the help or advice given. Most of us have poor listening skills. We listen to the first part of what we are being told and then spend the next few seconds waiting for the other person to stop speaking so that we can say the next thought that has come into our heads. During this latter part of the other person's speech, we have totally switched off from what is being said.

Without effective listening, there can be no effective communication. It has been discovered that people forget most of what they have heard within a couple of days. This can be improved by better messages, repeated messages and also by helping the receiver to learn to be a more efficient listener.

> Among the many ideas for better listening are the following:
> (a)  concentrate on what is being said, not on the person saying it
> (b)  ask for something to be repeated if you do not understand
> (c)  try to concentrate on the meaning of the message
> (d)  do not become emotionally involved
> (e)  remember that thoughts are quicker than words and you can evaluate what is being said without missing anything
> (f)  do not take many notes, just the key points.

Listening is not the same as hearing. It involves a more conscious assimilation of information and requires attentiveness on the part of the interviewer. Failure to listen properly to what someone is saying will mean that probing questions (in an interview) may become a worthless exercise. In preparing to listen you should ask 'What new things can I learn from this person?'

Barriers to listening include the following:
· scoring points – relating everything you hear to your own experience
· mind-reading
· rehearsing – practising your next lines in your head
· cherry-picking – listening for a key piece of information then switching off
· daydreaming – you can think faster than people can talk and there is a temptation to use the 'spare' time to daydream
· labelling – putting somebody into a category before hearing what they have to say
· counselling – being unable to resist interrupting and giving advice
· duelling – countering the other's advances with thrusts of your own, e.g. 'Well at least this department is never over budget'
· side-stepping sentiment – countering expressions of emotion with jokes or hollow clichés, such as 'Well it's not the end of the world'.

There are also health factors that may cause difficulties in concentrating on what is being said. People who are suffering from stress, who are in pain or are anxious about something will not be at their best when it comes to effective communications.

If you are to do your job properly then it is important that you listen carefully to all instructions, help and advice.

KAPLAN PUBLISHING

## 6 Teams

### 6.1 Introduction

A **work team** can be a department, section or group with a set of common tasks. It is a part of a larger organisation with one person in charge of it, although every member of the team has some input into the way it operates.

Teams are groups of people who show the following characteristics:
· They share a common goal, and are striving to get a common job done.
· They enjoy working together, and enjoy helping one another.
· They have made a commitment to achieve the goals and objectives of the project by accomplishing their particular portion of the project.
· They are very diverse individuals having all kinds of different disciplinary and experiential backgrounds who must now concentrate on a common effort.
· They have great loyalty to the project as well as loyalty and respect for the project manager, and have a firm belief in what the project is trying to accomplish.
· They have attained a team spirit and very high team morale.

### 6.2 Team performance

An important aspect of work is that it is usually done in groups or teams. It does not matter whether the work is developing a corporate strategy for an organisation, checking insurance claims in an office or building cars in a factory. A team is quite simply a number of individuals working together to achieve a common task.

There are a number of factors that contribute to the performance of teams; for instance, the organisational structure within which the team works, the type of task to be accomplished, resources available and the characteristics of the team and the team members.

Many jobs within an organisation are impossible on an individual basis and take place as part of a team or a group. Although it is necessary to have such a group, for example a department such as the accounts department or a production group within the manufacturing area, it is also necessary to recognise that group relationships can be even more complex than individual relationships.

The main factors to take into consideration when working within a group or closely knit department are as follows:
· The varying members of the group are likely to have a wide variety of personalities. You will have to work closely, possibly even constantly, with this group of people and therefore must be prepared to put up with the various types of personality within the group.
· **Individual aptitudes and skills** – again it is likely that any team will be made up of a group of people with a variety of different aptitudes and skills. The group will require each of these aptitudes and skills and this should be remembered when dealing with other members of the group.

· **Goals** – it is likely that each work group will have particular goals or aims. If the goals or aims of the individual members of the group do not coincide with those of the group as a whole then there is likely to be conflict and pressures affecting members of the group. Wherever possible a student should try to tie in his/her own goals with those of the group. For example if the group concerned is the accounting department then provision of accurate and relevant information will be the group's goal and a student studying for AAT levels of competence should also have similar types of goals regarding accuracy and relevance.

· **Communication** – a group can only operate effectively if there is full communication at all levels and between all parties in the group. If you do work as part of a group then you should ensure that you understand exactly what the group is doing, why it is being done and what part you are required to play in this.

· **Deadlines** – deadlines in general have been considered earlier in the study text. In a group or team context you should be even more aware of the importance of deadlines. If you are asked to produce information or a piece of work by a particular time or date then if this deadline is not met it is likely to affect the workings of the entire group.

Organisations are increasingly becoming aware of the importance of teams working effectively, and how in doing so this can contribute to the organisation's success. One way of doing this is by considering how an existing group can be developed into a team. Some organisations use team-building courses to help with this process. The objective of team building is to improve the team's performance by:

· encouraging effective working practices
· reducing difficulties the team encounters
· improving work procedures
· improving interpersonal relationships between team members.

The benefits of team building are:

· it increases the chances of real improvement in performance because the whole team is involved
· it gives the team a chance to stop and think about the way the work is done.

### 6.3 Teamwork

There are very few jobs in which it is not necessary to work as part of a team.

Being part of a team means dealing with people at all levels within your organisation and building professional relationships with them. It takes time to build this association with people but there are a few guidelines, which might get you off to a good start:

(a) be tactful and courteous
(b) treat with respect people who are your senior in either age or position
(c) have a pleasant and helpful manner

(d)  make allowances for others having personal problems which may affect their work, but do not joke about it or expect them to tell you why they might be having a 'bad day'

(e)  communicate with people using the correct words and tone.

### 6.4  Commitments to others

It is firstly necessary to consider what a commitment actually is. 'A commitment is a firm agreement to do something within a particular time scale or at a particular time'.

A commitment is therefore binding, within a business context. The main reason for this is that the person to whom the commitment has been made has probably made corresponding commitments to other parties either within the organisation or outside of the organisation based upon your commitment.

We can also describe commitment as something that happens when team members see themselves as belonging to the team instead of as individuals acting on their own initiative. It is evident when the team members are committed to the team goals over and above their own personal goals.

### 6.5  Agreed time scales

In most organisations if you are required to produce information then the time scale for producing it will be discussed with you rather than simply being imposed.  If you believe that the time scale proposed is unrealistic then you should say so, explaining why you hold this belief.  You should never make promises that you cannot keep.  The consequences of not producing work for a specified deadline are far worse than those of admitting that a deadline currently being set is unrealistic.  It is far better to ensure that a reasonable deadline or time scale is set at the outset of the project rather than having to extend the deadline, or indeed not meet it, later in the project.

It is appreciated that it is sometimes difficult to speak up when dealing with those of a higher authority than yourself.  However the final consequences should be borne in mind in all situations.

### 6.6  Personality differences

Having a professional relationship with someone is different from a social relationship. In a social relationship you can choose how well you get to know someone, even whether or not you get to know them in the first place.

At work you will inevitably have to deal with people whom you would not necessarily choose as friends. This does not mean that you have to treat them as friends, but as colleagues. This means being polite to other people and speaking to them in an appropriate tone of voice. It also means offering to help them if you can see they need help.

It can be difficult if you do have a personality clash with someone at any level, but you must keep it in proportion. One of the worst things you can do is to dwell on the problem. You will quickly become unpopular with your other colleagues if you talk continually about your problems with another member of staff. It may also mean that the other person hears about your complaints, which makes the matter worse.

### 6.7 Complaints

Staff morale is very important wherever you work and you can contribute to it. In the short term, everyone likes to complain about things, but in the long term this can cause tensions within the office.

In some cases, however, you may have a genuine cause for complaint. You should discreetly arrange to see your manager or personnel manager to discuss the problem. Remember that they will not necessarily have all the answers but will expect you to suggest solutions. Think carefully first about what you want to say and be positive.

## 7   Handling disagreements and conflicts

### 7.1 Disagreements and conflicts

Although one would hope that the vast majority of work time would pass without disagreement between individuals or conflicts within a team there will be circumstances in which such disagreements or conflicts do occur. There is no avoiding such situations and students should think carefully about how to deal with them.

The general rule should be that if there is a disagreement or conflict with a fellow employee then this should be dealt with at a higher level of management rather than between the individual employees. There is little to be gained from two employees losing their tempers with each other if a manager can solve the problem or produce some sort of compromise.

A second important consideration is that it is usually far more constructive to recognise any conflict and discuss this with a manager rather than try to avoid or simply smooth over the problem.

There are likely to be simple personality conflicts between students and other employees, but these should be dealt with on a polite and professional basis. Any disagreement or conflict on a work matter should normally, however, be taken to a higher authority through the organisation's Grievance Procedure. Grievances can include unfair treatment by managers e.g. being passed over for promotion because of gender or race, unfair pay – men being paid more than women and unfair dismissal (an extreme case).

KAPLAN PUBLISHING

## 7.2 Managing disagreements and conflicts

There are many ways of managing conflict and disagreements and the suitability of any particular action will be determined by the situation. Several possible ways of resolving conflicts and disagreements are detailed below:

(i) **Problem solving** – the individuals/team are brought together to find a solution to the particular problem.

(ii) **Common goal** – finding a common goal that is more important than the differences of team members/individuals.

(iii) **Allocating resources** – ending conflict over resources e.g. use of computers, by giving extra resources.

(iv) **Compromise** – finding a solution without there being a defined winner or loser.

(v) **Management decisions** – management making a decision.

(vi) **Altering the team/individual's role** – changing team members and/or their roles.

To be successful in resolving conflicts and disagreements you must understand the reason for it, why the team/individual is behaving in such a way and what their expectations are.

## 7.3 Negotiation

Disagreements and negative conflict lead to:

·   the misuse of resources, time, energy and creativity
·   an increase in hostility
·   a decrease in trust and openness
·   a decrease in the ability of groups and the organisation as a whole to achieve the set objectives.

The best way of managing negative conflict is by negotiation, because the potential outcome is much more positive than with any other approach. The ultimate goal when resolving a conflict is for both parties to be satisfied with the outcome. Ideally, this means that both individuals get what they want. In reality, both individuals may have to compromise and get most of what they want, especially if their goals are mutually exclusive. This type of solution is called WIN-WIN because both individuals feel satisfied with the outcome, they both win. This type of solution involves a commitment by both parties to work out the problem fairly via compromise. However, there are times when this commitment is absent. When that happens, less ideal solutions are probable. These solutions may take the following forms:

**WIN-LOSE** – one party gets what it wants but the other does not.

**LOSE-WIN** – the first party does not get what it wants but the other does.

**LOSE-LOSE** – neither party gets what it wants.

Everyone negotiates – almost every day – and certain principles seem to be present which anyone can learn.

- **Ask questions** – before stating a position or making proposals, it is very helpful to inquire about the other side's interests and concerns. This will help you understand what is important to the other side and may provide new ideas for mutual benefit. Ask clarifying questions to really understand the other's concerns in this negotiation. This will also help you determine their approach to negotiations: win-lose or win-win. You can then make more realistic proposals.

- **'Win-win' negotiations** involve understanding each other's interests and finding solutions that will benefit both parties. The goal is to co-operate and seek solutions so both parties can walk away winners. If you come to the table thinking only one person can win (win-lose), there won't be an effort to co-operate or problem solve. By the same token, if you come to the table expecting to lose (lose-win), you play the martyr and resentment builds.

- **Respect** – when the other side feels that you respect him or her, it reduces defensiveness and increases the sharing of useful information, which can lead to an agreement. When people feel disrespect, they become more rigid and likely to hide information you need.

- **Trust** – people tend to be more generous toward those they like and trust. An attitude of friendliness and openness generally is more persuasive than an attitude of deception and manipulation. Being honest about the information you provide and showing interest in the other side's concerns can help.

### 7.4 The skills of a negotiator

The skills of a negotiator can be summarised under three main headings:
- **Interpersonal skills** – the use of good communicating techniques, the use of power and influence, and the ability to impress a personal style on the tactics of negotiation.
- **Analytical skills** – the ability to analyse information, diagnose problems, to plan and set objectives, and the exercise of good judgement in interpreting results.
- **Technical skills** – attention to detail and thorough case preparation.

In most situations a negotiation strategy is not an easy option but it is one that has much more of a positive outcome than an imposed solution. The first step is to get the parties to trust you. Next, you can try to find as much common ground as there is between the parties and encourage them to arrive at a middle ground. If neither party get what they want then you have a lose-lose situation. This is a very common situation where compromise comes in. Unfortunately, compromises result in needs not being satisfied. You are aiming for a win-win situation, where both parties get as close as possible to what they really want. This situation is not always possible but working towards it can achieve mutual respect, co-operation, enhanced communication and more creative problem solving. You need to start by identifying what both parties really want - as opposed to what they think they want. The parties also need to explain what they want it for and what will happen if they do not get it. This procedure is a severe test of a manager's interpersonal skills, but it could bring about the best solution.

## 7.5 Negotiating styles

Negotiating styles that can be used are competing, collaborating, compromising, accommodating, and avoiding.

**Competing** – 'hard bargaining' or 'might makes right'

Pursuing personal concerns at the expense of the other party. Competing can mean 'standing up for your rights' defending a position that you believe is correct or simply trying to win.

**Collaborating** – 'sharing tasks and responsibilities' or 'two heads are better than one'
Working with someone by exploring your disagreement, generating alternatives, and finding a solution that mutually satisfies the concerns of both parties.

**Compromising** – 'splitting the difference'

Seeking a middle ground by 'splitting the difference', the solution that satisfies both parties.

**Accommodating** – 'soft bargaining' or 'killing your enemy with kindness'

Yielding to another person's point of view – paying attention to their concerns and neglecting your own.

**Avoiding** – 'leave well enough alone'

Not addressing the conflict, either by withdrawing from the situation or postponing the issues.

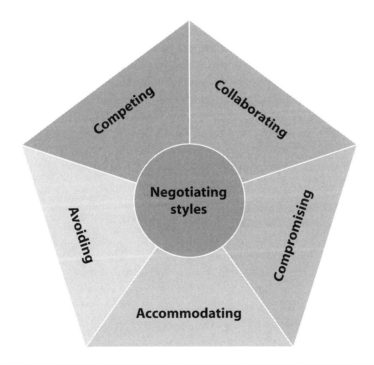

## ▷ ACTIVITY 2                                    ▷ ▷ ▷ ▷

You work in quite a large accounts department. Your manager has three deputies and the rule is that only one of them can be away on holiday or attend a course at a time. All three approach him in March asking for the same two weeks off in June. Tom, who is the most senior of the three, wants to do a sponsored bike ride in Cuba. Dick wants to take his family to Las Vegas for his brother's wedding. Harry has been accepted on a special course that will enhance his promotional prospects.

Each of them hears about the other's applications and they have a furious row and now only talk to each other about work-related matters.

Outline five different ways the manager can deal with this situation.

[Answer on p. 194]

### 7.6  Maintaining good relationships

Once you have created a good relationship with other staff, this must be maintained because it is important for the following reasons:
(a)   staff who are happy and co-operate with each other work harder and are more productive
(b)   morale and motivation are improved.

Be the ideal member of staff that everyone appreciates by:
(a)   communicating with people in a mature and professional manner
(b)   thinking through the consequence of your words and actions before you say or do anything that you might later regret
(c)   carrying out requests promptly and willingly, explaining fully and politely when you are not able to help
(d)   asking others for help and assistance politely and only when necessary
(e)   informing others about anything you have said or done on their behalf
(f)   bearing no grudges, not being moody or difficult to work with
(g)   knowing the difference between telling tales and reporting unethical behaviour or problems to your superior
(h)   finding solutions for any conflicts and dissatisfaction that could reduce personal effectiveness and team effectiveness.

## 8  Test your knowledge   ▷ ▷ ▷

1   What is meant by social skills?

2   List three of the Acts that make up the legislation on equal opportunities.

3   Describe the provisions of the Equal Pay Act.

KAPLAN PUBLISHING

4 Communication is the process of passing information and understanding from one person to another. What are the six basic elements of the communication process?

5 What might hinder the transmission of a message?

6 Give another name for the informal communication network.

7 Outline the main advantage of written communication.

8 What would you do to build rapport?

9 List four barriers to listening.

10 Briefly describe three negotiating styles

[Answers on p. 195]

## 9 Summary

This chapter has demonstrated the need to be sensitive to the responsibilities and commitments of your colleagues' workloads. It has also described how communication between individuals and within teams can be improved and how communication can be altered according to the goals and context of the situation. You should now understand how empathy and sensitivity to the needs, background and position of colleagues (both more junior and more senior) will improve professionalism and performance of the whole organisation and how this can help to establish constructive working relationships.

### Answers to chapter activities & 'test your knowledge' questions

### △ ACTIVITY 1 △ △ △ △

**Scenario 1**
The quotations manager is currently in a meeting with a prospective customer. He is presenting a quotation to that customer for a series of contracts; however the price is based upon the existing price of XX5, which is £2.65 per kg.

If this information does not reach the quotation manager during this meeting there is a possibility that the prospective customer will be lost to a competitor, as the price quoted will not be low enough.

**Scenario 2**
The quotations manager is currently in his office making a number of telephone calls. He is in fact telephoning a variety of alternative suppliers in order to find a lower price than the current £2.65 per kg for XX5.

If this information does not reach the quotations manager promptly then he may agree a price higher than £2.42 with an alternative supplier.

**Scenario 3**

The quotations manager is just about to enter a meeting with the production manager. At that meeting they will discuss the use of an alternative product to XX5 that can be purchased at a price cheaper than the current £2.65 per kg of XX5. It is suspected that the product is of inferior quality to XX5 but the needs of cost cutting are too great to ignore.

If the information regarding the reduced price of XX5 does not reach the quotations manager then there is a possibility that future production may use an inferior product, which can be purchased at a price cheaper than the current £2.65 per kg.

## △ ACTIVITY 2  △△△△

Your manager you could deal with the situation in the following ways.

- Call them all together and explain they must sort the matter out themselves but, if they fail to do so, you will sort the matter out for them by exercising your right to determine the holiday rota, and that no one will be allowed to go that fortnight anyway. If you go for this option, you are choosing the power route. This is fine if jobs are scarce, but highly risky. If you win, they all lose!
- Call them all together and tell them they must sort the matter out themselves. By choosing this option and letting them sort it out themselves you are avoiding the situation.
- Talk the matter over with each of them separately to discuss the facts with them. Make a decision as to whose need is the most pressing, then get them all together and announce your decision. This option is an attempt at a compromise, although not allowing very much input from them.
- Tell them individually not to be silly, and suggest they take an afternoon off and talk the matter over with their families/friends/training officer. This solution of patting them on the head and telling them to talk to others is trying to defuse the situation.
- Discuss all the problems the situation raises with each fully and, if the matter still cannot be sorted out, go to the training officer and see if there is an alternative course; and the Chief Officer to see if on this occasion two deputies can be allowed on holiday at the same time. Bring them all back to hear the outcome. Only this option begins to address the problems. Even though there is no knowing there will be a successful outcome, you are trying to resolve all the conflicting needs.

A team-building approach can promote openness and discussion of problems like these, meaning that there will be fewer destructive conflicts to cope with.

## Test your knowledge △ △ △

1 Social skills are the ways in which we discuss work-related matters with others, or obtain information from them.

2 The Acts that make up the legislation on equal opportunities include The Sex Discrimination Act of 1975, The Race Relations Act of 1976, The Equal Pay Act 1970, The Disability Discrimination Act 1995 and The Rehabilitation of Offenders Act (1974) .

3 The Equal Pay Act 1970 is concerned with equality of pay and related matters. The Act aims to ensure that, where men and women are employed in 'like work' or 'work of equal value' or 'rated as equivalent', they will receive the same basic pay.

4 The six basic elements of the communication process are: sender (encoder), message, channel, receiver (decoder), noise and feedback.

5 Within the communication 'noise' is anything in the environment that hinders the transmission of the message. Noise can arise from many sources, e.g. factors as diverse as loud machinery, status differentials between sender and receiver, distractions of pressure at work or emotional upsets.

6 The informal communication network is called the grapevine.

7 Written methods of communication have the advantage that, being in permanent or hard-copy form, they are less open to misinterpretation.

8 Rapport is about actively making sure that we have some shared message that we both send and receive. We can build rapport by being aware of the non-verbal messages we communicate. If we make eye contact, use a friendly tone of voice, turn towards them, look relaxed and smile, we create the impression of being someone easy to deal with.

9 Barriers to listening include scoring points, mind-reading, rehearsing, cherry-picking, daydreaming, labelling and counselling.

10 Negotiating styles that can be used are competing, collaborating, compromising, accommodating and avoiding.

# IMPROVING YOUR OWN PERFORMANCE

**INTRODUCTION**

The appraisal of performance should identify your strengths and weaknesses and this can be the starting point for a career plan. Your strategy will then be designed to use your strengths and overcome any weaknesses so that you can take advantage of career opportunities.

A competence is an observable skill or ability to complete a particular task. It also includes the ability to transfer skills and knowledge to a new situation. The general purpose of any assessment or appraisal is to improve the efficiency of the organisation by ensuring that the individual employees are performing to the best of their ability and developing their potential for improvement.

**KNOWLEDGE & UNDERSTANDING**

· Where to access information about new developments relating to your job role (Item 3)
· Ways of identifying development needs (Item 9)
· Setting self development objectives (Item 10)
· Development opportunities and their resource implications (Item 11)
· Ways of assessing own performance and progress (Item 12)
· Where to access information that will help you learn including formal training courses (Item 33)
· The people who may help you plan and implement learning you may require (Item 34)

**CONTENTS**

1 Identify your own development needs
2 Career planning
3 Process of competence assessment
4 Learning to improve your importance
5 Methods used to acquire skills and knowledge
6 Review and evaluate your performance and progress

**PERFORMANCE CRITERIA**

· Identify your own development needs by taking into consideration your current work activities and also your own career goals (Item A in Element 23.3)
· Define your own development objectives and, where necessary, agree them with the appropriate person (Item B in Element 23.3)
· Research appropriate ways of acquiring new skills and knowledge (Item C in Element 23.3)
· Ensure that development opportunities are realistic and achievable in terms of resources and support from relevant persons (Item D in Element 23.3)
· Review and evaluate your performance and progress and also to agreed timescales (Item E in Element 23.3)
· Monitor your own understanding of developments relating to your job role (Item F in Element 23.3)
· Maintain and develop your own specialist knowledge relevant to your own working environment (Item G in Element 23.3)
· Undertake learning that will help you improve your performance (Item H in Element 23.3)

# 1 Identify your own development needs

## 1.1 Becoming an accounting technician

There are many reasons to become an accounting technician. If you think you deserve a better career with improved prospects and a higher earning potential, then becoming an accounting technician is an ideal first step to achieving these goals and more.

You will be qualified to work in any number of accounting roles, in a wide range of industries – you do not have to work for an accounting firm.

As an AAT qualified accounting technician you will have an internationally recognised and respected qualification that shows potential employers that you have been trained to a high standard.

In addition, as the AAT's qualification is founded on actually doing the work, they will know that as well as the underpinning knowledge, you have the skills and practical experience not just to perform in an accounting role, but also to excel in it.

And if you are thinking of training to be a chartered or certified accountant then the AAT is an ideal route to these qualifications. All the main UK CA bodies offer exemptions to AAT qualified members.

## 1.2 What is development?

Development is the growth or realisation of a person's ability and potential through the provision of learning and educational experiences.

Organisations often have a training and development strategy based on the overall strategy for the business.

Development activities include:

·   career planning
·   training – both on and off the job
·   appraisal
·   other learning opportunities e.g. job rotation.

Training can be described as the planned and systematic modification of behaviour through learning events, programmes and instruction which enable individuals to achieve the level of knowledge, skills and competence to carry out their work effectively.

All training and development is self-development, whether it is provided by the organisation or not. If you do not want to learn, acquire new skills, change attitudes or behaviour or are not sufficiently motivated to do so, you will not manage it. If the outcome of an appraisal programme or promotion planning incorporates training that is imposed it cannot lead to effective development.

Some organisations make a commitment to individual development, which requires the setting of individual objectives and the negotiation of a learning contract between the organisation and the employee. It allows the individual to select the way in which learning will take place, the provision of support and guidance by the organisation and joint assessment of the results.

### 1.3  Development opportunities

Your manager should be able to refer you to others who can assist you in achieving your development and suggest appropriate referral sources both within and outside the department e.g. books, journals, professional associations or people who might be willing to serve as mentors.

You can do your own research into developments relating to your job and also relating to the AAT and where it will lead you.

Make a note of useful addresses and look out for publications that keep you up-to-date with developments relating to your job role.

**Association of Accounting Technicians**

140 Aldersgate Street,
London EC1A 4HY

Tel: +44 (0)20 7397 3000

Fax: +44 (0)20 7397 3009

Website: www.aat.org.uk

The AAT – ACA fast track is a direct route to qualification as a Chartered Accountant – from the AAT.

For the first two years of the Fast Track, you train for the AAT as normal, making sure you have completed certain units and kept a record of your work experience. After that, if you obtain an ACA training contract and pass a Top Up paper, you effectively bypass the first year of training, leaving you just two years away from a top financial business qualification.

**The Institute of Chartered Accountants in England & Wales**

Chartered Accountants' Hall
PO Box 433
London EC2P 2BJ

Tel 020 7920 8100

Fax 020 7920 0547

There are many on-line resources that will give you more information:
AAT - www.accountingtechnician.co.uk

Financial Times Self-Assessment – http://ftcareerpoint.ft.com/YourCareer/developyourself

Financial Times – Mastering Management – www.ftmastering.com

Financial Times – Business Education – www.ft.com/surveys/businessed

Your People Manager – www.yourpeoplemanager.com

Many colleges will run courses that you might consider. They also have websites, or will send you brochures, which you might find interesting.


## 2 Career planning

### 2.1 Why plan?

Today emphasis is on lifelong learning and multiple job/career transitions. The aim of career development is to help you understand your potential and to help you maximise this potential in the work force today and in the future. From the start, you will need to have a clear idea of the kind of career path you would like to follow. Good career planning can lead to a satisfying career. People who do not career plan usually get sick from stress working in fields they do not like, and students waste time and money pursuing educational areas in which they have no interest. The decisions we make about careers and leisure activities throughout our life span are critical to our sense of well being. Satisfaction in our work can be a key ingredient to our feelings of self-worth. Happiness can be contingent upon a role as productive and worthwhile employer or employee. Conversely, excessive stress on the job can interfere with our health and personal relationships. Many believe that a person who balances work with life roles find fulfilment in the work place as well as in his or her other life roles as citizen, student, parent, etc. When planning your future you need to understand that career development is often a lifetime project and may require continuous learning.

## 2.2 Preparing a SWOT analysis

One of the most difficult tasks is to gain insight into yourself – your strengths and weaknesses - yet this is an essential first step in developing a career plan. You need to know whether you are an introvert or an extrovert and whether you have the right approach towards achievement, work, material things, time and change. Different personal skills are required for interacting with other people, goal planning, self-development, motivation and performance. Many firms evaluate people on such personality factors as aggressiveness, co-operation, leadership and attitude.

Capabilities or skills may be categorised as:
· **technical** – involves working with tools and specific techniques
· **human** – the ability to work with people; it is co-operative effort; it is team-work and the creation of an environment in which people feel secure and free to express their opinions
· **conceptual skill** – is the ability to see the 'big picture', to recognise significant elements in a situation and to understand the relationships among the elements
· **design skill** – is the ability to solve problems in ways that will benefit the organisation.

The relative importance of these skills differs for the various positions in the organisational hierarchy, with technical skills being very important at the supervisory level, conceptual skills being crucial for top managers and human skills being important for all positions.

It is also important to make a careful assessment of the external environment, including its opportunities and threats. For example, joining an expanding company usually provides more career opportunities than working for a mature company that is not expected to grow.

E-learning might make it easier for some people to achieve their qualifications than attending classes at colleges etc.

| Strengths | Weaknesses |
|---|---|
| – What are your advantages? (colleagues will identify these) <br><br> – What do you do well? (competence analysis will identify strengths and development needs) | – What could be improved? (assessment by supervisor will identify any weaknesses) <br><br> – What is done badly? <br><br> – What should you avoid? |
| **Opportunities** | **Threats** |
| – What are the interesting trends? (keep up-to-date with courses, colleagues and managers as well as publications) <br><br> – Does your organisation have high turnover of managerial staff? (appraisals will outline the range of opportunities | – What obstacles do you face? <br><br> – Is changing technology threatening your position? <br><br> – Is your job changing? |

### 2.3 Career strategy

The most successful strategy would be to build on your strengths and take advantage of opportunities. For example, if you have an excellent knowledge of computing and many organisations are looking for accountants who are also computer literate, you should find many opportunities for a satisfying career. On the other hand, if there is a demand for accountants with computing skills and you are interested but lack the necessary skills, the proper approach would be to develop the skills so that you can take advantage of the opportunities.

People do not always choose the most obvious career because it might not be the most fulfilling one. The choice involves personal preferences, ambitions and values. For example, although you might have certain computing skills demanded in the job market, that type of job may not interest you and it might be preferable to broaden your knowledge and skills or deal more with people.

You must also consider whether your choice is realistic and achievable in terms of resources and support from relevant people. You may be thinking of undertaking this entirely on a distance-learning basis or you may need to attend college on a day release or full time basis. You may be receiving support from your organisation for this in terms of money and time or you may be entirely self-financing. The qualification may just be one element in a complex and highly structured development programme. Some accountancy career paths take a long time, are quite expensive and require a lot of spare time to be devoted to study. If you have a family to consider, this must be discussed thoroughly before you broach the subject at work. An effective career strategy requires that consideration be given to the career of your spouse. Dual career couples sometimes have to make very stressful choices, especially when it comes to opportunities for promotion that require relocation.

Even without a family there might be constraints in terms of personal relationships that would suffer if you did not give them your full attention.

Career choices require trade-offs. Some alternatives involve high risks, others low risk. Some choices demand action now; other choices can wait. Your plans are developed in an environment of uncertainty and the future cannot be predicted with great accuracy. Therefore, contingency plans based on alternative assumptions should also be prepared. For example, while you might enjoy working for a fast-growing venture company, it might be wise to prepare an alternative career plan based on the assumption that the venture might not succeed.

### 2.4 Growth

Your objective should be to ensure 'growth' during your career. This objective can obviously benefit your organisation as well as you. The growth should be triggered by a job that provides challenging, stretching goals. The clearer and more challenging the goals, the more effort you will exert, and the more likely it is that good performance will result. If you do a good job and receive positive feedback, you will feel successful (psychological success). These feelings will increase your feelings of confidence and self-esteem. This should lead to you becoming more involved in your work, which in turn leads to the setting of future stretching goals. This career-growth cycle is outlined below:

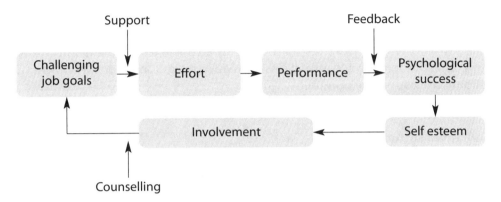

The above cycle can only be successfully completed if you receive support from your supervisor or manager.

### 2.5 Development goals/objectives

Once the direction of your career has been identified, the strategy has to be supported by objectives and action plans.
Short-term goals should be attainable within one year; medium-term goals within three years; and long-term goals within five years. Each goal should have a specific target and the deadlines by which these targets should be achieved should be stated, although flexibility should be retained to allow for unforeseen circumstances.

Your goals and objectives will be aimed at:
· performance in the current job
· future changes in the current role
· moving elsewhere within the organisation
· developing specialist expertise.

Your manager can support your career development by informing you about options for improvement and possible barriers to career movement, encouraging you to focus on clear, specific and attainable career goals or suggesting steps you might take to improve existing skills and knowledge.

Some organisations make a commitment to individual development, which requires the setting of individual objectives and the negotiation of a learning contract between you and the organisation. It allows you to select the way in which learning will take place, the provision of support and guidance by the organisation and joint assessment of the results.

If you are seeking membership of one of the accountancy bodies the selection of the most appropriate qualification and methods of study will have to be determined by discussions between you, the accountant and the training officer (this may have been agreed at the selection interview). In addition a training programme must be initiated so that the correct practical experience is obtained to satisfy the requirements of the accountancy body. This will include the identification of the skills and competences that are required and the alternative training and development strategies that can be employed to meet your objectives.

For some people this will be discussed during their performance appraisal process. The objectives must be measurable e.g., to have completed a part of the AAT course by September with a high grade. The action plans to achieve this objective might be to attend classes, read study guides and text books and submit the coursework on time.

### 2.6  Monitoring progress

Monitoring is the process of evaluating your progress towards career goals and making necessary corrections to the aims or plans. Having embarked on your career path you must demonstrate effective time-management and efficient task-achievement so that you can accomplish your objectives in the time you have allowed yourself.

As well as self-monitoring, you will hopefully be receiving help, encouragement and feedback from your supervisor or manager. During your performance appraisal, your progress will be discussed and you will be encouraged to review your performance against objectives in the operating areas of your job and also to review the achievement of milestones in your career path.

## 3    Process of competence assessment

### 3.1  Competences

A competence is an observable ability to complete a specific task successfully. Competencies are the critical skills, knowledge and attitude that a jobholder must have to perform effectively. There are three different types of competence:
·    behavioural competences include the ability to relate well to others
·    occupational competences cover what people have to do to achieve the results in the job
·    generic competences that apply to anyone, e.g. adaptability, initiative.

They are expressed in visible, behavioural terms and reflect the skills, knowledge and attitude (the main components of any job) which must be demonstrated to an agreed standard and must contribute to the overall aims of the organisation.

The term is open to various interpretations because there are a number of competence-based systems and concepts of competence. As a general definition, a competent individual can perform a work role in a wide range of settings over an extended period of time.

Some competence-based systems are achievement-led – they focus on assessment of competent performance – what people do at work and how well they do it. Others are development-led – they focus on the development of competence and are linked to training and development programmes to develop people to a level of performance expected at work. Actual training needs may be categorised on the basis of the following competencies:

**Work quality:**
· technical and task knowledge
· accuracy and consistency
· exercise of judgement and discretion
· communication skills
· cost consciousness.

**Work quantity:**
· personal planning and time management
· capacity to meet deadlines or work under pressure
· capacity to cope with upward variations in work volume.

**Supervisory and managerial skills and competencies:**
· planning and organising
· communication and interpersonal skills
· directing, guiding and motivating
· leadership and delegation
· co-ordination and control
· developing and retaining staff
· developing teamwork.

### 3.2  National Vocational Qualifications (NVQs)

NVQs are qualification frameworks based on standards of competence. There is one single employment-led standard in each occupational area and they are offered at levels to indicate the extent of a person's competence in that occupational area.

There are five levels in each occupational area.

| Level 1 | Foundation level dealing with work activities that are routine and predictable. |
| --- | --- |
| Level 2 | More demanding, dealing with work activities, which involve greater responsibility. This level is aimed at normal jobs in offices, retail or on the shop floor. |
| Level 3 | More complex, dealing with non-routine activities; supervisory duties may be included at this level. |
| Level 4 | Supervisory or management level, dealing with professional and technical work activities. |
| Level 5 | Tasks and jobs performed by very senior staff; the equivalent of the current postgraduate level. |

Were there is more than one awarding body that wants to offer an NVQ in a particular area then each must base their award on the same standards.

### 3.3 Process

Competences are defined by means of a competence (or capability, or functional) analysis. This process describes:
· the job's main tasks or key result areas
· the types and levels of knowledge and skill that these require
· the acceptable standard of performance in each task or result area
· how performance is assessed.

Installing a competence-based system means:
· establishing the elements of competence – activity, skill or ability required by the job holder to perform the job
· establishing the criteria of performance of the skill or ability required and setting standards to measure it by
· measuring the actual performance against the standard
· taking corrective action where there is any deviation from the standard.

The control element of the system allows feedback to change the elements of competence or the criteria of measurement in the light of actions taken and feedback given by the job-holder.

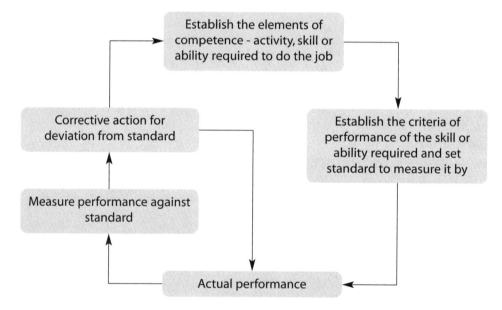

Although it is not a work-based activity, think of the process of passing a driving test. It is an observable skill that is measured against set standards. In the case of failure a list that outlines the failed areas is given to the learner driver and is used to form the basis of any corrective action needed before re-applying for the test.

The Lead Body guidelines for the AAT units that make up your course, are written as statements incorporating:

- elements of competence – specific activities a job holder should be able to perform
- performance criteria – how well it should be performed
- a range statement – in what context and conditions
- the knowledge and understanding that underpins the competence.

---

## ▷ ACTIVITY 1     

After studying this section you should be able to explain the process of competence assessment.

[Answer on p. 216]

---

# 4    Learning to improve your performance

### 4.1   Management of learning

Managing learning is about your ability to learn efficiently and be aware of your learning strategies, whether as an individual or as part of a group. You need to reflect on your own abilities and style as a learner, and how you can take responsibility for improving your own learning.

These skills represent possibilities – but feel free to use any other ideas and descriptions that you have:
- use, evaluate and adapt a range of learning skills (analysis, synthesis, evaluation, argument, justification, problem-solving, etc)
- purposefully reflect on own learning and progress
- demonstrate awareness of learning processes
- use learning in new or different situations/contexts
- assist/support others in learning and learn from peers
- develop, evaluate and adapt learning strategies
- carry out agreed tasks
- work productively in a co-operative context
- learn through collaboration
- provide constructive feedback to colleagues
- assist/support others in learning
- interact effectively with supervisor/wider group
- develop business awareness
- evaluate own potential for employment.

### 4.2   Self-management

Self-management is about your personal organisational skills and being able to cope with the demands of managing your work, your studying, your college life, and beyond. It might also include addressing your personal values and commitments. You need to ask yourself, whether you:
- manage time effectively
- set realistic objectives, priorities and standards
- listen actively and with purpose

· show intellectual flexibility and creativity
· take responsibility for acting in a professional/ethical manner
· plan/work towards long-term aims and goals
· purposely reflect on own learning and progress
· take responsibility for own learning/personal growth
· demonstrate awareness of learning processes
· clarify personal values
· cope with physical demands/stress
· monitor, evaluate and adapt own performance.

## 4.3 Communication skills

Communication obviously underpins all aspects of life. At work it will often be oral but written and visual communication is equally important. How good are you at expressing ideas and opinions, at speaking or writing with confidence and clarity, at presenting yourself to a variety of audiences? You should be able to:
· use appropriate language and form in a range of activities (reports, presentations, interviews, etc)
· present information/ideas competently (oral, written, visual)
· respond to different purposes/contexts/audiences
· persuade rationally by means of appropriate information
· defend/justify views or actions
· take initiative and lead others
· negotiate with individuals/the group
· offer constructive criticism
· listen actively and effectively
· evaluate and adapt strategies for communication.

## 4.4 Team/group work/management of others

Do you fit well into a team? Are you a leader? Have you had a wide experience of working with different types of group, whether formal or informal? Have you been on a team development course? Do you work in study groups, or project groups, or manage meetings for a club or society? Consider your skills of co-operation, delegation or negotiation. How have you worked and learned with others? The following skills would indicate your group working abilities:
· carry out agreed tasks
· respect the views and values of others
· work productively in a co-operative context
· adapt to the needs of the group/team
· defend/justify views or actions
· take initiative and lead others
· delegate and stand back
· offer constructive criticism
· take the role of chairperson
· learn through collaboration
· negotiate with individuals/the group
· assist/support others in learning from peers
· interact effectively with tutor/wider group
· monitor, evaluate and assess processes of group/team work.

KAPLAN PUBLISHING

### 4.5 Problem-solving

Do you like tackling and solving problems? How do you manage your job tasks? Can you identify the main features of a problem and develop strategies for its resolution? Are you able to monitor your performance and improve on strategies? Some subjects may traditionally be perceived as related to problem-solving (say, computing), but, for most of us, in any subject area, assignments such as reports or presentations present us with a variety of problems to be solved.

Problem-solving skills means you need to be able to:
· identify key features of the problem/task
· conceptualise issues
· identify strategic options
· plan and implement a course of action
· organise sub-tasks
· set and maintain priorities
· think laterally about a problem
· apply theory to practical context
· apply knowledge/tools/methods to solution of problems
· manage physical resources (tools/equipment)
· show confidence in responding creatively to problems
· show awareness of issues of health and safety
· monitor, evaluate and adapt strategies and outcomes.

## 5 Methods used to acquire skills and knowledge

### 5.1 Personal development plan (PDP)

Basically there are four main options you should consider for each of the development needs within your PDP:
· **Education** – this option will most likely lead to a qualification and will provide you with a broad based body of knowledge, which in turn you need to be able to apply in the work place. With the introduction of more flexible delivery methods you can mix and match between taught modules, self-study and open learning and an increasing availability of e-learning facilities.
· **Training** – this option will be most useful when you need to focus on a particular skill or skill set and can be delivered in many ways: in house, off the job, on the job, by instructors or trainers, or by self-learning.
· Development – this option is a combination of all the other options and should be planned with clear learning goals and measurable outcomes. Ideally the PDP will be aligned with the organisations objectives and your career aspirations.
· **Experience** – we know that there is no substitute for experience, but we also know that many experiences can be painful. Throwing someone in at the deep end may work for some but it is a lot safer if the person doing the throwing knows how deep it is and is on the sideline if difficulties arise. Setting stretching goals and objectives and having coaching and mentoring support will provide a really powerful way of growing and developing yourself.

### 5.2 Training solutions

A training needs analysis addresses the following:
·   What skills does my organisation need me to have to perform my current tasks effectively?
·   What skills do I need to ensure are maintained?
·   What aspects of my work do I enjoy and wish to develop?
·   What personal qualities do I need to enhance?
·   What training resources are available to me?
·   What learning methods suit me best?
·   Where do I expect to be in five years' time?

The training plan is constructed from an investigation into training needs and includes the identification of the skills and knowledge required by the labour force, the identification of the skills and knowledge already possessed - the difference between the two providing a picture of the job-centred training needs. This is then incorporated into the organisation's training plan and decisions are taken on priorities, location, duration, timing and content of training.

Training objectives should be specific and related to observable targets that can be measured. They will cover:
·   **behaviour** – what you should be able to do
·   **standard** – the level of performance
·   **environment** – the conditions.

Once the training objectives are identified, the training funds available and the priorities established in relation to the urgency of the training, the training decisions must be made. These include decisions on the scale and type of training system needed, and whether it can best be provided by the organisation's own staff or by external consultants. Training methods, timing and duration, location and the people actually doing the training also needs to be decided.

Training may be carried out 'in-house' or externally. If any of the training is done in-house, decisions will need to be made on such things as:
·   training workshops
·   location and equipping of classrooms
·   selection of training officers.

Colleges, universities, training organisations and management consultants may provide external courses. There are also open and distance learning facilities via the Open University and other programmes.

To make sure that the training needs are being met, separate training and development co-ordinators may be allocated the responsibilities for training within the firm and for any external training. They may also be responsible for reviewing the system on a regular basis to ensure that it is still satisfying those needs.

KAPLAN PUBLISHING

## 5.3 Researching training and development methods

Training and development methods vary tremendously depending on the person, the job, the resources, the organisation and the economic environment. You can divide them into on-the-job and off-the-job training methods, structured or unstructured, participatory or self development, sitting in front of a computer screen or 'sitting with Nellie'. The methods that you might be looking at include: training courses, both external and in-house; on-the-job training; mentoring; coaching; computerised interactive learning; planned experiences; and self-managed learning.

Business games, either in the sophisticated format of the computer based-profit-seeking program or as the simple leadership games centred around packs of playing cards, are also effective tools of management development. The list of games available is endless; all involve high participation levels.

## 5.4 Internal training and development methods

You can research the types of training and development that can take place at work. These include:

- **Job instructions** – are a systematic approach to training for a particular job, normally used by supervisors when training those who report to them. It can be a cost-effective way of satisfying training needs and can also be linked to a competence-based qualification such as NVQ, which is supervised by the trainee's immediate superior.
- **Internal training centres** are sometimes used to provide customised training programmes e.g. where there would be a risk if the trainee made a mistake.
- **Job rotation** – the training idea of moving an employee from one job to another is that it broadens experience and encourages the employee to be aware of the total activity.
- **Films and closed circuit television** (CCTV) – Films are used to describe company situations, how the different functions of an organisation relate to one another, or for presenting an overview of production. CCTV is used increasingly in management training to illustrate how managers behave and to show how such behaviour can be modified to enable beneficial changes in their interpersonal and problem solving skills.
- **Computer-based training** (CBT) and computer assisted learning (CAL) – user-friendly systems enable trainees to work at their own pace, working on set programmes.
- **Programmed learning** – consists of the presentation of instructional material in small units followed immediately by a list of questions the trainee must answer correctly before progressing to more difficult work.
- **Coaching** – is a specialised form of communication with support being given from the planning stage and continuing during the learning process, with the value of constructive criticism being particularly relevant.
- **Mentoring** – the mentor is expected to guide the new recruit through a development programme and 'socialise' them into the culture of the enterprise. It is a route for bringing on 'high flyers' by allowing them to make mistakes under supervision.

- **Secondments** are temporary transfers to another department or division to gain a deeper understanding or learn more about certain aspects within an organisation.
- **Work shadowing** is a method where one employee shadows another, often more senior, to experience what it is like working at that level.

---

### ▷ ACTIVITY 2 ▷▷▷▷

What type of training is most suitable for the following people?
- Senior lecturer in a university
- The son of the managing director taking over his father's business in the family firm
- New recruit into the payroll section of the account department
- Bank clerk needing to brush up on selling techniques

[Answer on p. 217]

---

### 5.5  Internal training and development methods for groups

Group training encourages participants to learn from each other through discussing issues, pooling experiences and critically examining opposite view-points. Instructors guide discussions rather than impart knowledge directly. They monitor trainee's understanding of what is going on, ask questions to clarify points and sometimes, but not always, prevent certain members from dominating the group. Some of the most popular methods follow:

1  **The lecture method** – is an economical way of passing information to many people. Lectures are of little value if the aim of training is to change attitudes, or develop job or interpersonal skills.

2  **Discussion methods** – are known ways of securing interest and commitment. They can shape attitudes, encourage motivation and secure understanding and can also underline the difficulties of group problem solving.

3  **Case study method** – learning occurs through participation in the definition, analysis and solution of the problem or problems. It demonstrates the nature of group problem solving activity and usually underlines the view that there is no one best solution to a complex business problem.

4  **Role playing** – This method requires trainees to project themselves into a simulated situation that is intended to represent some relevant reality, say, a confrontation between management and a trade union. The merit of role-playing is that it influences attitudes, develops interpersonal skills and heightens sensitivity to the views and feelings of others.

5  **Business games** – simulate realistic situations, mergers, take-overs, etc in which groups compete with one another and where the effects of the decision taken by one group may affect others.

6  **T-group exercises** (the T stands for training) leave the group to their own devices. The trainer simply tells them to look after themselves and remains as an observer. The group itself have to decide what to do and, understandably, the members feel helpless at first and then they pool their experiences and help each other. They eventually form a cohesive group, appoint a leader and resolve any conflicts within the group. They exercise interpersonal communication skills and learn to understand group dynamics.

### 5.6 Self development

Self-development is taking personal responsibility for your own learning. This is an ongoing process that takes place wherever you are and that will continue throughout your life.

A very rich ground for learning, however, is in the workplace. You can have significant learning experiences by doing, being thrown in at the deep end, undertaking challenging new projects and even making mistakes! You can:

· learn ways to improve what you do now
· learn new skills to meet the changing needs of your employer or
· prepare to move on to a new job.

Effective self-development means you need to focus on the following:

· Assess your current skills and interest through paper-and-pencil career tests or through computer programs that analyse skills and interests.
· Maintain a learning log or diary to help you analyse what you are learning from work experiences.
· Develop a personal development plan that identifies your learning needs and goals.
· Consciously seek out learning opportunities to meet your goals e.g. by watching colleagues and asking relevant questions.
· Actively seek feedback on performance/abilities/actions.
· Find a mentor who can provide you with support, advice, and assistance in your career direction.
· Become involved in professional organisations.
· Be opportunistic – look for learning opportunities outside of formal activities e.g. home, social, voluntary, etc.
· Read books, professional journals and trade magazines to keep current on the latest developments in your field.
· Use the Internet to browse for interesting sites and different views on subjects that interest you.

## 6 Review and evaluate your performance and progress

### 6.1 Assessment

In all organisations someone assesses the performance of each employee. Often this is a casual, subjective and infrequent activity where the manager or supervisor spontaneously mentions that a piece of work was done poorly or well. The subordinate then responds in an appropriate manner. It encourages desirable performance and discourages undesirable performance before it becomes ingrained.  But increasingly, many organisations (particularly larger ones) have decided to formalise the assessment process and use it to improve performance, assess training needs and predict the potential of employees.

If you are studying for an NVQ you are assessed on your standards of competence; the focus being on what you have achieved – can you do what is being assessed? There are only three possible outcomes of an assessment:

· pass
· not yet competent
· insufficient evidence upon which to make a judgement.

The majority of the assessment is done at work and when you are ready for it. Assessment methods at NVQ level 3 may be practical, written and oral:
· **practical** – from observing performance within an organisation or department
· **written** – from examining entries in log books
· **oral** – from assessment of oral presentations or observation of leading discussions.

This method of assessment allows you to gain the level of competence required for your jobs in stages. The successful completion of a unit is recorded in the National Record of Achievement.

### 6.2 Appraisal

Performance appraisal is a formal proce-dure to ensure that employees receive objective feedback on their performance, in the context of organisational goals and enabling them to improve themselves. It is often used:

· to audit an employee's competences
· to identify potential and agree targets
· to review achievements
· to communicate and align plans and priorities, both personal and the organisation's
· to identify training and development needs, and monitor career progression
· to exchange feedback and motivate an employee.

### 6.3 Techniques of appraisal

Appraisal techniques include the following:
· **Employee ranking** – Employees are ranked on the basis of their overall performance. This method is particularly prone to bias and its feedback value is practically zero. It does, however, have the advantage that it is simple to use.
· **Rating scales** – Graphic rating scales consist of general personal character-istics and personality traits such as quantity of work, initiative, co-operation and judgement. The judges rate the employee on a scale whose ratings vary, for example from low to high or from poor to excellent. It is called 'graphic' because the scale visually graphs performance from one extreme to the other.
· **Description/Report** – This is a qualitative method of assessment where the manager writes a brief description of the employee under a number of headings.

## 6.4 Self-appraisal

Self-appraisal is assessing your own capabilities and personal characteristics. Occupational Standards and Key/Core Skills provide a framework and language to describe them.

It is a vital component in managing your own professional development and will help you:

· plan and manage your career
· improve your job performance
· improve your capacity to learn
· increase your self confidence and present yourself more effectively
· identify and take advantage of job and learning opportunities
· obtain support from mentors and managers
· manage and provide support to others.

With a realistic self-appraisal you are more likely to be loyal to a supportive environment and committed to improving your own and colleagues' performance. It will enable you to develop yourself to your full potential, reliably managing your work and career. You are also more likely to make use of your training, development and experience as lifelong learning and provide good role models to others.

Steps to self-appraisal

1   **Clarify personal aims** – focus on your objectives - how much is your self-appraisal for: improved work performance, enhanced career development or personal growth? Record your aims.

2   **Manage the appraisal** – find sources of help. Use the professional guidelines to identify relevant standards and key/core skills. Gather insights from others inside and outside the organisation according to personal circumstances. Record the results.

3   **Review personal experience** – look at CV, performance appraisal records, portfolios of evidence, and significant events. Assess values, interests, competences, motivation and contacts. Know yourself.

4   **Assess your own competencies** – assess yourself against occupational standards and key/core skills. Identify strengths, weaknesses, opportunities and threats. Analyse your job. Use diagnostic tools. Identify your priority competences in terms of relative importance of career competence needs and ease of access/opportunities for achieving.

5   **Assess what helps and hinders your development** – identify your learning style and forces for/against personal change.

6   **Review self-appraisal process** – identify the benefits. Record the results and improve the process.

## 7 Test your knowledge ▷ ▷ ▷

1 What do development activities include?

2 When developing your SWOT analysis, what are the four categories of skills you will outline?

3 What will a competence analysis identify?

4 List three different types of competence.

5 What is an NVQ?

6 Describe the competence (or capability, or functional) analysis process.

7 What will the training objectives cover?

8 What types of appraisal techniques are there?

[Answers on p. 217]

## 8 Summary

This chapter has looked at ways of improving your own performance at work. Now that you have studied this chapter you should be able to identify your development needs and research appropriate ways of acquiring skills and knowledge. Training and development need to be reviewed from time to time, just as any other procedures. Some organisations have continuous assessment of training in general; others will have annual appraisals to monitor performance and review achievements.

## Answers to chapter activities & 'test your knowledge' questions

### △ ACTIVITY 1                              △△△△

Your explanation should include the fact that it is a way of measuring what people do at work and how well they do it.

After analysing a job, there should be a statement drawn up by the supervisor or manager establishing both the specific activities a jobholder should be able to perform and the performance criteria detailing how well it should be performed.

The assessment is predominantly by observation – the jobholder demonstrating how well he or she performs the activity. Feedback is given and assistance with corrective actions required where the performance does not match the standard set.

△ **ACTIVITY 2**   △ △ △ △

The type of training that is most suitable:
- Secondment might be considered for a senior lecturer in a university.
- Mentoring or coaching could be the best solution for the son of the managing director taking over his father's business in the family firm.
- Job instructions might be the quickest way to get the new recruit up to scratch on the payroll system.
- Programmed learning or computer-based training could give the bank clerk the ability to brush up on selling techniques.

**Test your knowledge**   △  △  △

1   Development activities include career planning, training - both on and off the job, appraisal and other learning opportunities such as job rotation.

2   Skills may be classed as
- technical – involves working with tools and specific techniques
- human – the ability to work with people; it is co-operative effort; it is teamwork and the creation of an environment in which people feel secure and free to express their opinions
- conceptual – is the ability to see the 'big picture', to recognise significant elements in a situation and to understand the relationships among the elements
- design – is the ability to solve problems in ways that will benefit the organisation.

3   A competence analysis will identify strengths and development needs.

4   There are three different types of competence. Behavioural competences include the ability to relate well to others; occupational competences cover what people have to do to achieve the results in the job; and generic competences apply to anyone, e.g. adaptability, initiative.

5   NVQs or National Vocational Qualifications are qualification frameworks based on standards of competence.

6   This process describes the job's main tasks or key result areas, the types and levels of knowledge and skill that these require, the acceptable standard of performance in each task or result area and how performance is assessed.

7   Training objectives should be specific and related to observable targets that can be measured. They will cover behaviour – what you should be able to do, standard – the level of performance and environment – the conditions.

8   Appraisal techniques include employee ranking rating scales and a description or report which is a qualitative method of assessment where the manager writes a brief description of the employee under a number of headings.

KAPLAN PUBLISHING

# USING AN ACCOUNTING PACKAGE

**INTRODUCTION**

The aim of this chapter is to give you an overview of a typical computerised accounting package. We will be looking especially at the market-leading packages designed for use by small and medium-sized enterprises (SMEs) and produced by **Sage**, but if you have **another package** then that can be used, too. The basic elements of most accounting packages are the same, and ways of operating them (tabbing, shortcut keys, lists and so on) are similar, although different packages may use different terms, icons, keyboard combinations, and so on.

This chapter covers the IT Knowledge and Understanding and Performance Criteria of Units 1 to 4 of the AAT Standards of Competence.

**UNIT 1**, RECORDING INCOME AND RECEIPTS

**UNIT 2**, MAKING AND RECORDING PAYMENTS

**UNIT 3**, PREPARING AN INITIAL TRIAL BALANCE

**UNIT 4**, SUPPLYING INFORMATION FOR MANAGEMENT CONTROL

We are including them in this book because the AAT tests these topics in the simulation for Unit 21.

## CONTENTS

1 Components of an accounting package
2 Control features
3 Standing data
4 Posting transactions
5 Recording cash transactions
6 Accounting for sales and debtors
7 Bank reconciliations and error corrections
8 Batch processing
9 Summary

# 1 Components of an accounting package

## 1.1 Well-known accounting packages

There are dozens of different accounting packages. Here are some of the names you are likely to encounter during your accounting career.

| | |
|---|---|
| Access (Foundations; Dimensions; Horizons) | MYOB |
| ACCPAC Advantage Series | OpenAccounts |
| Baan Financials | Oracle Financials |
| CODA – DREAM; CODA – Financials | Pegasus (Capital Gold; Opera II) |
| DO$H Cashbook | PeopleSoft Financials |
| Exact | QuickBooks |
| Exchequer Enterprise | Sage (Instant; Line 50; Line 100 etc.) |
| JD Edwards One World | SAP R/3 |
| Lawson | SunSystems |
| Microsoft (Axapta; Great Plains; Navision) | VT Transactions |

**Sage Line 50** is the market leader amongst small to medium sized businesses in the UK, followed by **QuickBooks**. Packages such as Oracle Financials and SAP R/3 are designed for very large organisations.

## 1.2 Accounting packages and manual systems

Within a computerised accounting system you will find almost all the same basic components as you have in a manual system – main ledger, sales ledger and so on – with two major exceptions.

· Most packages **do not have an analysed cash book**: cash is simply an account in the main ledger.
· The components are likely to have **different names**, depending upon the program you use.

Here are some typical differences in names. See if you can find the relevant buttons in the screen illustrations on the next page. Note in particular that the main ledger is more commonly called the **Nominal Ledger** or simply the **Chart of Accounts** and that some packages base their terminology on the people involved (e.g. 'Customers') while others refer to transactions (eg 'Sales').

| AAT Term | Sage | QuickBooks | MYOB |
|---|---|---|---|
| Main Ledger | Nominal Ledger | Chart of Accounts | Accounts |
| Subsidiary Sales Ledger | Customers Ledger | Customers Ledger | Sales Ledger |
| Subsidiary Purchases Ledger | Suppliers Ledger | Vendors Ledger | Purchases Ledger |
| Invoice | Invoice | Invoice/Bill | Invoices/Purchases |
| Stock | Products | Item | Stock Control |
| Prime entry/day books | These are not components in most accounting packages. Day books do not really exist although equivalents may be available as reports. | | |

Since most of this chapter takes its illustrations from the market leading package, Sage, try to get used to the Sage terms listed above.

### Sage Instant/Line 50

### QuickBooks

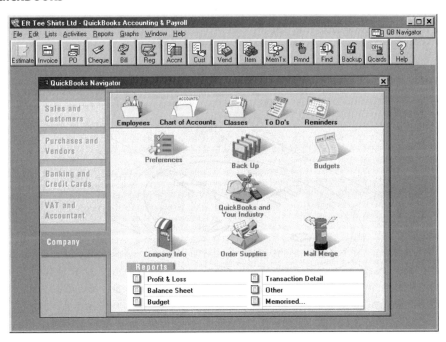

**MYOB**

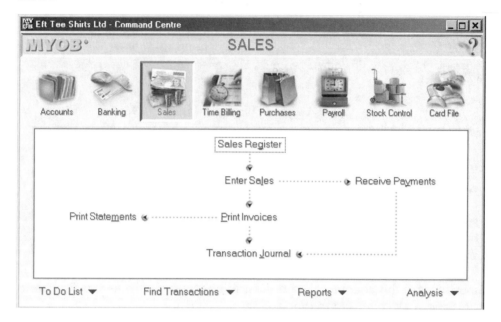

Apart from the variable terminology the principal difference between manual and computerised accounting is that a computerised package does most of the double entry (and many other routine tasks) **automatically**, with little or no effort from the accountant.

Accounting software also offers **better reporting** and **more reliable data analysis** capabilities than manual systems, as we will see later.

### 1.3 Credit sales

Let us look first at credit sales. In a computerised system the customers (debtors) ledger and nominal (main) ledger are updated from a single source. You only have to input the details of credit sales into an invoicing screen and the program will prepare invoices and update both ledgers automatically.

**Posting a credit sale**

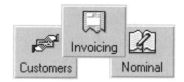

### 1.4 Credit purchases

The system for recording credit purchases is similar to the system for recording credit sales, except of course that you don't need to prepare an invoice, merely post the details of an invoice you have received from one of your suppliers. Again the suppliers (or creditors) ledger and the nominal (main) ledger are updated automatically.

**Posting a credit purchase**

### 1.5 Cash receipts

As we have mentioned most packages do not have a separate cash book, only a cash account in the nominal ledger. A receipt from a debtor is input through a cash/bank posting screen which automatically records the receipt in the debtor's individual account in the customers ledger and in the debtors control account and bank account in the nominal ledger. Other receipts such as bank interest can also be input through the cash/bank posting screen, but these only affect the nominal ledger.

**Receipt of cash from a debtor**          **Receipt of bank interest**

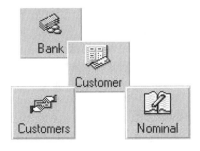    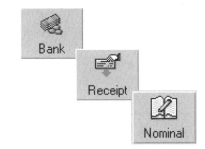

### 1.6 Cash payments

Cash payments (whether from a bank account or petty cash, or another source) are also divided into two types: payments to suppliers and other payments. Once again these are input via options (the Supplier button or the Payment button) in the cash/bank posting screen.

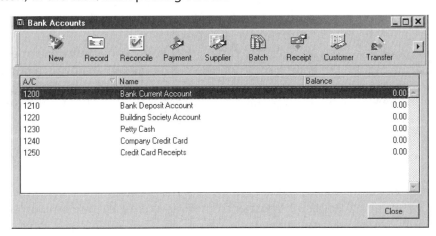

> ▷ **ACTIVITY 1**                                                    ▷ ▷ ▷ ▷
>
> Look at the illustration above. Which button would you click on to record the receipt of a payment from a debtor?
>
> [Answer on p. 260]

## 2    Control features

One of the key features of accounting software is that it encourages good control over data, particularly at the input stage, because it has facilities for verification and validation of data.

### 2.1  Validation

Validation is the application of pre-programmed tests and rules by the accounting package to make sure that the data input is reasonable.

There are a number of different forms of validation control.  Some examples are as follows:

· **Range checks** – test that the data is within an appropriate range, for example all product prices should be between £10 and £100. This will prevent some-body keying in a price of £22.99 as £2,299 in error. These checks can also be applied to dates: for instance you won't be able to enter a date of 31 February, and you won't be able to enter a 2006 transaction in the accounting records for any other year.

· **Existence checks** – compare the input data with some other piece of data in the system, to see if it is reasonable.  For example a customer code might be compared with a list from the customer records file and if the code does not exist the computer would give you the options of amending your entry or creating a new customer account.

· **Format checks** – test the data in each input area against rules governing whether it should be numeric, alphabetic or a combination of the two.  For example the software would not allow letters to be entered in a box desig-nated for the quantity of items sold.

· **Completeness or sequence checks** – ensure that all data items in a series have been processed.  For example if the next invoice number you want to create is number 13455 but 13450 was the previous invoice raised the soft-ware may force you to confirm this is correct.

· **Check digits** – may be built in to certain data items. For instance the operator may be required to enter a code such as 211-2 where the final 2 is a number that the computer can check by performing calculations on the first three digits. If the operator accidentally entered 212-1 instead of 211-2 this would generate an alert that the number was not valid.

### 2.2  Codes

To improve the speed and accuracy of the processing, data is normally organised using a system of codes.  In most accounting systems all the nominal ledger accounts, suppliers, customers, stock items and documents are referenced using codes. This allows more of the validation checks to be carried out. Coding systems also help to make all the necessary postings from a single data input. Each input field can be set up to perform both sides of the appropriate double entry automatically.

In Sage Instant and Sage Line 50, for instance, all the nominal ledger accounts are given a unique four-digit code. As you will see later, all the Working Capital codes begin with 1, the Stock with 10, the Debtors with 11 and so on. This is known as a hierarchical code structure, and makes it easier for the user to find items on a code list, as the related accounts are grouped together.

## 2.3 Verification

Verification is the comparison of input data with the source document. Computers can't yet see in the way that humans can but they can encourage the operator to check the accuracy of their inputs. For instance if the operator is posting an invoice for Postage and enters a nominal code of 7600 the computer can automatically display the name of the account with the code 7600 (eg 'Legal Fees'): this should alert the operator that they have made a mistake that needs to be corrected before the transaction is recorded in the accounts.

However it is important to recognise that accounting software is not capable of enforcing accuracy in a case like this, as it cannot see the source document. It can check to see if the input is reasonable, according to pre-defined parameters, but if the operator wilfully posts an item to the wrong account the computer won't be able to prevent this.

> **ACTIVITY 2**

Can you think of any way in which computers could check source data?

[Answer on p. 260]

## 2.4 Error messages and warnings

Where the accounting system is computerised, certain errors cannot occur:
· single entries (the computer will not accept them)
· casting errors (the computer will total accounts automatically)
· transposition errors (the computer posts the double entry automatically)
· extraction errors (the computer posts the double entry automatically).

But **human errors** can still occur:
· errors of original entry
· errors of commission
· errors of principle.

When you are learning to use an accounting package it is likely that you will occasionally do something that is not allowed or is not what you intended. If that happens a message will appear either asking you to confirm that you want to process the transaction or telling you what you have done wrong.

Here are some examples.

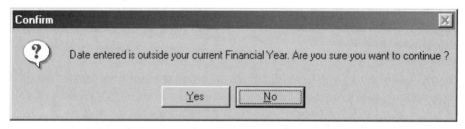

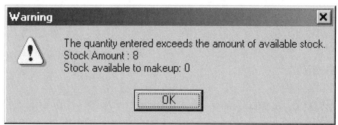

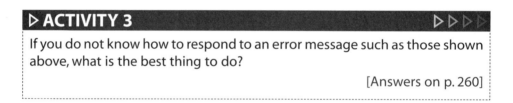

## ▷ ACTIVITY 3 ▷ ▷ ▷ ▷

If you do not know how to respond to an error message such as those shown above, what is the best thing to do?

[Answers on p. 260]

## 3 Standing data

### 3.1 Standing data

A great deal of the information used in an accounting package is known as standing data, in other words data that does not change or changes very rarely. Examples are:

· the name of the company and its address, VAT number, etc
· the names and codes of the accounts in the nominal ledger
· names and addresses of customers and suppliers
· names, descriptions and prices of stock items,

The beauty of an accounting system is that you only have to enter these details once and then whenever you want to use them again you simply have to enter a short code which will automatically reproduce all the other details on your screen, without any further typing from you.

To help you become familiar with an accounting package, you are going to look at the early life of a small business as it might be reflected in **Sage Instant** or **Sage Line 50**. (We'll refer to both packages as 'Sage' in future: **it does not matter which version you use**.)

First of all we will need some standing data.

> **ACTIVITY 4**

We have provided enough illustrations and explanations in the rest of this chapter for you to get a good understanding of how a typical accounting package works just by reading, but ideally you should be sitting at a computer equipped with Sage and following the instructions given, **hands-on**.

Even the cheapest accounting package costs around £100 (the basic version of Sage Line 50 costs around £500), so it is unlikely that you have your own, even if you have your own computer. Most colleges, however, have computers equipped with Sage or a similar package.

Your task in this activity is to find out what arrangements **your college** makes to allow you to complete the computerised accounts aspects of Units 1 to 3. If there are any special instructions that you need to follow to get access to your college's accounts training facilities make a note of them and keep them with this book.

[There is no answer to this activity]

### 3.2  Eft Tee Shirts Ltd

The business we are going to look at is a fictional one set up by a fictional person called William Eft.

His company was set up to sell custom printed adult and children's leisurewear, and it is called **Eft Tee Shirts Ltd**.

Assume the company started trading on 1 January in the current year, i.e. the year in which you are working on this chapter. In the examples the date will be shown as 200X

The company is registered for VAT and it intends to make both cash and credit sales and purchases.

### 3.3  Setting up company details

It is extremely unlikely that you would be asked to set up a company on an accounting system from scratch – at least not at this stage of your career – but you can still get an overview of how the standing data about a business can be entered.

Like most other modern accounting packages Sage has a number of **Wizards** to take you through common tasks, step by step. In Sage you set up and change company details by clicking on **File** and using the **Easy Startup Wizard**.

Your progress through the start up procedure is controlled using the Next, Back and Cancel buttons. Any fields that you are unsure of can be left as they appear in the Wizard: for instance in the **Bank Accounts** screen just accept that the name of the Current account is 'Bank Current Account' and in **Bank Defaults** do not alter the options that are ticked or unticked: just click on Next when you get to this screen.

Here are the details of the company, Eft Tee Shirts Ltd, which we are going to look at in this first case study. If these details have been input for you already or restored from a backup file, check them carefully on screen.

| | |
|---|---|
| Nominal account structure | General Business – Standard Chart of Accounts (you won't get the option to set or change this unless you have a multi-company version of Sage). |
| Company name | Eft Tee Shirts Ltd |
| Address | 123 Greenwood Road<br>Withington<br>Manchester<br>M20 4TF |
| Telephone | 0161 460 7488 |
| Fax | 0161 460 3442 |
| Financial Year Start Month | January |
| Financial Year Start Year | Use the current year when you are reading this. |
| VAT reg. no.<br>(Standard VAT accounting) | 456 3344 12 |
| Standard Nominal Code for Customers | 4000 |
| VAT Rate | 17.50% (The standard rate is given a code of T1) |
| Standard Nominal Code for Suppliers | 5000 |
| VAT Rate | 17.50% (Again this is given a code of T1) |

Once you have checked the company's standing data, you can enter other information about the business and the people it does business with, such as: customer names and addresses and nominal ledger codes, if they do not exist in the default settings or you want to change them.

### 3.4 Customers

You will need to set up the names and addresses of the customers you are dealing with and give each one a code. The details can be amended whenever necessary, for instance if a customer moves or appoints a new person as your contact.

For customer codes Sage uses up to eight characters (letters, numbers or punctuation marks, but not spaces). By default Sage enters the first eight letters of the customer's name as a code, although you can change this to any other coding system if your company has a different one.

| | | |
|---|---|---|
| FREDBROW | Fred Brown Associates<br>234 Barlow Moor Road<br>West Didsbury<br>Manchester  M19 5DG | Telephone: 0161 456 8833<br>Contact: Fred Brown<br>VAT No: 999 0101 22<br>Terms agreed: Yes |
| EVERETTE | Everett Enterprises<br>122 Wilbraham Road<br>Chorlton<br>Manchester<br>M21 9JK | Telephone: 0161 860 3345<br>Contact: Sid Francis<br>VAT No: 545 2233 01<br>Terms agreed: Yes |
| THORNWOO | Thornwood Manufacturing Ltd<br>89 Glendale Street<br>Ancoats<br>Manchester<br>M1 3GH | Telephone: 0161 236 1903<br>Contact: Sarah Marshall<br>VAT No: 200 6666 05<br>Terms agreed: Yes |
| TAYLORAN | Taylor and Atkins<br>34 Lightbowne Road<br>Moston<br>Manchester<br>M15 1TF | Telephone: 0161 556 4785<br>Contact: Steve Hardy<br>VAT No: 456 7777 88<br>Terms agreed: Yes |
| WHITEBRO | White Brothers<br>239 Darnell Way<br>Oldham<br>OL1 4NM | Telephone: 0161 940 3782<br>Contact: Heather Thomas<br>VAT No: 600 1234 55<br>Terms agreed: Yes |

Using Sage, you can set up new customers' details with a Wizard or you can start up an empty Record to fill in without help. **We strongly recommend that you use the Wizard.** Click on Customers then New and fill in the details given. Enter Manchester as the county (the system will just ignore any address lines you leave blank). The credit limit for each account is £1,000. There are no opening balances. **All other options** in the Wizard can be left as they are.

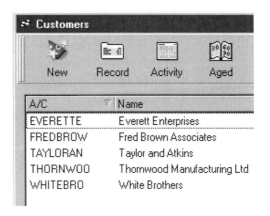

### 3.5 Printed output

You can produce a report to check that all these customers have been entered onto the system correctly. Click on the Reports button in the Customers window (be careful not to click the Reports button in the main toolbar). This opens the Customer Reports Window. Scroll down until you find **Customer Address List**, and click on it.

At the bottom of this Window, you will see five boxes: New, Edit, Delete, Run and Close. Choose **Run**.

If you click on **Preview**, a **Criteria** box is displayed which allows you to specify specific customers for whom you want a report.

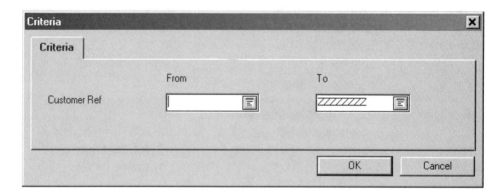

If you leave the options as initially displayed you will get a report for **all** customers.

The report will then be produced as a print preview. After viewing it on the screen by scrolling down the page, you can save it to a file or print it if you wish.

Check all the details you have entered against the information shown in this book and make a note of any corrections that you need to make.

Close the report by clicking on **Close** at the bottom of the window. Do the same with any other windows that are open until you get back to the main screen.

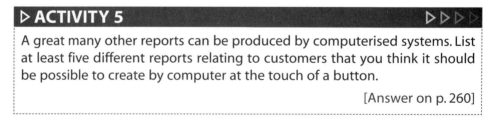

▷ **ACTIVITY 5**     ▷ ▷ ▷ ▷

A great many other reports can be produced by computerised systems. List at least five different reports relating to customers that you think it should be possible to create by computer at the touch of a button.

[Answer on p. 260]

### 3.6 Suppliers

This section contains the names and addresses of the suppliers.
Again suppliers' details can most easily be entered by clicking on **Suppliers** then **New** and using the **Wizard**.

| TREVORMA | Trevor Manufacturing Ltd<br>345 Taylforth Road<br>Sale<br>Manchester   M24 2KN | Telephone: 0161 345 2234<br>Contact: Harold Goodman<br>VAT No: 444 5555 66<br>Terms agreed: Yes |
|---|---|---|
| OLYMPICD | Olympic Design Studio<br>34 Weaver Street<br>Withington<br>Manchester M20 2JL | Telephone: 0161 404 4654<br>Contact: Betty Davies<br>VAT No: 888 9999 01<br>Terms agreed: Yes |
| JOSEPHPA | Joseph Parker & Sons<br>7 Hillside Drive<br>Chorlton<br>Manchester   M21 4DF | Telephone: 0161 403 5712<br>Contact: Laura Jackson<br>VAT No: 333 4545 66<br>Terms agreed: Yes |
| HILLANDS | Hill and Saint<br>566 Burton Road<br>Withington<br>Manchester   M20 8JN | Telephone:  0161 723 3887<br>Contact: Kevin Birch<br>VAT No: 888 9090 11<br>Terms agreed: Yes |
| DRYERSUP | Dryer Supplies Ltd<br>899 Regency Way<br>Bolton<br>BL1 4RT | Telephone: 01204 573413<br>Contact: David Warren<br>VAT No: 345 6789 22<br>Terms agreed: Yes |

Start each account with a nil opening balance and leave the default entries for all the other fields.

## ▷ ACTIVITY 6                                        ▷ ▷ ▷ ▷

Identify which part of your program you need to use to input standing data about customers and suppliers. Make a note of the procedure followed.

Once you have input all the details, print out a list of customers and a list of suppliers.

[There is no feedback to this activity]

### 3.7 Nominal codes

Many nominal codes are created automatically when you first set up a company. The nominal codes that we will be using initially are as follows.

| | | | |
|---|---|---|---|
| 0030 | Office Equipment | 2200 | Sales Tax Control Account (VAT) |
| 1100 | Debtors Control Account | 3000 | Ordinary Shares |
| 1200 | Bank Current Account | 4000 | Sales Type A |
| 1230 | Petty Cash | 5000 | Materials Purchased |
| 2100 | Creditors Control Account | 7600 | Legal Fees |

Although there are many default nominal codes like this, you may need to add others to cater for your particular type of activities. We'll be doing this later. Transactions that need to be recorded in the Debtors, Creditors and Tax (VAT) **control accounts** are generally done **automatically** for you when you post an invoice, so you won't actually realise that you are 'using' these accounts.

### 3.8 VAT rates

In some packages you may have to set up **rates of VAT** which are currently charged, including codes for **exempt** and **outside of scope**.

Tax codes are used to identify the rate of VAT to be applied to a given transaction. You can specify up to 100 VAT rates, each one identified by a code from T0 to T99. You can then select which rates are to be included in the VAT Return calculations and which relate to EC (European) transactions.

On installation, Sage automatically sets up the following VAT rates for you.

T0      zero rated transactions
T1      standard rate  (currently at 17.5%)
T2      exempt transactions
T9      transactions not involving VAT

There are also default codes for transactions with organisations in the EC (outside the UK), because these need to be shown separately on a VAT return, but we won't be using those.

You can change all the VAT codes if the occasion arises, by clicking on the **Settings** menu and then **Tax Codes**.

### 3.9 Program date

When you start up an accounting package it will assume that the date is the computer's system date, ie today's date, assuming your computer is properly set up.

Normally this is exactly what you want, because you will enter transactions on the day when they occur. However, smaller companies may have so few transactions that it is not worth starting up the accounts package each time. They may save up all their invoices, and employ an accountant to come in and enter them into the system once a month, say.

In Sage you can change the default date that the program uses by clicking on **Settings** and then **Change Program Date**.

In the case of Eft Tee Shirts Ltd, when you make the opening entries detailed below, you should start by changing the program date to **1 January** in the current year . As you work through the remainder of the chapter, you should change the dates to the date given in the text.

Dates are important because they affect how the system accounts for VAT, how it produces aged debtors and creditors reports, monthly trial balances, and other reports, whether settlement discounts are due or can be taken, and so on. Don't be tempted to use the system date if you know it is not correct.

# 4 Posting transactions

## 4.1 Opening balances

Before you begin posting transactions to a new accounting system, you may need to transfer the current balances from your existing system to the new one. Outstanding customer and supplier balances must be entered to reflect what is owed from customers and to suppliers.

This is not necessarily as laborious as it sounds: it is usually possible to export data from one system (QuickBooks, say) and import it to another (say, Sage), without much retyping or reformatting, although doing this is well **beyond the scope** of your current studies.

## 4.2 Journal entries

After the ledgers have been set up and any opening balances sorted out, then the day-to-day transactions can be entered into the ledgers.

Most of these transactions are going to be routine, eg purchase and sales on credit and transactions affecting the company's cash. Transactions other than these routine ones do occur, but they are not so numerous as to warrant special ledgers for each class. This is where the journal is used.

The entries into the journal are different because both aspects of each transaction are recorded. As you know from your experience of manual accounting, it is important to add an **explanatory note (narrative)** with each entry.

If you have postings that need to be made on a regular basis, such as standing orders, direct debits, depreciation postings, etc then most accounting packages will allow you to set these up as journals once and then post them automatically.

Recurring journals can be repeated continuously or set for a number of postings, after which they will be cancelled.

### 4.3 Posting journal entries

As Eft Tee Shirts Ltd is starting from scratch it has **no opening balances** to transfer for suppliers or customers. The first entry you need to post is a journal for the **capital introduced** by the owner, William Eft. He has bought £10,000 of share capital. He spent £100 to register the company with Companies House and he has introduced £7,400 in cash and some office equipment (a computer) that cost £2,500.

Before you read on see if you can work out what the double entry for this transaction would be, using the nominal codes supplied on the previous page.

These initial transactions will be recorded as Journal entries and will be posted to the appropriate accounts in the Nominal Ledger. For every journal transaction, there will be a debit entry in one Nominal Ledger account and a corresponding credit entry in another Nominal Ledger account.

**It is vitally important to provide a reference number**. Eft Tee Shirts has decided that these will all begin with a J followed by five digits, starting at J00001.

Here is what the journal might look like in a manual system.

| JOURNAL ENTRY | | **No: J00001** | |
|---|---|---|---|
| **Date:** 1 January 200X | | | |
| **Narrative:** Capital introduced by William Eft | | | |
| *Account* | Code | Debit | Credit |
| Legal Fees | 7600 | 100.00 | |
| Office Equipment | 0030 | 2500.00 | |
| Cash at Bank | 1200 | 7400.00 | |
| Shares | 3000 | | 10,000.00 |
| TOTALS | | 10,000.00 | 10,000.00 |

And here it is again as it would appear in Sage.

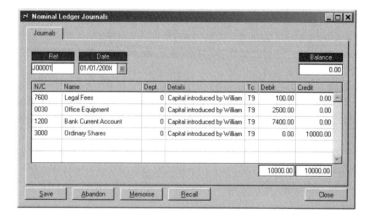

KAPLAN PUBLISHING

Don't be tempted to enter these details yet, if you are working hands-on. Read the next section first.

▷ **ACTIVITY 7**                                        ▷ ▷ ▷ ▷

What do you think the **Memorise** and **Recall** buttons in the above illustration might be used for? What might be the advantage of such facilities in an accounting package?

[Answer on p. 260]

### 4.4 Saving time using shortcut keys

At first sight you might think that the above involves a lot of clicking and typing: it is probably not clear what the advantage of using a computer system is. However there are lots of little tricks you can use to minimise the effort involved. The general idea is that you should take your hands off the keyboard as little as possible, because using the mouse slows you down.

For instance, in almost all accounting packages to **move around the screen** between the different **fields** (boxes to fill in) just press the **Tab** key. To move back to the previous field hold down the Shift key and press Tab. You will quickly get used to this and it saves you a great deal of time and wrist-ache!
Other features in Sage include the following.

Whenever you need to **enter a date** in a field just press the function key **F4**. A mini calendar will appear and you can select the date you want by using the up, down, right or left arrow keys. When you find the date you want press **Enter**. (A further option is to set a default 'program date', as described earlier.)

·   Whenever you need to look something up such as the nominal code for an account you simply tab to the relevant field and press the function key F4. A list of all available codes appears and you can simply scroll through it (using the arrow keys or the PgUp and PgDn keys) until you find the one you want, then press Enter or click on OK. The account code and its name are filled in automatically.

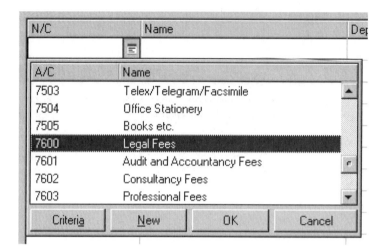

You can speed this up still further if you know part of the code. For instance in the illustration above you could **just type 7** in the N/C box and then press F4. The list will scroll automatically to accounts beginning with 7. Likewise, if you want a customer or supplier code you can simply type the first letter or first few letters of their name and then press F4.

· You can quickly **duplicate items** from the line above by pressing the function key **F6**. So in the example of a journal above the user only typed 'Capital introduced by William Eft' in the first line. In the second, third and fourth lines the user would simply press F6 when they got to the Details box. (You can also press **Shift+F6** if the item in the previous line ends with a number and you want to increase the number by 1.)

· Whenever you are about to **enter debits or credits** you can press F4 and a mini calculator will appear. You can operate this using the numeric keypad and operators (+, * etc) on your keyboard. You don't have to do this, but it is sometimes useful when you need to calculate the amount to enter, for instance when working out the VAT on an invoice with settlement discount.

If you enter debits or credits directly you won't be allowed to enter a pound sign. If it is a whole number such as 150.00 you do not need to enter the decimal point or the final two 0s. The program will do this for you.

Most of these features are not exclusive to Sage – similar shortcuts are available in other packages, although the precise key combinations will be different. For instance, where you would press F4 in Sage, you might press the **Enter** key or some combination such as **Control+L** in other packages.

KAPLAN PUBLISHING

▷ **ACTIVITY 8**

Enter the journal, using as many keyboard shortcuts as you can (try not to use the mouse at all!). Enter the current year  if you have decided to use that as the current financial year. Here are the details again. Leave the field headed Tc as T9. Make sure you include the journal reference number.

| JOURNAL ENTRY | No: J00001 | | |
|---|---|---|---|
| **Date:**       1 January 200X | | | |
| **Narrative:** Capital introduced by William Eft | | | |
| *Account* | Code | Debit | Credit |
| Legal Fees | 7600 | 100.00 | |
| Office Equipment | 0030 | 2500.00 | |
| Cash at Bank | 1200 | 7400.00 | |
| Shares | 3000 | | 10,000.00 |
| TOTALS | | 10,000.00 | 10,000.00 |

Once you have entered all the necessary data, press the 'Save' button (if you are using Sage) to process the journal.

[There is no feedback to this activity]

## 4.5  Prime entry, Day Books and accounting packages

The concepts of prime entry and Day Books are **anachronisms** in the context of computerised accounting packages, although many accounting packages still offer facilities for 'computerised' day book **reports**.

As you know, the key idea in a **manual system** is that Day Books contain the detailed (prime) entries, while the **ledgers** contain a **summary** of those entries, by means of page totals, or date totals, or the like – and in a manual system this certainly saves time and effort.

In a **computerised** system, however, **all the details** of everything you record can automatically be recorded, **both** as a **prime** (detailed) entry –  though it will probably not be called anything like that, in any modern package – **and** in **summary** form, posted directly to the **ledgers**.

A computerised system has access to all of the information recorded, all of the time, and so it can **assemble reports on request**, with any details you want – day books or whatever –  in any form you like. Just click on **Reports** and take your pick.

▷ **ACTIVITY 9**

Explain in your own words how an accounting package has facilities that allow a user to enter a gross amount and generate net and VAT amounts without further input from the user. Give a simple numerical example.

[Answer on p. 261]

### 4.6 Posting supplier invoices

Here is the first batch of supplier invoices. Some information is not given deliberately: see the next paragraphs.

| Date | Supplier | Ref | N/C | Details | Net | VAT | Gross |
|------|----------|-----|-----|---------|-----|-----|-------|
| 2 January | Trevor Manufacturing Ltd | 00001 | 5000 | 84 women's tee shirts | 231.00 | 40.43 | |
| 2 January | Hill and Saint | 00002 | 5000 | 72 men's tee shirts | 234.00 | 40.95 | |
| 2 January | Joseph Parker & Sons | 00003 | 5000 | 36 children's tee shirts | 77.40 | Zero | 77.40 |
| 3 January | Dryer Supplies Ltd | 00004 | 7504 | Stationery | | | 19.72 |
| 5 January | Olympic Design Studio | 00005 | 5000 | Graphic design | 68.34 | 11.96 | |

To post details of purchase invoices received from Suppliers to the accounts, you click on **Suppliers** then **Invoice** and simply enter the details, as illustrated below.

Use the **F4, F6** and **Shift+F6** shortcut keys as much as you can to look up codes and dates and duplicate or increment previous entries.

The box labelled **Ex.Ref** is for a code such as the supplier's invoice number. In this case you can leave it blank. Eft Tee Shirts is too small to have separate departments, so you can leave the **Dept** box blank, too.

When you enter the **Net** figure the package will calculate VAT for you automatically, but make sure you change the Tax code to T0 for the zero-rated transaction.

If you have an invoice that does not show the VAT amount you can enter the gross amount in the **Net** box and before tabbing on press the F9 function key. This will automatically calculate the net figure and the VAT (£16.78 and £2.94 in the case of the **Dryer Supplies** invoice above.) There is also a **Calculate Net** button at the foot of the screen, which does the same thing.

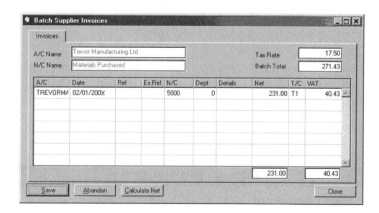

KAPLAN PUBLISHING

You can click on **Save** after entering each line of details or you can wait until you have entered all five invoices. You will be reminded to Save if you try to **Close** the screen without doing so. If you get things terribly wrong you can click on **Abandon** and start again.

Remember that although you have only input the purchase invoice details into a screen, **clicking on Save completes all the double entry** for you and also **updates the individual accounts** in the creditors ledger.

### 4.7  Posting customer invoices (without creating a printable invoice)

Some organisations create sales invoices in a separate package such as a word processing program and only use their accounting package to record the details. We'll assume that Eft Tee Shirts does this for its first few sales invoices.

To enter sales invoices into the program you click on **Customers** and then **Invoice**. The screen looks exactly like the one for posting supplier invoices and works in exactly the same way.

Here are the sales invoices for the first month of trading. In each case the nominal code is 4000 (Sales Type A). The VAT code (T/C) is T1 except for the children's tee shirts where the code is T0.

The net figure you should get for invoice 10004 is £115.08. Remember the **F9** key.

| Date | Customer | Ref | Details | Net | VAT | Gross |
|---|---|---|---|---|---|---|
| 7 January | Everett Enterprises | 10001 | Tee shirts: 6 men's, 15 women's | 151.98 | 26.60 | 178.58 |
| 7 January | Taylor and Atkins | 10002 | Tee shirts: 20 children's | 107.60 | 0.00 | 107.60 |
| 8 January | Thornwood Manufacturing Ltd | 10003 | Tee shirts: 12 women's | 82.56 | 14.45 | 97.01 |
| 8 January | White Brothers | 10004 | Tee shirts: 4 men's, 12 women's | | | 135.22 |
| 9 January | Taylor and Atkins | 10005 | Tee shirts: 20 men's | 162.60 | 28.46 | 191.06 |

Remember that although you have only input the sales invoice details into a screen, clicking on Save completes the double entry for you and updates the individual accounts in the debtors ledger.

### 4.8  Trial balance

You have now completed posting the first batches of transactions. As a quick check on your work you can produce a trial balance. Using Sage you do this by clicking on **Financials** then **Trial**.

You are asked for the criteria, i.e. the month (January, Month 1) and the type of output. You can choose to have a preview, to print or to save it as a file. If you have entered all the transactions so far correctly your preview should be the same as the trial balance below.

**Eft Tee Shirts Ltd Trial Balance**

| N/C | Name | Debit £ | Credit £ |
|---|---|---|---|
| 0030 | Office Equipment | 2,500.00 | |
| 1100 | Debtors Control Account | 709.47 | |
| 1200 | Bank Current Account | 7,400.00 | |
| 2100 | Creditors Control Account | | 723.80 |
| 2200 | Sales Tax Control Account | | 89.65 |
| 2201 | Purchase Tax Control Account | 96.28 | |
| 3000 | Ordinary Shares | | 10,000.00 |
| 4000 | Sales Type A | | 619.82 |
| 5000 | Materials Purchased | 610.74 | |
| 7504 | Office Stationery | 16.78 | |
| 7600 | Legal Fees | 100.00 | |
| | **Totals:** | 11,433.27 | 11,433.27 |

### 4.9  Backing up

It is a good idea to take regular backups of your work. We suggest that you do so at least at the end of each section of this chapter.

To make a backup just click on **File** and **Backup** …. By default Sage may try to backup to a floppy disk, but (as the backup screen explains) if you want to save your backup to the hard disk you can do so by clicking on a button labelled Setup and choosing another location.

By default Sage will suggest the **file name** SAGEBACK.001, but you should always change this, otherwise you may end up overwriting an earlier backup file.

We suggest you use a name such as **ABC.059**, where ABC are your initials and 059 refers to the heading number in this book when you made the backup (write the name you used in the margin).

## 5   Recording cash transactions

### 5.1  Cash receipts

Let us move on in time. Let us assume the customers all pay the full amount. The information required to record a receipt includes:
·    the nominal code for the bank ledger account
·    the customer's account code
·    the amount
·    a reference number.

To enter a customer receipt click on **Bank** and make sure the correct account (1200) is highlighted. Then click on the **Customer** button in the Bank Accounts row of icons. The Customer Receipt window is displayed.

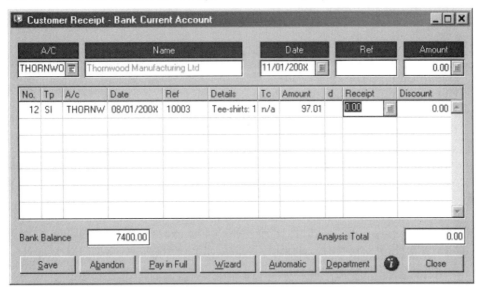

If you enter a customer account code all the items that you have invoiced to that customer which are not fully paid, appear automatically.

Eft Tee Shirts has received the following customers' payments. You may want to change the program date to 11 January to save typing it each time. You will need to use your package's **allocation** facility to pay off each invoice. The easiest way to do this in Sage is to tab through the Amount box without making an entry and when you get to the **Receipt** column press **Alt+P** (or click on the **Pay in Full** button). This updates the Amount box and allocates the payment automatically.

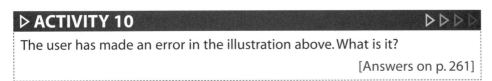

The user has made an error in the illustration above. What is it?

[Answers on p. 261]

Enter the following receipts into the program.

| 11 Jan | R00001 | Thornwood Manufacturing Ltd | 97.01 |
|--------|--------|-----------------------------|--------|
| 11 Jan | R00002 | Everett Enterprises | 178.58 |
| 11 Jan | R00003 | White Brothers | 135.22 |
| 11 Jan | R00004 | Taylor and Atkins | 298.66 |

Note how the receipt from Taylor and Atkins pays off two invoices.

Clicking on Save for each receipt will post the entries to all the relevant ledgers. You can check this by clicking on Customers in the main window and looking at the list of balances (they should all be 0.00). You can also check the balance on the bank account by clicking on Nominal and scrolling down to account 1200. It should be £8,109.47 (the original £7,400 plus the above amounts).

### 5.2 Recording cash payments

The information required to record a payment includes:
· the cheque number
· the amount paid
· the amount of discount
· the supplier's account code
· the nominal code for the bank account.

To record a supplier payment, choose the **Bank** button again. The **Bank Accounts** Window is displayed. Select the account that you are using to pay this invoice (1200) and then select the **Supplier** button from the toolbar.

The supplier payment posting screen works in exactly the same way as the customer receipt screen, but it looks a little different.

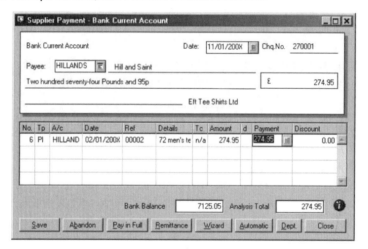

The top half of the Supplier Payment Window looks like a cheque. The cheque number is an essential identifier when it comes to reconciling the bank accounts. Use F4 to enter the account code of the supplier. Amounts for all supplies that have been invoiced but not paid for appear automatically in the table in the bottom half. Once again the quickest way to enter a payment is to tab straight through to the **Payment** box and press **Alt+P** (or click on **Pay in Full**). The cheque amount should be entered automatically and the program even writes it out for you in words automatically (see the illustration above).

Eft Tee Shirts' cheque book shows the following payments.

| 11 Jan | 270001 | Hill and Saint | 274.95 |
|--------|--------|----------------------|--------|
| 11 Jan | 270002 | Joseph Parker & Sons | 77.40 |
| 11 Jan | 270003 | Olympic Design Studio | 80.30 |
| 11 Jan | 270004 | Trevor Manufacturing | 271.43 |

Enter these payments into the program and press Save to process them.

### 5.3 Settlement discounts offered to customers

To improve cash flow let us offer a 2% settlement discount to trusted customers who pay within seven days. The customers in question are Everett Enterprises, Fred Brown Associates, and Taylor and Atkins.

To set this up on the computer click on **Customers** and select the one you want then click on **Record** and choose the **Credit Control** tab.

Enter the 2% discount for the three trusted customers and press Save to process them.

---

## ▷ ACTIVITY 11    ▷ ▷ ▷ ▷

Look at the illustration above. What do you understand by the term Defaults and what information do you think might be shown on the Defaults tab?

[Answer on p. 261]

---

Here is the next batch of sales invoices to input.

| Date | Customer | Ref | Details | Net | VAT | Gross |
|------|----------|-----|---------|-----|-----|-------|
| 13 January | Everett Enterprises | 10006 | Tee shirts: 15 men's, 16 women's | 232.03 | 39.79 | 271.82 |
| 13 January | Fred Brown Associates | 10007 | Tee shirts: 7 women's | 48.16 | 8.26 | 56.42 |
| 13 January | Taylor and Atkins | 10008 | Tee shirts: 5 men's, 12 women's | 123.21 | 21.13 | 144.34 |

The VAT charge is based on the lowest amount the customer could pay i.e. 98% of the net value. For Everett Enterprises this is £232.03 x 0.98 x 0.175 = £39.79.

Enter and **Save** these transactions using the screen identified earlier. When you get to the VAT box you will have to **overwrite** the amount calculated by the program with the amount shown above. Sage **does not do this automatically** when you enter sales invoices in batch mode.

We later have the following receipts, each customer taking the 2% discount.

| Date | Reference | Customer | Cash | Discount |
|------|-----------|----------|------|----------|
| 16 January | R00005 | Everett Enterprises | 267.18 | 4.64 |
| 17 January | R00006 | Fred Brown Associates | 55.46 | 0.96 |
| 17 January | R00007 | Taylor and Atkins | 141.88 | 2.46 |

For Everett Enterprises this is calculated as (£232.03 x 0.98) + £39.79 = £267.18.

You post these transactions in Sage using the screen identified earlier (**Bank … Customer**). The easiest way to post an invoice where discount has been taken is to tab straight through to the Discount box and enter the money amount of the discount taken. The other amounts will then be filled in automatically. Alternatively you could enter the cheque amount in the Receipt box and then use the mini calculator in the Discount box to calculate the difference between the cheque amount and the original gross (271.82 - 267.18 = 4.64).

**Save** these transactions to process them.

### 5.4  Taking advantage of settlement discounts

Let us look at an invoice from a new supplier who is prepared to give a settlement discount if Eft Tee Shirts settles its account within ten days. There is a 1.5% settlement discount.

Here is the purchase invoice from the supplier.

| **Invoice 00006** | **Net £** | **VAT £** | **Gross £** |
|-------------------|-----------|-----------|-------------|
| 17 January | 150.00 | 25.86 | 175.86 |
| Tee Shirts: 25 men's, 25 women's | | | |
| Farmer Manufacturing Ltd | | | |
| 122 High Lane | | | |
| Gorton | | | |
| Manchester | | | |
| M8 2DJ | | | |
| Phone: 0161 345 7766 Contact: Wendy Hillby | | | |
| VAT No: 654 3210 12 | | | |
| Terms agreed 30 days. Credit limit: £1,000. No trade discount. 1.5% settlement discount for payment within 10 days. | | | |

You will have to set up a new supplier account first, before processing this invoice. If you use the **Wizard** to do this make sure you wait until you get to the **Sett.Disc.** screen before entering the discount information.

When you post the invoice be careful to overwrite the VAT amount calculated by the program with the amount shown above. **Save** the invoice to process it.

## 5.5 Sending out remittance advices

Let's pay Dryer Supplies the amount we owe them (£19.72) with cheque number 270005 and prepare a remittance advice to send them.

There is an option to print remittance advices in Sage when you post a payment: just enter the details and then choose the **Remittance** button at the bottom of the screen. Note that you **must** do this **before** you click on Save. (You can't create a remittance advice after you have posted the transaction: this is to help avoid fraud.)

If you actually intend to print a remittance advice select whichever layout is appropriate (probably A4) and select Printer as the output, then click the Run button. Otherwise just choose Preview as output to view the advice on screen. If you think you might print the remittance advice later click on **Save As** in the Preview screen to save it to a report file.

## 5.6 Cash sales and purchases

There may be occasions where customers pay immediately for their goods or services. The transaction does not need entering in the Customers Ledger.

The transaction is recorded as a sale and a bank receipt. Select the **Bank** button on the toolbar and then select **Receipt** and enter the details. The bank account code is 1200 and the nominal code for Sales is 4000.

| Date | Ref | Details | Net | VAT | Gross |
|------|-----|---------|-----|-----|-------|
| 18 January | 10009 | Cash sales. Tee shirts: 25 men's, 20 women's | 340.85 | 59.65 | 400.50 |

The principle is the same for payments through the bank, which are made to non-credit suppliers.

Select the Bank button on the toolbar and then select **Payment** and enter the details.

Here are some payments for you to post, paid on 18 January.

| Narrative | Ref | Net | VAT | Gross |
|-----------|-----|-----|-----|-------|
| Motor Expenses | 00008 | 98.56 | 17.25 | 115.81 |
| Miscellaneous Expenses | 00009 | 34.44 | nil | 34.44 |

The nominal code for Motor Expenses is 7304 and for Miscellaneous Expenses it is 6900. The 'expenses' payment is zero-rated. Use T0 as the VAT code.

▷ **ACTIVITY 12**                                    ▷ ▷ ▷ ▷

How could you find out the nominal code for Motor Expenses in an accounting package?

[Answer on p. 261]

### 5.7 Petty cash payments

Petty cash comes initially from the main bank account. It has been estimated that the business needs £150 a month petty cash to cover minor cash expenses.

The business maintains a manual **petty cash book** in which payments are recorded (including the analysis of VAT where applicable).

To transfer the float from the current bank account to petty cash, you need to click on the **Nominal** then **Journals**. The entries are shown below:

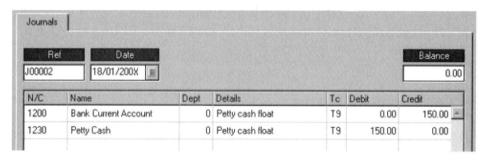

Once you have created the float you can post some petty cash payments. Select the Bank button then Payment and enter the details. The date for these transactions is 18 January.

| Reference | Bank | Narrative | Net | VAT | Gross |
|-----------|------|-----------|-----|-----|-------|
| C0001 | 1230 | Envelopes (7504) | 22.34 | 3.91 | 26.25 |
| C0002 | 1230 | Tea, coffee, milk etc.(7406) | 11.38 | 0.31 | 11.69 |

### 5.8 Trial balance

You have now completed posting the second batch of transactions.

Once again as a quick check on your work you can produce a trial balance. Using Sage you do this by clicking on Financials then Trial.

You are asked for the criteria, ie the month (January, Month 1) and the type of output. You can choose to have a preview, to print or to save it as a file. If you have entered all the transactions so far correctly your preview should be the same as the trial balance over page.

| N/C | Name | Debit £ | Credit £ |
|------|------|---------|----------|
| 0030 | Office Equipment | 2,500.00 | |
| 1200 | Bank Current Account | 7,950.44 | |
| 1230 | Petty Cash | 112.06 · | |
| 2100 | Creditors Control Account | | 175.86 |
| 2200 | Sales Tax Control Account | | 218.48 |
| 2201 | Purchase Tax Control Account | 143.61 | |
| 3000 | Ordinary Shares | | 10,000.00 |
| 4000 | Sales Type A | | 1,364.07 |
| 4009 | Discounts Allowed | 8.06 | |
| 5000 | Materials Purchased | 760.74 | |
| 6900 | Miscellaneous Expenses | 34.44 | |
| 7304 | Miscellaneous Motor Expenses | 98.56 | |
| 7406 | Subsistence | 11.38 | |
| 7504 | Office Stationery | 39.12 | |
| 7600 | Legal Fees | 100.00 | |
| | **Totals:** | 11,433.27 | 11,433.27 |

Don't forget to **backup** before moving on.

> **ACTIVITY 13**                            ▷ ▷ ▷ ▷

Why should you make regular backups when using an accounting package or in any other computer processing?

[Answer on p. 261]

## 6    Accounting for sales and debtors

### 6.1  Better analysis

You have probably noticed that the sales invoices we have created so far are all lumped together into one sales account, which is not very good practice as far as controlling the business is concerned. You are probably also fed up with typing 'tee shirts' all the time!

We can do two things to improve matters: create some new nominal accounts, and use the accounting package's stock facilities. Then we will look at the **debtors ledger** in more detail, in particular **producing sales invoices**.

### 6.2  Nominal accounts

To create or rename a nominal account you simply click on **Nominal** and either use the Wizard or do it manually. We'll do it manually, because it is quicker.

Click on Nominal and scroll down until you have account 4001 selected. Click on Record and alter the name from 'Sales Type B' to 'Sales Men's Tee Shirts' and click on Save. (We'll leave account 4000 as it is for now.) Account 4002 should be renamed as 'Sales Women's Tee Shirts'. Then tab back into the N/C box and type 4003.

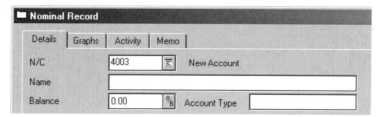

The words New Account will appear next to the N/C box, and in the name box below you should type 'Sales Children's Tee Shirts'. Then click on **Save**.

### 6.3 Setting up product categories

To save typing out the items sold on each individual invoice you can set up a product file. Here are the products for you to input. These prices exclude VAT.

| Product code | Description | Nominal | Unit of sale | Unit Price | VAT rate |
|---|---|---|---|---|---|
| TS001 | Tee Shirts – Men's – Green | 4001 | Each | 8.13 | Standard |
| TS002 | Tee Shirts – Men's – Blue | 4001 | Each | 8.13 | Standard |
| TS003 | Tee Shirts – Men's – Red | 4001 | Each | 8.13 | Standard |
| TS004 | Tee Shirts – Men's – Yellow | 4001 | Each | 8.13 | Standard |
| TS005 | Tee Shirts – Women's – Green | 4002 | Each | 6.88 | Standard |
| TS006 | Tee Shirts – Women's – Blue | 4002 | Each | 6.88 | Standard |
| TS007 | Tee Shirts – Women's – Red | 4002 | Each | 6.88 | Standard |
| TS008 | Tee Shirts – Women's – Yellow | 4002 | Each | 6.88 | Standard |
| TS009 | Tee Shirts – Children's – Green | 4003 | Each | 5.38 | Zero |
| TS010 | Tee Shirts – Children's – Blue | 4003 | Each | 5.38 | Zero |
| TS011 | Tee Shirts – Children's – Red | 4003 | Each | 5.38 | Zero |
| TS012 | Tee Shirts – Children's – Yellow | 4003 | Each | 5.38 | Zero |

To enter these details click on **Products** then on **New** and you will start up a Wizard. As usual on completion of each screen, click **Next** to continue. You can ignore any questions where you have no information to enter.

Before you can actually use these details to invoice customers you will have to put some goods into stock.

| Product code | Quantity | Cost £ |
|---|---|---|
| TS002 | 12 | 3.25 |
| TS004 | 10 | 3.25 |
| TS007 | 10 | 2.75 |
| TS008 | 5 | 2.75 |
| TS009 | 5 | 2.15 |
| TS010 | 11 | 2.15 |

To do this click on **Product** then highlight all the items with the codes above. Then click on **Record** and you will be taken straight to product code TS002. On this screen there is a blank box labelled **In Stock** and next to it a button labelled **O/B** (for Opening Balance).

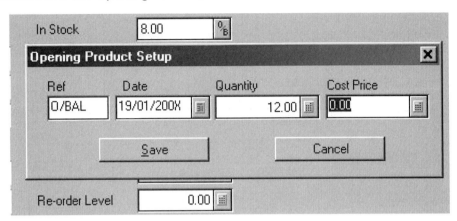

Click on the **O/B** button (or use the **F4** shortcut) and enter and **Save** the details. For the date use 19 January each time. To move to the next record just click on **Next**.

You might want to take another backup at this point, because you have already entered quite a lot of new data.

### 6.4 Generating an invoice

Up to now we haven't actually produced any physical invoices to send to customers. Let's now do this and take advantage of all the new features we've set up.

You are required to invoice **Thornwood Manufacturing Ltd** as follows.

| | | | |
|---|---|---|---|
| Date | 19 January | | |
| Invoice number | 10010 | | |
| Order number | Leave blank | | |
| Product no. | TS002 | TS008 | TS009 |
| Quantity | 3 | 4 | 5 |

To generate an invoice click on the **Invoicing** icon in the main window and then **Product**.

The package will allocate the number 1 to this invoice by default but you can change it to the next number in sequence (10010). You only need to do this once. In future the package will remember your most recent invoice number and increase it by one.

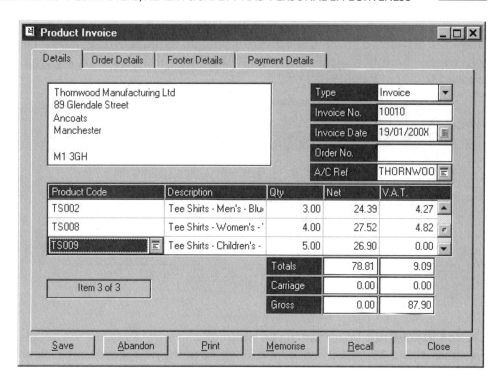

**Tab through** the boxes entering the above details, using F4 to pick items from lists at every opportunity. You should find this much faster than our previous efforts to post invoices because there is much less typing to do.

> ## ▷ ACTIVITY 14    ▷ ▷ ▷ ▷
>
> Why might the Memorise and Recall facilities be a very useful feature of an accounting package when posting invoices?
>
> [Answer on p. 262]

When you have finished click on **Save** and **Close**. Unlike every other occasion when you have clicked on Save **this does not post the transaction** to the ledgers: you can see that this is so if you look at the main Invoicing screen, which has two columns on the right showing whether the invoice has yet been printed and posted.

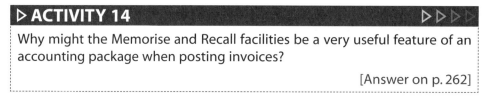

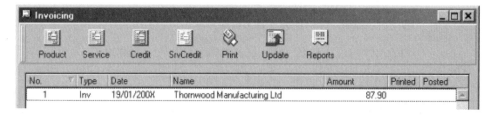

To print out the invoice simply select it in this window and click on **Print**. You may be presented with a long list of possible layouts. The one you want is most likely to be one of the **A4 Prod Inv** options. As usual you can either print it to your printer or just look at a **Preview**.

We suggest that you just look at a preview, because the various layouts are meant for **pre-printed invoice stationery**, and you probably don't have any of this.

When you close the preview window and the layout window and go back to the Invoicing screen you should see that the **Printed** column now says **Yes** next to this invoice.

## 6.5  Updating the ledgers

You might need to get your supervisor to approve the draft invoice you just printed. At this point you could still make changes to the invoice, for instance add more items or insert special delivery details.

Let's assume it has been approved as it is. To actually post this invoice, simply select it and then click on the **Update** button. This always produces an **Update Ledgers** report, though you can just preview this and then close the preview window if you don't want to print it.

Note that when you return to the Invoicing screen there is a **Yes** in the **Posted** column. You can confirm this if you wish by clicking on **Customers**, calling up the **Record** for Thornwood Manufacturing and clicking on the **Activity** tab.

## 6.6  Offering settlement discounts

Thornwood Manufacturing has found out that they are not getting the 2% settlement discount that is offered to some other customers. We will offer them a 2% discount if they settle their invoices within 10 days.

You can set this up by changing their customer record (the **Credit Control** option is the one you want).

When you've done this use the Invoicing option in the main window to generate an invoice for Thornwood Manufacturing with the following details.

| | | |
|---|---|---|
| Date | 21 January | |
| Invoice number | 10011 | |
| Order number | Leave blank | |
| Product no. | TS002 | TS008 |
| Quantity | 1 | 1 |

The net amount is £15.01, but when you use the Invoicing option the package **automatically applies the discount.** You will find that VAT has been calculated as £15.01 x 0.98 x 0.175 = £2.57. What's more, if you click on the **Footer Details** tab you will see information about the settlement discount available to Thornwood Manufacturing. If they pay within ten days they can deduct £0.30 and only need pay £17.28.

When you've checked these points on your screen you can **Save** the invoice and don't forget to **update** the ledgers.

### 6.7 Aged debtors

Next we want to see how to create an aged debtors' report. We'll assume it is now the end of February. Change the program date (**Settings ... Change Program Date**) to 28 **February**.

To see how ageing works properly we will need transactions in more than one period so we'll begin by entering and posting the following invoice to Fred Brown Associates.

| | | | |
|---|---|---|---|
| Date | 28 February | | |
| Invoice number | 10012 | | |
| Order number | Leave blank | | |
| Product no. | TS004 | TS007 | TS010 |
| Quantity | 10 | 3 | 2 |

Make sure you update the ledgers.

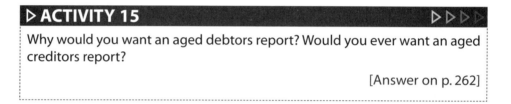

### ▷ ACTIVITY 15 ▷▷▷▷

Why would you want an aged debtors report? Would you ever want an aged creditors report?

[Answer on p. 262]

In Sage there are two ways that you can produce an aged debtors' report. The simplest is to click on **Customers**, then **Aged** and then specify the dates that you are interested in:

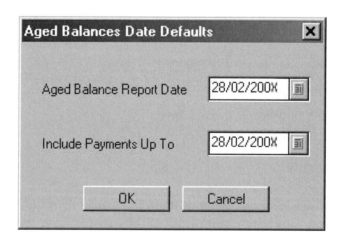

The screen shown below will be the result. This shows a variety of information, for instance that by now Thornwood Manufacturing have owed an amount for more than 30 days (even after they made a fuss about early settlement discount!).

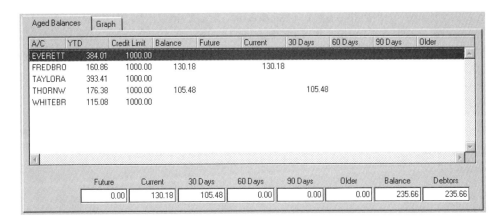

The second way is to click on **Customers** then **Reports** and choose one of several suggested layouts for **Aged Debtors Analysis.** For instance you can get a list that includes contact numbers (so you can phone up late payers) or you can have the information sorted by account name or by balance (so you can phone up the customers who owe the largest amounts first), and so on.

### 6.8  Statements

As you know, the first thing to do when customers owe you money is to send them a statement, as a gentle reminder of the situation. A statement is essentially the same as the ledger accounts, but you would print them on special stationery to make them look more professional.

From the **Customers** window select the customers with outstanding balances and click the **Statement** button. The Customer Statements window appears and you can choose from a variety of options (you probably want one of the A4 options).

As usual you have the choice of previewing the statement before printing, and as usual this is probably the best option if you don't have any pre-printed stationery. When you click on Run a Criteria screen will appear, but you can ignore the options there if you wish and just click OK.

### 6.9  Posting credit notes

As with sales invoices, there are two methods of posting credit notes issued by the company. These are:
· generating credit notes for printing out by using the option within the program, or
· inputting the details of credit notes generated by some other means, such as a word processing program.

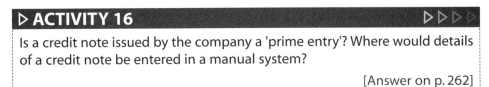

▷ **ACTIVITY 16**  ▷ ▷ ▷ ▷

Is a credit note issued by the company a 'prime entry'? Where would details of a credit note be entered in a manual system?

[Answer on p. 262]

In a computer system like Sage you can raise and print out a credit note for the products you have invoiced a customer, in exactly the same way that you would raise a product invoice. All postings to the Nominal Accounts are the opposite of those made when an invoice is raised.

To produce a credit note click on **Invoicing** and then **Credit**.

From your program, generate the following credit note for Thornwood Manufacturing to refund the customer for an item on invoice no. 10010, which was faulty.

| | |
|---|---|
| Date | 28 February |
| Credit note number | 1 |
| Order number | Leave blank |
| Product no. | TS008 |
| Quantity | 4 |

Remember that the original invoice **did not offer a settlement discount**, but Thornwood's account is now set up to do this automatically. You will therefore need to click on Footer details and set the Settlement **Discount** % to 0% to ensure that the VAT is correct. (This does not alter the customer's record permanently.)

Don't forget to **update the ledgers** when you have created the credit note.

If you display the individual ledger account the credit note will appear as a negative entry. And the overall amount due from Thornwood Manufacturing in respect of invoice 10010 will have reduced to £55.56.

Let's assume we receive payment of this amount on 28 February. You can post this (reference R00008) in exactly the same way as you posted other customer receipts. Click on **Bank**, then **Customer** and pick Thornwood's account. Tab through the Amount box and when you get to the **Receipt** box for invoice 10010 press **Alt+P** or click on **Pay in Full**. Then tab down to the Receipt box for the credit note and press Alt+P again. Note that the program nets off the credit note and the original invoice.

**Save** this customer receipt in order to process it.

### 6.10 Bad debts

**Bad debts** must be written off within the **debtors ledger** if the debt clearly cannot be recovered.

Four types of bad debts can be written off in Sage – accounts; transactions; transactions below a specified value; and overpayments. All the appropriate adjustments to the nominal ledger are generated automatically, and customer and supplier account transactions are added accordingly.

Note that the VAT and sales accounts in the nominal ledger are unaffected by the write-off. The VAT account is unaffected because the company cannot generally reclaim the VAT unless the customer has gone into liquidation. If this is so then the company must fill out certain forms and receive permission from HM Customs & Excise.

If you are using an automatic bad debt routine, the system will post the entries to the correct accounts for you. The double entry involves debiting the Bad debt write off account and crediting the Debtors control account.

Let us say we want to write off invoice 10011, which we now have to admit will not be paid. The original invoice totalled £17.58, including VAT of £2.57.

To do this in Sage click on **Tools** then **Write Off, Refund, Return**.

The result is a Wizard that goes through the steps to produce the write off. In this case you want to make amendments to the sales ledger, and write off a customer transaction with Thornwood Manufacturing as at 28 February.

### 6.11 Trial balance and backup

Produce a trial balance and compare it with the one shown below. Don't forget to take a backup before carrying on.

### Eft Tee Shirts Ltd Trial Balance

| N/C | Name | Debit £ | Credit £ |
|---|---|---|---|
| 0030 | Office Equipment | 2,500.00 | |
| 1100 | Debtors Control Account | 130.18 | |
| 1200 | Bank Current Account | 8,006.00 | |
| 1230 | Petty Cash | 112.06 | |
| 2100 | Creditors Control Account | | 175.86 |
| 2200 | Sales Tax Control Account | | 242.80 |
| 2201 | Purchase Tax Control Account | 143.61 | |
| 3000 | Ordinary Shares | | 10,000.00 |
| 4000 | Sales Type A | | 1,364.07 |
| 4001 | Sales Men's Tee Shirts | | 113.82 |
| 4002 | Sales Women's Tee Shirts | | 27.52 |
| 4003 | Sales Children's Tee Shirts | | 37.66 |
| 4009 | Discounts Allowed | 8.06 | |
| 5000 | Materials Purchased | 760.74 | |
| 6900 | Miscellaneous Expenses | 34.44 | |
| 7304 | Miscellaneous Motor Expenses | 98.56 | |
| 7406 | Subsistence | 11.38 | |
| 7504 | Office Stationery | 39.12 | |
| 7600 | Legal Fees | 100.00 | |
| 8100 | Bad Debt Write Off | 17.58 | |
| | **Totals:** | 11,961.73 | 11,961.73 |

## 7 Bank reconciliations and error corrections

### 7.1 Checking the bank statement

On 5 February Eft Tee Shirts received the following bank statement.

| date | details | | paid out £ | | paid in £ | | balance £ | |
|------|---------|--|-----------:|--|----------:|--|----------:|--|
| | Opening balance | | | | | | 0 | 00 |
| 1 JAN | SUNDRY CREDIT | 500001 | | | 7400 | 00 | 7400 | 00 |
| 11 JAN | | 270002 | 77 | 40 | | | 7322 | 60 |
| 12 JAN | SUNDRY CREDIT | 500002 | | | 709 | 47 | | |
| | | 270003 | 80 | 30 | | | 7951 | 77 |
| 13 JAN | | 270001 | 274 | 95 | | | 7676 | 82 |
| 17 JAN | SUNDRY CREDIT | 500003 | | | 267 | 18 | 7944 | 00 |
| 18 JAN | | 270004 | 271 | 43 | | | | |
| | SUNDRY CREDIT | 500004 | | | 197 | 34 | 7869 | 91 |
| 22 JAN | | 27006 | 150 | 00 | | | | |
| | SUNDRY CREDIT | 500005 | | | 400 | 50 | | |
| | ESSO-GRANADA391604 | 3117DC | 115 | 81 | | | | |
| | ASDA SUPERSTORE | | | | | | | |
| | MANCHESTER | 3117DC | 34 | 44 | | | 7970 | 16 |
| 2 FEB | CHARGES 1 JAN TO 31 JAN | | | | | | | |
| | SERVICE CHARGE | | 10 | 43 | | | 7959 | 73 |
| | TOTAL PAYMENTS/RECEIPTS | | 1014 | 76 | 8974 | 49 | | |

If you click on Bank you will see that there is a **Reconcile** button. Click on this and compare the screen that appears with the above statement.

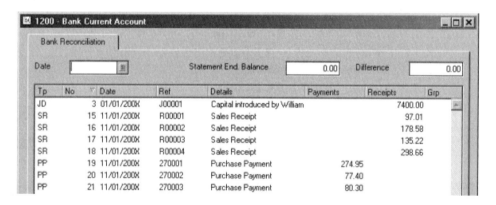

You'll note that some of the items are exactly the same, but the bank statement's SUNDRY CREDIT for £709.47, for instance, does not appear anywhere on the computer screen.

In fact if you add up the first four Sales Receipts you will find that the total is indeed £709.47. The bank has treated them as one item because all the cheques were paid in on the same paying-in slip (numbered 500002).

Obviously this is rather inconvenient for the purpose of doing a bank reconciliation, but fortunately we can do something about it in recent versions of Sage. You may remember that when you set up the company details you had various options under **Bank Defaults**. To see them again click on **File ... Easy Start Up Wizard** and just click on **Next** until you get to this screen.

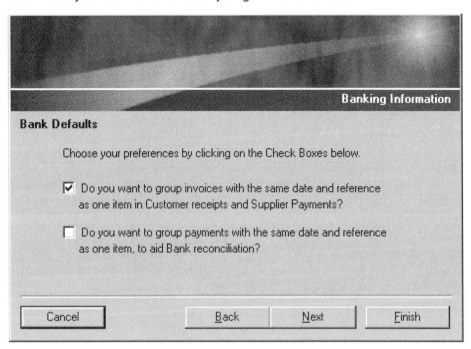

Put a tick in the second box in this screen, then click on Finish and confirm you want to save your changes. We'll see the effect in a moment.

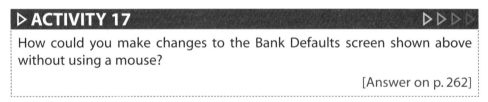

> **ACTIVITY 17**                                                    ▷ ▷ ▷ ▷

How could you make changes to the Bank Defaults screen shown above without using a mouse?

[Answer on p. 262]

### 7.2 Corrections

We still have a problem, though, because we did not use the paying in slip reference when posting the receipts. Fortunately you can change this. Click on **File... Maintenance... Corrections** and you will see a list of all the transactions you have posted so far. Scroll around until you find the transactions with the references R00001 to R00004. Select the first and click on Edit and change the reference to the one shown on the bank statement (500002). Then click on Save and confirm you want to post the change. Do the same for each of the receipts paid in on slip number 500002. Make sure you type the correct number of zeros each time!

You will also need to change any transactions with the reference R00005 to slip number 500003, and any transactions with reference R00006 and R00007 to slip number 500004.

Be aware that some corrections that you can make have a larger impact than ones that simply involve changing a reference number. For instance if you changed dates or amounts or account codes for a transaction the program will **automatically post a record of the deleted transaction:** this is to avoid fraud.

### 7.3 Computerised bank reconciliation

Once you have corrected the references click on **Bank** and **Reconcile** and enter the date (5 February) and you should see a screen that much more closely resembles the bank statement. In future you should always use the relevant paying-in slip number as the reference for receipts!

To perform a reconciliation type in the statement end balance (£7,959.73) and then click on each item on screen that you can see in the bank statement. As you do so you will the see the amount in the difference box change until eventually it reaches £10.43.

Your cheque number 270005 has not yet been presented, so leave it unhighlighted. The difference is due to the bank charges shown on the bank statement. The entry that is needed is as follows.

| 2 Feb | Cr | Bank Account (1200) | £10.43 |
| 2 Feb | Dr | Bank Charges (7901) | £10.43 |

You haven't posted this yet because you did not know about it until the bank statement arrived, but you can do so now. At the foot of the reconciliation screen there is an Adjustment button which you can use to post payments (e.g. charges) or receipts (e.g. bank interest) directly to the bank account.

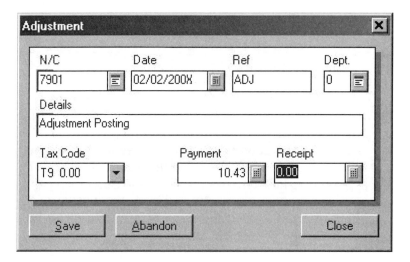

Enter these details and click **Save** and **Close** and you should now find that the bank reconciliation difference is nil. Click on **Save** and confirm that you want to mark the transactions as reconciled.

If you click on **Reports** in the **Bank** window you will see that there are a variety of Bank Reports that you can run relating to reconciled transactions. You might like to preview some of these.

### 7.4 Backup

Take a final backup so you can look through all the transactions you have posted. The final trial balance will be almost the same as the previous one, except that it will include the £10.43 bank charges.

> **▷ ACTIVITY 18** ▷ ▷ ▷ ▷
>
> Find out how to generate an audit trail of all the transactions you have posted. How many are there in total?
>
> [Answer on p. 262]

## 8 Batch processing

### 8.1 Introduction

In very old computer systems a strong distinction is made between batch processing and real time processing (i.e. processing transactions immediately when they occur), but the distinction is not terribly important any more, thanks to huge advances in computing power and networking technology. The terms are still used in some systems, however, so it is worth being aware of them.

### 8.2 Batch processing

In batch processing, large numbers of similar transactions (e.g. sales invoices) are grouped together and processed at the same time. This has some advantages.

· Systems can use control or batch totals which can help prevent errors. The amounts on the documents are totalled manually and this total is input to the computer. The computer also totals the documents and will not accept the batch if the totals do not agree.

· It is flexible in that, if necessary, part of the data could be processed now, the remainder later.

· It may make it easier to organise work, for instance if an organisation only needs to employ an accountant on a part-time basis.

## 9 Summary

You have simulated the first month's trading for a small company. In that time, you have created the company, set up the standing data, entered transactions and produced reports.

You should now be in a position where you could demonstrate your competence in the computerised aspects of accounting in Units 1 to 4.

## Answers to chapter activities & 'test your knowledge' questions

△ **ACTIVITY 1**    △ △ △ △

You would click the Customer button (not the Receipt button, which is for receipts from sources other than customers). The terminology in Sage is a little confusing at first but this is a common feature in accounting packages.

△ **ACTIVITY 2**    △ △ △ △

Computers can check source data if it is given to them in digital form. For this reason many companies use Electronic Data Interchange (EDI) or trans-actions via the Internet, whereby the customer inputs the data on their own computer and their input can be automatically read by the receiving organisation's computer. Other possible answers include bar code scanners, credit card readers and computerised tills.

△ **ACTIVITY 3**    △ △ △ △

You should press the Esc key and this will make the message disappear and take you back to the position you were in before you did whatever it was that caused the message to appear in the first place.

△ **ACTIVITY 5**    △ △ △ △

Here are some of the many reports that Sage can produce.
(i)      Aged Debtors Analysis
(ii)     Day Books (Customer Invoices)
(iii)    Top Customer List
(iv)     Customer Address List
(v)      Time Taken to Pay Sales Invoices
(vi)     Sales Accounts Credit Limit Exceeded
(vii)    Customers on Hold Report
(viii)   EC Sales List

△ **ACTIVITY 7**    △ △ △ △

These buttons can be used to save the details of a recurring journal to the system (Memorise) and call it up again (Recall) the next time it is needed. The advantage is that you only need to type the details and work out the double entry once. When you know the memorised details are correct you can just repost them effortlessly whenever the need arises.

## △ ACTIVITY 9   △△△△

A computerised accounting package stores details of rates of VAT as part of its standing data, and therefore if you enter one figure (a gross amount of £117.50, say) the computer can automatically calculate 100/117.5 x £117.50 to give the net amount (£100) and 17.5/117.5 x £117.50 to give the VAT amount (£17.50). This works in any combination, of course. If you enter the net amount the package can work out the VAT and gross amount by itself.

## △ ACTIVITY 10   △△△△

You can see from the highlighted field (Receipt) that the user has tabbed beyond the Ref box without giving the transaction that is being posted a reference number. This may make it difficult to trace the transaction through the system later if a query arises. References may be a slight irritation when you are posting transactions but they are very useful when you, or more senior staff than you, are reviewing them! We'll see an example later in this chapter.

## △ ACTIVITY 11   △△△△

Defaults are pre-selected options adopted by a computer system when the user specifies no alternative. For instance the default date for a computer is today's date.

Typical customer default items are the usual nominal code to which transactions are posted, standard discount percentages, default VAT rate, the usual currency for the transaction and so on.

## △ ACTIVITY 12   △△△△

You would select the option that lists Nominal codes or the Chart of Accounts and scroll through it. It is helpful to know what category of account you are looking up because accounting packages generally group them under the same initial character(s). For instance, in Sage, Miscellaneous Motor Expenses (7304) is part of the 7000 to 7999 series of codes (Overheads) which includes other accounts in the range 7300 to 7399 like Fuel, Vehicle Insurance, Repairs and Servicing and so on.

## △ ACTIVITY 13   △△△△

Backups are vital to prevent loss of data. This can occur due to damage to the computer or to a removable disk, but it is much more common for operator error or a software glitch to be to blame.

For instance a user may post some transactions (perhaps hundreds) and forget to take a back up. The next time the system is used it would be very easy to restore an old backup and lose all the user's hard work.

## △ ACTIVITY 14 △△△△

It can be very useful to have an easily retrievable record of the entries necessary to post invoices because repeat customers often buy standard items and quantities each month or each week, say. If this data has been 'memorised', to use Sage terminology, the details can very easily be recalled and posted with the minimum of effort and maximum accuracy.

## △ ACTIVITY 15 △△△△

This is a revision question: see earlier in this text. Aged debt analysis is used to identify debtors who need chasing for payment or who may be a problem in terms of credit control. You may very well also use an aged creditors report to identify invoices that you need to pay soon (e.g. to avoid suppliers putting your account on hold), and invoices you will need to pay in the coming months (to keep control of cashflow).

## △ ACTIVITY 16 △△△△

Credit notes are recorded in their own book of prime entry, the sales returns day book, then in individual customer's accounts and in the nominal ledger. The double entry is DR Sales returns and VAT; and CR Debtors Control Account.

## △ ACTIVITY 17 △△△△

You can **move** between each of the options and buttons on screen by pressing the **Tab** key or **Shift+Tab**. In Sage (and many other programs, such as web browsers) you can tick or untick a check box or a radio button by pressing the **Space bar**. To **activate** a button using the keyboard (rather than clicking on it with the mouse) you can tab to it and then press **Enter**. You can operate some buttons by means of shortcut key combinations: for instance in this case you could do the equivalent of clicking on the **Back** button by pressing **Alt+b** (in other words Alt plus the underlined letter).

These features are not exclusive to Sage. They are standard in almost all Windows programs. (Apple Mac programs and Unix programs also have similar features, though possibly different shortcut keys.)

## △ ACTIVITY 18 △△△△

To create an audit trail in Sage, simply click on **Financials** and click the **Audit** button.

There should be 52 transactions if you have entered everything correctly. There may be more if you have made mistakes, but there should not be fewer than 52.

# KEY TECHNIQUES QUESTIONS

## UNIT 21

## Working with computers

## Chapter 1

### ▷ ACTIVITY 1

Arrange the following into increasing levels of detail: files, disks and folders.

### ▷ ACTIVITY 2

The grandfather/father/son is a technique for:

    A    maintaining back-ups

    B    filing certain company information

    C    distinguishing between different generations of application software

    D    setting up directories.

### ▷ ACTIVITY 3

To demonstrate that you understand how it works, draw a diagram to show the grandfather/father/son method of backing up files.

### ▷ ACTIVITY 4

Files can be set up into directories, sub-directories and sub-sub-directories. Which of the following would you consider the right order (starting with the directory level)?

    A    AAT, Units 21,22 and 23, Foundation level

    B    AAT, Foundation level, Units 21,22 and 23

    C    Foundation level, AAT, Units 21,22 and 23

    D    Units 21,22 and 23, AAT, Foundation level.

## Chapter 2

### ▷ ACTIVITY 5

What measures can an organisation take to reduce the risk of equipment being stolen?

### ▷ ACTIVITY 6

Give examples of the type of fraud that might be perpetrated.

## ▷ ACTIVITY 7

Consider the system at your place of work and list all the security threats to hardware and software. Indicate those risks that might be accidental and those that could be malicious.

What steps can you take to minimise these risks? Consider procedural steps, such as back-up routines, job specifications, physical locations, extra hardware, passwords, etc.

Explore your back-up procedures.

## ▷ ACTIVITY 8

Copyright law covers:
  (a) reference books, sound recordings, film and broadcasts, computer programs, dramatic and musical works
  (b) books of all kinds, sound recordings, film and broadcasts, computer programs, dramatic and musical works
  (c) books of all kinds, sound recordings, film and broadcasts, computer programs written in the UK, dramatic and musical works
  (d) books of all kinds, sound recordings on CD, film and broadcasts, computer programs, dramatic and musical works.

Which one is correct?

## ▷ ACTIVITY 9

One of your friends at work has told you that she can't remember her password unless it is easy, so she uses her forename, Mary. Can you think of a password that is equally easy but could not be guessed by anyone else?

## ▷ ACTIVITY 10

A small company's computer system comprises five desktop personal computers located in separate offices linked together in a local network within the same building. The computers are not connected to a wide area network and employees are not allowed to take floppy disks into or out of the building. Information that the owner of the business wishes to keep confidential to herself is stored in one of the computers.

Which ONE of the following statements can be concluded from this information?

The company's computer system does NOT:
  (i) need a back-up storage system
  (ii) need a password access system
  (iii) receive e-mails from customers and suppliers
  (iv) include virus detection software.

## UNIT 22

## Contribute to the maintenance of a healthy, safe and productive working environment

## Chapter 3

▷ **ACTIVITY 11**

Which details do you think should be recorded in an accident book?

▷ **ACTIVITY 12**

Mitchell & Co is a partnership of solicitors. They have five offices situated in various parts of the country.

(a) What information would you expect to find in their health and safety manual, a copy of which is provided for all new employees?

(b) What conditions and facilities do you think Mitchell & Co should provide for their employees?

▷ **ACTIVITY 13**

What do you think are the causes of most accidents in the workplace?

▷ **ACTIVITY 14**

Describe your actions in the following situations:

(a) if you discover a fire

(b) if you hear the fire alarm.

KAPLAN PUBLISHING

## ▷ ACTIVITY 15

It is Wednesday 9 April and Vanessa Wilson is approaching your desk carrying a large pile of papers. She does not notice the waste paper basket that a colleague has left in the path between the two desks. She trips over it and hurts her wrist.

Complete the accident report form below:

| ACCIDENT REPORT FORM | | |
|---|---|---|
| Name(s) of injured person(s) | | |
| Date of accident | | |
| Place of accident | | |
| Details of accident | | |
| Names of witnesses | | |
| Completed by | Block capitals | Signature |
| First aid treatment given (to be completed by First Aid Officer) | | |
| Action taken to prevent ecurrence (to be completed by Safety Officer) | | |

## ▷ ACTIVITY 16

List the kinds of incidents that must be reported under the RIDDOR regulations. What form should the report take in each case?

## ▷ ACTIVITY 17

An accident report form covers which of the following:

- A    employees and other people on the employer's premises and incidents away from the employer's premises if they occur in the course of an employee's duties
- B    employees and other people on the employer's premises
- C    employees on the employer's premises and incidents away from the employer's premises if they occur in the course of an employee's duties
- D    employees on the employer's premises.

▷ **ACTIVITY 18**                                               ▷ ▷ ▷ ▷

As part of a training exercise, everyone in your department has been asked to draw a fire alarm notice. Your manager will choose the best one which will be displayed on all notice boards throughout the building. The winner will also receive a small cash prize.

## Chapter 4

▷ **ACTIVITY 19**                                               ▷ ▷ ▷ ▷

Draw up a checklist of questions/points to note that you could use to help deal with a bomb threat over the telephone.

▷ **ACTIVITY 20**                                               ▷ ▷ ▷ ▷

Each employee should take steps to become familiar with the emergency procedures within his or her organisation. What might this involve?

## Chapter 5

▷ **ACTIVITY 21**                                               ▷ ▷ ▷ ▷

Draw a plan of your office, outlining your position and that of your supervisor in it. Does it follow the criteria laid out above?

## UNIT 23

## Achieving personal effectiveness

## Chapter 6

▷ **ACTIVITY 22**                                               ▷ ▷ ▷ ▷

In which example below does the assistant have the authority and ability to delegate to the operatives?

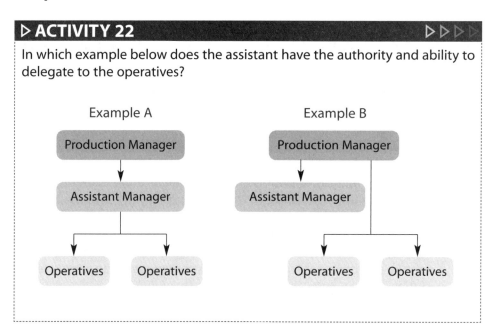

## ▷ ACTIVITY 23

Prepare a checklist of information you would store relating to a meeting at some other organisation's premises.

## ▷ ACTIVITY 24

Today is Friday.

Thomas has three tasks to complete, each of which will take two hours. His supervisor is expecting him to have completed them all by 10am on Monday.

Thomas was unable to perform any of the tasks on Friday morning because the computer was not working. It is now 2pm on Friday. Thomas normally goes home at 5pm.

What should Thomas do in these circumstances?
- A  Complete one of the tasks and start one of the others. He should be able to complete all of them by noon on Monday.
- B  Complete the most urgent task and take home the other two tasks. He is bound to be able to find time to finish them over the weekend.
- C  Contact his supervisor immediately and explain the problem. He should suggest that he finishes what he considers to be the most urgent task first before starting one of the others.
- D  Start all of the tasks and do parts of each of them. This way he has at least done something towards each of them before he goes home.

## ▷ ACTIVITY 25

The 'laid-down' or 'established' procedures are generally written into some form of office procedure manual, or in the form of a duty list issued to staff. What would you expect them to contain? Give an example of an administrative procedure.

## ▷ ACTIVITY 26

Which one of the following statements about an organisation is NOT true?
- (i)  An organisation chart provides a summary of the structure of a business.
- (ii)  An organisation chart can indicate functional authority but not line authority within a business.
- (iii)  An organisation chart can improve employees' understanding of their role in a business.
- (iv)  An organisation chart can improve internal communications within a business.

## Chapter 7

### ▷ ACTIVITY 27

What type of information might be contained in your organisation's procedures manual?

### ▷ ACTIVITY 28

Darren is the supervisor of a travel shop. When his staff take a customer booking, they have to add on a charge for airport taxes. The charges are different for each airport but are found in the company's fares manual.

One afternoon Fiona, who has worked in the shop for six weeks, asks Darren for the charge for Oslo airport. Darren gets angry. What could explain his outburst?

### ▷ ACTIVITY 29

Diana's supervisor is explaining a new accounting procedure to her. Suggest some things that Diana might do which would suggest that she is not listening properly.

How might her supervisor react to these?

### ▷ ACTIVITY 30

Can you think of any advantages and disadvantages associated with the preparation of office manuals?

### ▷ ACTIVITY 31

Your boss is currently overseas negotiating an extension of a sales contract with one of your existing customers. You receive the following fax message from him:

> 'Urgent – we've agreed that the trade discount applying to the future contracts will be based on a formula related to sales volumes over the last two years. Please fax me the details of monthly sales volumes to this customer over that period immediately.'

Outline the likely consequences if you fail to act quickly on this message.

KAPLAN PUBLISHING

## ▷ ACTIVITY 32

There are various ways in which a business can communicate information electronically. A facility whereby a duplicate copy of a document can be sent electronically is known as:
- (i) electronic mail or e-mail
- (ii) internet
- (iii) telex
- (iv) facsimile or fax.

## Chapter 8

## ▷ ACTIVITY 33

Draw up your own SWOT analysis using the following type of cruciform diagram:

| Strengths | Weaknesses |
|---|---|
| Opportunities | Threats |

## ▷ ACTIVITY 34

Why are staff appraisals important?

## ▷ ACTIVITY 35

You work in the bought ledger department of a large company – Global Supplies Ltd. The purchasing manager is due to meet a potential new supplier of product PF123. In preparation for the meeting you have been asked to provide an analysis of Global Supplies' purchases of this product over the last few months, showing the unit price charged by two different suppliers the company has used in the past.
- (i) What sources of information would you be likely to access to fulfil this request?
- (ii) The meeting is scheduled for 4pm this Friday coming. It is now 5pm on Wednesday and you have not been able to begin assembling the information because you have had to cover for a colleague who is off sick. You begin to doubt whether you will be able to produce the information on time. What action should you take?

KAPLAN PUBLISHING

# MOCK SIMULATION 1
# QUESTIONS

## Data and tasks

### Instructions

This mock simulation is designed to test your ability to maintain financial records and prepare accounts.

The situation and tasks you are required to complete are set out below.

This booklet also contains data that you will need to complete the tasks. **You should read the whole mock simulation before commencing work so as to gain an overall picture of what is required.**

Your answers should be set out in the answer booklet provided. If you require additional answer pages, ask the person in charge.

You are allowed **four hours** to complete your work.

A high level of accuracy is required. Check your work carefully before handing it in.

Correcting fluid may be used but it should be used in moderation. Errors should be crossed out neatly and clearly. You should write in black ink, not pencil.

You are reminded that you should not bring any unauthorised material, such as books or notes, into the mock simulation. If you have any such material in your possession, you should surrender it to the assessor immediately.

Any instances of misconduct will be brought to the attention of the AAT, and disciplinary action may be taken.

## The situation

Mr Osmond, your accountant at Turner & Sons Ltd realises that computers have improved the speed, accuracy and scope of information processing. However, he is also aware that security problems have mushroomed. Although most procedures are done through automated systems at Turner's, the issues of handling, maintaining and security of information have never been addressed systematically. Mr Osmond is planning to review the procedures and is currently asking different members of staff their opinions on certain issues. As Charlie Smith you have been given the following tasks:

## Tasks to be completed

### TASK 1

Most of the work you are due to perform next week will involve you sitting in front of a computer screen updating the organisation's customer database. What hazards does this kind of work expose you to? How can they be minimised?

## TASK 2

All machines can go wrong – often when you are in the middle of a rush job. The following chart shows some common printer problems. Identify the probable cause in each situation and the action you would take to sort the problem out.

| Fault | Probable cause | Action |
|---|---|---|
| No response from printer when command to print given | | |
| Print is gibberish | | |
| Print quality poor | | |
| Print wrong size | | |
| Paper jam | | |
| Print crooked on paper | | |
| Printing with incorrect pitch or line spacing | | |

## TASK 3

List ways that the physical security of computer equipment can be improved.

## TASK 4

Outline the problems that are associated with passwords and the precautions that should be adopted to protect passwords and user numbers against discovery.

## TASK 5

Explain the principle of the grandfather/father/son method of backing up files.

## TASK 6

Information held on computers is usually stored in a file. In order to find this file, directories exist. Explain the system of directories on your computer.

## TASK 7

One of your friends is starting his own car valeting business and has asked you to help him out. As you are not too busy today you are copying some software for him – he needs a bookkeeping package. He also wants you to copy the manual that goes with it. You also suggested that he might find the database of Turner's customers useful, so you are sending him that too.

Are you breaking any laws by doing this?

KAPLAN PUBLISHING

# MOCK SIMULATION 2
# QUESTIONS

## The situation

Charlie Smith works in the accounts department of Turner & Sons Ltd – a manufacturing company that produces components for the car industry. The accountant, Mr J Osmond, who recently joined the company was quite concerned at the lack of interest in health and safety regulations. He organised a series of training sessions and has devised the following series of tasks for certain employees to assess whether any more training is required.

## The tasks to be completed

You are to assume the role of Charlie Smith and undertake the following tasks:

**TASK 1**
Both the employer and the employee have legal responsibilities with regards to health and safety at work. What are your responsibilities?

**TASK 2**
One of the key points when observing health and safety regulations is that you must understand the limits of your own responsibilities and obligations. What sources of information would provide this information?

**TASK 3**
You have a headache and a colleague suggests you get an aspirin from the first aid box. Examine the first aid box for your department (make sure you wash your hands first) and make a list of the contents. Did you find the aspirins? If not, why not?

**TASK 4**
You have been asked to design an accident report form to be used in your organisation's accident book. The information that will be required includes the time and place of the incident, whether anyone was injured – with details of the injury and names of any witnesses, as well as details of any first aid given by the first aid officer. It should also include a section to be completed by the safety officer of any action to be taken to prevent recurrence of the incident.

**TASK 5**
It is 10.15 am on 1 May 2006. One of your colleagues, Joe Bloggs, has just fallen off his chair. He was standing on his swivel chair trying to reach a box on top of a cupboard when it rolled backwards and he lost his balance. He says he is not hurt but is rubbing his leg and his elbow. Mary Holden, who also saw him fall, is making him a cup of tea because he is shaken.

Using the accident report form that you have just designed, record the details of the accident. You may use your imagination to supply details that you have not been given.

**TASK 6**
The printer in your office has been in use all day and you have noticed that there is a smell of burning and sparks shooting out from the back of it. Near where you are sitting is a fire extinguisher (see below). There is also a notice on

how and under what circumstances to use the range of fire extinguishers. Describe what you would do.

Type of fire and fire extinguishers:

| | Dry Powder | Water | Aqueous Film Forming Foam | Foam | Carbon Dioxide | Fire Blanket |
|---|---|---|---|---|---|---|
| **Wood & Textiles** | YES | YES | YES | YES | NO | NO |
| **Flammable Gases** | NO | NO | NO | NO | YES | YES |
| **Flammable Liquids** | YES | NO | YES | YES | NO | YES |
| **Electrical Fires** | NO | NO | NO | NO | YES | NO |
| **Kitchen Fires** | NO | NO | NO | NO | NO | YES |

How To Use a Fire Extinguisher:

Remember the phrase **'P.A.S.S'**:
· **P**ull out the pin.
· **A**im the extinguisher nozzle at the base of the flames.
· **S**queeze the trigger while holding the extinguisher upright.
· **S**weep the extinguisher from side to side, covering the area of the fire with the extinguishing agent.

## TASK 7
Why is it important for you to use the correct type of extinguisher on a fire?

## TASK 8
What signs would indicate that the electrical equipment that you are using is in a potentially dangerous state?

## TASK 9
In your opinion, what are the main health, safety and security risks facing a person like you working in the accounts department of Turner & Sons Ltd?

## TASK 10
Apart from fire risk, outline the security risks that Turner & Sons' assets (tangible and intangible) might be exposed to.

## TASK 11
Because Turner & Sons Ltd has a retail shop attached to the factory it keeps large amounts of cash on the premises. What types of security procedures and devices might be in use to reduce the risks that might have been identified?

## TASK 12
True or false?
(i)   Buildings can be evacuated for other reasons besides fire.
(ii)  All fire extinguishers are red.

(iii) An employee who wedges open a fire door is committing an offence under the Health and Safety at Work Act.

(iv) An employee who falls in a busy area should be moved immediately.

(v) It is essential you read the instructions thoroughly before operating a new piece of equipment.

### TASK 13

Under the Health and Safety at Work Act organisations must produce a health and safety document for their employees giving the organisation's rules, regulations and procedures. What basic information would you expect to find in this document?

### TASK 14

Would you say that the person shown in the picture below is working efficiently?

Why is it important to be organised at work?

Test yourself by seeing how quickly you can find:

· a piece of work you completed last week

· a handout you received last month.

### TASK 15

You have recently had some training on how to make your work area comfortable. Using the diagram below, suggest some practical tips that you could pass on to a new recruit in your department.

KAPLAN PUBLISHING

# MOCK SIMULATION 3
# QUESTIONS

## The situation

Charlie Smith works as a sales ledger clerk in the accounts department of Turner & Sons Ltd – a manufacturing company that produces components for the car industry. Over the past few months Mr Osmond, the accountant at Turner & Sons Ltd and Charlie's manager, has shown an interest in his/her career development and invited Charlie into his office at least once a week to discuss progress, help with course work and to ask his/her opinion on several matters. Assuming the role of Charlie answer the following questions that Mr Osmond might have raised over the last few months:

### QUESTION 1
Can you think of three reasons why deadlines are important?

### QUESTION 2
How can you organise your work so that you meet your deadlines?

### QUESTION 3
What kinds of information might be regarded as confidential in Turner & Sons Ltd?

### QUESTION 4
How can the company safeguard confidential information?

### QUESTION 5
What types and sources of technical, organisational and personal information might be required by an accounting technician working in the product costing and budgeting department at Turner & Sons?

### QUESTION 6
What types of planning aids can help you plan your work and prioritise urgent tasks?

### QUESTION 7
Which of the following would you **not** analyse when drawing up a staff planning chart?

A    Timesheet
B    Personnel records
C    Holiday rotas
D    Individual employee's contracts

### QUESTION 8
Which of the following does copyright law not cover?

A    Computer programs
B    Sound recordings
C    Business letters

KAPLAN PUBLISHING

## QUESTION 9

Mr Osmond knows that planning your work and managing your time are an important part of your course and he has devised a few tasks to help you complete the performance criteria for Unit 23.

### Task 1

You (as Charlie Smith) work in a section that has a team of three people. The senior and most experienced is Mary Holden; the intermediate is Joe Bloggs and Charlie Smith is the junior. All three have plenty of work associated with their own section but occasionally they are involved with special work to get specific jobs done.

Late on Friday afternoon, Mr Osmond allocates some special work to Mary's team, which he wants finished by Wednesday week. It must be done by Friday week at the latest.

Mary plans and schedules the work as follows:

| Job | | Experience level | Time required |
|-----|--------------------------------|------------------|---------------|
| (i) | Database extraction | Junior | 2 days |
| (ii) | Analysing information | Senior | 1/2 day |
| (iii) | Data entry | Junior | 2 days |
| (iv) | Grouping results | Senior | 1/2 day |
| (v) | Transferring to production schedule | Senior | 1 day |
| (vi) | Report produced | Intermediate | 1 day |

Joe and Mary can do Charlie's work, although it is to be avoided because it does not save time. Staff development is encouraged and Joe and Charlie can gain new experience by doing work at the next level up but this doubles the normal time taken to do the work, which is then subject to review by a person at the next level up - taking an additional half-day. None of the tasks can be completed before the previous one is done and sharing the tasks generally works out to be inefficient.

The team members will be available to spend time on the special work over the next two weeks on the blank days shown below:

| | Mon | Tues | Wed | Thur | Fri | Mon | Tues | Wed | Thur | Fri |
|---------|-----|------|-----|------|-----|-----|------|-----|------|-----|
| Mary | ■ | | ■ | | | | | | | |
| Joe | | | | ■ | ■ | | ■ | ■ | ■ | |
| Charlie | ■ | | | | | | | | | |

(a) Plan how the team can complete the special work in the time available.

(b) Charlie has a sore throat and is feeling quite poorly. Should Mary take any action?

### Task 2

It is Monday morning and Mary has rung in to say that she is ill and will not be able to report for work, possibly for the whole of the week. She mentions that her main work commitments for the week are noted in her desk diary and suggests that you (Charlie Smith) look at this and then ring her back if you need clarification.

On opening her desk diary you find the following:

| | |
|---|---|
| Monday: | Arthur Barnes joins<br>Jupiter payment received? Action required? |
| Tuesday: | 10am – Departmental meeting<br>3pm  – Report due with Mr Osmond<br>4pm  – Credit controller re Jupiter |
| Wednesday: | Chase Kathy on new product codes |
| Thursday: | 10.30am – Review overdue accounts with Mr Osmond |
| Friday: | Joe on holiday next week. Temp?<br>Send updated product codes out |

### Required

As Charlie Smith, what can you deduce from these entries and what further clarification would you request from Mary?

# MOCK SIMULATION 4
# QUESTIONS

## Introductory note

This scenario question offers practice in the use of accounting packages on a computer. It illustrates the market-leading program Sage Line 50 and will be of most benefit to students who can get access to a computer with Sage Line 50 installed. However, if you use another accounting package, or indeed if you have no access to a computer at all, you should still find this question useful.

The question is divided into ten tasks. You are recommended to complete each task in turn, then back up your work, and refer to the answer to make sure that you are still on track.

## Data relating to the tasks

At the end of the ten tasks there is a bank of data that relates to the tasks. You are recommended to read all the tasks and the data before starting the tasks.

## The situation

| | |
|---|---|
| Business name | A-80 Ltd |
| Location | Office space in the managing director's home in Cumbernauld, Lanarkshire, Scotland |
| Business | Supply and installation of GPS (Global Positioning by Satellite) systems in motor vehicles |

**BUSINESS PROFILE**
A-80 Ltd is a start-up business that started trading in January 2006.

The company will supply and install GPS tracking and navigation systems in its customers' vehicles.

**PERSONNEL**

| | |
|---|---|
| Managing Director | Mr Lee McGregor |
| You | You work for Mackays, a local firm of accountants, and you have been appointed to visit A-80 Ltd's premises and maintain the computerised accounts on a once-monthly basis until Mr McGregor is ready to operate the system himself or employ somebody to do so. |

**COMPANY'S PROCEDURES**
It has already been agreed that you will use all the accounting package defaults regarding nominal ledger codes, supplier and customer codes, VAT codes, terms of trade and so on, unless otherwise instructed. If your accounting software does not allocate customer, supplier and stock codes automatically, use the first eight letters of the full name.

Sales invoices are prepared and printed out to send to customers using a word processor, not the accounting package.

Purchase invoices will be internally numbered in a sequence starting from P00001. Journals will be numbered in a sequence beginning J0001. Sales invoices will start at 1.

Computer hardware and electrical tools will be treated as fixed assets. Computer software expenditure will be written off in the year in which it is incurred. You may need to set up new nominal ledger account(s) for this purpose.

**TERMS OF TRADE**
Some of the company's customers will be offered settlement discounts.

A-80 Ltd is registered for VAT and uses Standard VAT accounting.

## The tasks to be completed

Your first visit is in the second week in January 2006. Relatively few transactions occur in this period because the managing director spends most of his time visiting local companies and explaining his company's offer. On your first visit the accounting software has been installed, but no company details have yet been set up on the system.

You are required to set up the computerised accounting system for A-80 Limited and process all of the transactions that have occurred at the dates of your visits, as instructed in the tasks below.

**TASK 1**
You are required to set up the company standing details on the computer. Refer to the letter in the data provided, and enter the following details:
· Company name
· Company address
· Nominal ledger structure (general business, standard accounts)
· Telephone number
· Fax number
· Financial year start
· Financial year end
· VAT number (using standard VAT accounting)
· Nominal ledger code for customers
· Nominal ledger code for suppliers
· VAT rate for inputs and outputs (all standard-rated)

(Using Sage, the quickest way to set up new company details is to use the Easy Start-up Wizard. It is recommended that you click on File and then New and then Company.. and follow the Wizard.)

When you have finished this task, be sure to back up your work and give the back up file an appropriate name: we suggest you use a format such as ABC.W01, where ABC are your initials and W01 indicates that this is the back up for Workbook Task 01. You may wish to write the file name you use in the table of back up files provided at the end of this scenario, to make sure that you don't forget it.

**TASK 2**

Refer again to the letter from Mr McGregor in the data provided.

Identify the initial accounting transaction necessary to record the company's issue of share capital for cash, and then enter a journal in the accounting package to record this. The journal should be dated 1 January 2006 and numbered J0001.

(Using Sage, a journal is set up by selecting Nominal, and then Journals. Enter the names of the accounts involved and the relevant amounts. Press the Save button to post your journal to the selected ledger accounts.)

Be sure to back up your work and give the back up file a name such as ABC.W02 (see Task 1). Write the file name you choose in the table of back up files.

**TASK 3**

Refer to the list of suppliers that the company is expecting to use. Enter the details of each supplier into the computer.

Each supplier account should be opened with a nil balance on 1 January 2006. (Using Sage, suppliers' details can be entered by clicking on **Suppliers** then **New** and using the **Wizard**.)

You may wish now to back up your work and write the name of the back up file in the table provided.

**TASK 4**

Today is 10 January 2006. Refer to the five purchase invoices received to date. Enter the totals of each of these invoices into the computer.

(Using Sage, to post the details of purchase invoices received, you click on **Suppliers** then **Invoice** and then enter the details including the relevant VAT amounts.)

Remember to back up your work.

**TASK 5**

Refer back to the letter used in Tasks 1 and 2. You should note that three invoices (for £99, £376 including VAT, and £450 plus VAT) have been paid from the bank current account. Record these payments onto the computer using a date of 5 January and cheque numbers 1001, 1002 and 1003.

(Using Sage, payments to suppliers are recorded by clicking on **Bank**, then selecting the account from which the payment is to be made, and clicking the **Supplier** button on the toolbar. For each supplier to be paid, you should click **Pay In Full** to write up the cheque, then **Save** to post the entries.)

Remember to back up your work.

KAPLAN PUBLISHING

**TASK 6**

It is still 10 January 2006. Refer to the invoice received from GPS Wholesale Supplies Ltd to identify the items of stock purchased. Set up stock accounts for each of the four lines of stock, including both quantities and values.

(Using Sage, stock records are set up by clicking on **Products**, then **New** and following the **Wizard**.)

Remember to back up your work.

**TASK 7**

Refer to the three sales invoices and one credit note in the documents provided. You must set up the customer details for each customer and then record each sale and the credit.

(Using Sage, customer details can be entered by clicking on Customers, then New, and following the **Wizard**. Invoices to customers can be entered in a number of ways. While it is possible to click on **Customers**, then **Invoice**, and fill in the totals, this has no link with the stock accounts, so they would have to be entered separately. It is better to record sales invoices by clicking on **Invoicing** and then **Product**. Filling in the details here will automatically update the stock records at the same time. Similarly, credit notes should be recorded by clicking on **Invoicing** and then **Credit**. Remember that to post the invoices and credit note to the ledgers, you must select each and click on the Update button.)

Remember to back up your work.

**TASK 8**

Refer to the two paying-in slips in the documents provided, showing receipts from Riddle Fencing and from Quickmet. Enter these two receipts into the computer.

(Using Sage, customer receipts are recorded by clicking on **Bank**, then **Customer** and filling in the details.)

Remember to back up your work.

**TASK 9**

It is now 9 February 2006. You are required to enter the establishment of a petty cash system into the computer records. A cheque for £300 has been written for cash, and three petty cash vouchers have been presented for payment. You are required to enter the journal to set up the petty cash float in the first place, and then record each of the three payments.

(Using Sage, you must click on **Nominal** and then **Journals** to record the transfer of the initial float from the bank account to the petty cash account. Each payment can be recorded by clicking the **Bank** button, and then **Payment** and filling in the details.)

Remember to back up your work.

**TASK 10**

It is still 9 February.

(a)  Produce and print out a trial balance as at this date.

(b)  Produce and print out a summary audit trail showing all the transactions to date.

(Using Sage, the trial balance is extracted by clicking on **Financials** and then **Trial**. The audit trail is produced by clicking on **Financials** and then **Audit**.)

Remember to back up your work.

**NOMINAL ACCOUNTS**

Here is a list of nominal ledger accounts that you **may** wish to use to complete this scenario question together with their codes in the Sage Instant/Line 50 package default accounts layout. You need not restrict yourself to this list if you think other accounts are more appropriate, and just because an account is listed here it does not necessarily mean that it is needed in the scenario.

Some of the accounts required for this test may not appear in the default layout: you will need to set up a new account in this case.

If your accounting package uses different names it is up to you to decide the most appropriate nominal accounts to use. Your tutor may provide guidance.

| | | | |
|---|---|---|---|
| 0020 | Plant and Machinery | 5002 | Miscellaneous Purchases |
| 0030 | Office Equipment | 5003 | Packaging |
| 0040 | Furniture and Fixtures | 5009 | Discounts Taken |
| 0050 | Motor Vehicles | 5100 | Carriage |
| 1001 | Stock | 5200 | Opening Stock |
| 1002 | Work in Progress | 5201 | Closing Stock |
| 1003 | Finished Goods | 6001 | Cost of Sales Labour |
| 1100 | Debtors Control Account | 6100 | Sales Commissions |
| 1101 | Sundry Debtors | 6900 | Miscellaneous Expenses |
| 1102 | Other Debtors | 7002 | Directors Remuneration |
| 1200 | Bank Current Account | 7003 | Staff Salaries |
| 1210 | Bank Deposit Account | 7009 | Adjustments |
| 1230 | Petty Cash | 7200 | Electricity |
| 2100 | Creditors Control Account | 7301 | Repairs and Servicing |
| 2101 | Sundry Creditors | 7400 | Travelling |
| 2102 | Other Creditors | 7406 | Subsistence |
| 2200 | Sales Tax Control Account | 7500 | Printing |
| 2201 | Purchase Tax Control Account | 7501 | Postage and Carriage |
| 2202 | VAT Liability | 7502 | Telephone |

| | | | |
|---|---|---|---|
| 3000 | Ordinary Shares | 7504 | Office Stationery |
| 3010 | Preference Shares | 7600 | Legal Fees |
| 3100 | Reserves | 7601 | Audit and Accountancy Fees |
| 3101 | Undistributed Reserves | 7603 | Professional Fees |
| 3200 | Profit and Loss Account | 7900 | Bank Interest Paid |
| 4000 | Sales Type A | 7901 | Bank Charges |
| 4001 | Sales Type B | 7905 | Credit Charges |
| 4002 | Sales Type C | 8100 | Bad Debt Write Off |
| 4009 | Discounts Allowed | 8102 | Bad Debt Provision |
| 4900 | Miscellaneous Income | 8205 | Refreshments |
| 4905 | Distribution and Carriage | 9998 | Suspense Account |
| 5000 | Materials Purchased | 9999 | Mispostings Account |

**BACK UP FILES**

Use this table to note down the name of your back up files. You may prefer to photocopy this page or write your list on a separate sheet of paper.

| Task | File name |
|---|---|
| Task 1 | |
| Task 2 | |
| Task 3 | |
| Task 4 | |
| Task 5 | |
| Task 6 | |
| Task 7 | |
| Task 8 | |
| Task 9 | |
| Task 10 | |

**DATA FOR TASKS 1 AND 2**

# A-80

**18, Ettrick Walk, Cumbernauld, Glasgow, Lanarkshire, G67 1NE**
**Tel: 01236 452123**
**Fax: 01236 452888**
**Email: LeeMcGregor@a-80.co.uk**

Mr F Mackay
Messrs Mackay & Co
27 Ettrick Road
Cumbernauld
Glasgow
G67 2NE

5 January 2006

Dear Mr Mackay

**A-80 Ltd**

Thank you for your telephone call yesterday. Here are the details you asked for.

The company started trading on 1 January this year and the year end will be 31 December. We have already had some letterhead, compliment slips and business cards printed so this letter gives most of the information you need (including company number and VAT number at the foot of the page).

We will be making four types of sales initially: GPS tracking devices, portable GPS navigation devices, in-dash GPS navigation devices and installation services. We can purchase the hardware devices on demand although we will be carrying a small stock.

I have put £15,000 of my redundancy money into the business: I have paid £99 for company set-up fees (no VAT applicable), £376 (including VAT) for stationery printing and £450 plus VAT for tools. The rest of the £15,000 is in the bank. We do not yet have an overdraft facility.

The issued share capital is also £15,000: a copy of all the company documents is enclosed.

I understand that your assistant will be visiting once a month to maintain our accounts, and we will have all the invoices and so on that you need ready for you. We expect to receive bank statements on or about 30th of each month.

I look forward to your visits.

Yours sincerely

Lee McGregor

**A-80 Ltd. Registered in Scotland. Registered office: 18 Ettrick Walk, Cumbernauld, Glasgow, Lanarkshire, G67 1NE. Registered number: SC3745863. VAT reg number: 627 1329 84**

## DATA FOR TASK 3

A-80 Ltd uses the following five suppliers.

| Name | Oswalds Ltd | Desco Industries Ltd |
|---|---|---|
| Address | 7 Telford Place | Dunnswood Road |
|  |  | Wardpark South |
|  | Cumbernauld | Cumbernauld |
|  | Glasgow | Glasgow |
| Post Code | G67 2NH | G67 3ET |
| Phone | 01236 851559 | 01236 262456 |
| Fax | 01236 878458 | 01236 197619 |
| VAT number | None | 885 2565 57 |

| Name | Cumbernauld Computer Print Ltd | GPS Wholesale Supplies Ltd |
|---|---|---|
| Address | 13 Tollpark Road | 1-9 Telford Road |
|  | Wardpark East | Lenziemill |
|  | Cumbernauld | Cumbernauld |
|  | Glasgow | Glasgow |
| Post Code | G68 0LW | G67 2AX |
| Phone | 01236 851229 | 01236 411391 |
| Fax | 01236 842741 | 01236 292618 |
| VAT number | 669 9102 80 | 948 9916 16 |

| Name | Matlock Systems |  |
|---|---|---|
| Address | 1–3 Duncan McIntosh Road |  |
|  | Cumbernauld |  |
|  | Glasgow |  |
| Post Code | G68 0HH |  |
| Phone | 01236 139051 |  |
| Fax | 01236 724254 |  |
| VAT number | 871 9216 79 |  |

**DATA FOR TASKS 4, 5 AND 6**

# SALES INVOICE

**TO:**
A-80 LTD
18 Ettrick Walk
Cumbernauld
Glasgow
G67 1NE

**Desco Industries Ltd**
Dunnswood Road
Wardpark South
Cumbernauld, Glasgow
G67 3ET
Tel: 01236 262456
Fax: 01236 197619
Invoice no:     A80-821676
Tax point:      15 December 2005
VAT reg no:    885 2565 57

| Description | Quantity | VAT rate % | Unit price £ | Amount exclusive of VAT £ |
|---|---|---|---|---|
| Professional Electrical Toolkit | 1 | 17.5% | 450.00 | 450.00 |
| Trade discount 0% | | | | 450.00 |
| | | | | 0.00 |
| | | | | 450.00 |
| VAT at 17.5% | | | | 78.75 |
| TOTAL | | | | 528.75 |

For your records only. Thank you for your payment

---

Sales invoice no 7114
# Oswalds Limited
7 Telford Place, Cumbernauld, Glasgow, G67 2NH
Telephone: 01236 851559 Fax 01236 878458

*Date:*    *12 December 2005*

Lee McGregor
18 Ettrick Walk
Cumbernauld
Glasgow
Lanarkshire   G67 1NE

Company formation expenses: A-80 Limited
Submission of documents to Companies House
   Total fee                                                                                £99.00

                                   £99.00

**Paid with thanks**
**This invoice is for your records**

# Cumbernauld Computer Print Ltd

**Sales invoice** SI8993

13 Tollpark Road
Wardpark East
Cumbernauld
Glasgow
G68 0LW

**Tax point** 20 December 2005

| Telephone | 01236 851229 |
| Fax | 01236 842741 |

**VAT Reg No** 669 9102 80

**Sale to:**
Lee McGregor
18 Ettrick Walk
Cumbernauld
Glasgow
G67 1NE

| Description | Quantity | Total £ |
| --- | --- | --- |
| Letterhead | Starter (250) | |
| Compliment slips | Starter (250) | |
| Business cards | Starter (250) | |
| Net total | | 320.00 |
| Value Added Tax at 17.5% | | 56.00 |
| | | 376.00 |

**Paid with thanks**

Sales invoice C15811

# Matlock Systems

1-3 Duncan McIntosh Road, Cumbernauld, Glasgow G68 0HH
Telephone 01236 139051; Fax 01236 724254

**Tax point 2/1/2006    VAT Reg No  871 9216 79**

**Supply by sale**

A-80 Limited
18, Ettrick Walk
Cumbernauld, Glasgow
Lanarkshire
G67 1NE

| Description | Unit price £ | VAT rate % | Total excl VAT £ | VAT £ |
|---|---|---|---|---|
| Desktop PC | 1,100.00 | 17.5 | 1,100.00 | 192.50 |
| Laser printer | 174.00 | 17.5 | 174.00 | 30.45 |
| Accounts software | 424.00 | 17.5 | 424.00 | 74.20 |
| | | | 1,698.00 | 297.15 |
| | | VAT | 297.15 | |
| | | | 1,995.15 | |

# GPS Wholesale Supplies Ltd

**SALES INVOICE**    5231/a80

**Address**
1-9 Telford Road
Lenziemill
Cumbernauld
Glasgow
G67 2AX
Phone: 01236 411391
Fax: 01236 292618

**Customer**
A-80 Limited
18, Ettrick Walk
Cumbernauld
Glasgow
Lanarkshire
G67 1NE

**VAT registration no**        948 9916 16

**Tax point**                2 January 2006

| Description | Quantity | VAT rate % | Unit price £ | Amount exclusive of VAT £ |
|---|---|---|---|---|
| Blaupunkt in-car tracking device | 10 | 17.5% | 255.30 | 2,553.00 |
| Garmin in-car GPS (portable) | 5 | 17.5% | 429.34 | 2,146.70 |
| Navman in-car GPS (portable) | 5 | 17.5% | 536.25 | 2,681.25 |
| Alpine GPS Navigation System (in-dash) | 3 | 17.5% | 740.42 | 2,221.26 |
| | | | | 9,602.21 |
| VAT at 17.5% | | | | 1,680.39 |
| TOTAL | | | | 11,282.60 |

KAPLAN PUBLISHING

**DATA FOR TASK 7**

# A-80 Ltd

18, Ettrick Walk, Cumbernauld, Glasgow, Lanarkshire, G67 1NE
Tel: 01236 452123 Fax: 01236 452888

### *SALES INVOICE*

**Invoice number: 1**
**Tax point 04/01/2006**    **VAT Reg No**    **627 1329 84**

TO:

Quickmet (Scotland)          Contact:
25-27 Napier Road            Phone: 01236 817528
Cumbernauld                  Fax: 01236 255924
Glasgow                      VAT: 847 3726 49
G68 0EF

| Description | Quantity | VAT rate % | Unit price £ | Amount exclusive of VAT £ |
|---|---|---|---|---|
| Blaupunkt in-car tracking devices | 10 | 17.5% | 425.50 | 4,255.00 |
| Installation charge (per hour) | 6 | 17.5% | 70.00 | 420.00 |
| | | | | |
| | | | | |
| | | | | |

| | |
|---|---|
| Net | 4,675.00 |
| VAT at 17.5% | 818.13 |
| TOTAL | 5,493.13 |

# A-80 Ltd

18, Ettrick Walk, Cumbernauld, Glasgow, Lanarkshire, G67 1NE
Tel: 01236 452123 Fax: 01236 452888

## *SALES INVOICE*

**Invoice number: 2**
**Tax point 07/01/2006**     **VAT Reg No**     **627 1329 84**

TO:

Riddle Fencing Ltd
Blairlinn Industrial Estate
11 Greens Road
Cumbernauld
Glasgow
G67 2TU

Contact:
Phone: 01236 242504
Fax: 01236 246315
VAT: 653 7546 74

| Description | Quantity | VAT rate % | Unit price £ | Amount exclusive of VAT £ |
|---|---|---|---|---|
| Garmin in-car GPS (portable) | 4 | 17.5% | 715.56 | 2,862.24 |
| Installation charge (per hour) | 2 | 17.5% | 70.00 | 140.00 |
| Alpine GPS Navigation System (in-dash) | 3 | 17.5% | 1,234.04 | 3,702.12 |
| Installation charge (per hour) | 8 | 17.5% | 70.00 | 560.00 |
| | | | | |

| | |
|---|---|
| Net | 7,264.36 |
| VAT at 17.5% | 1,271.26 |
| TOTAL | 8,535.62 |

KAPLAN PUBLISHING

# A-80 Ltd

18, Ettrick Walk, Cumbernauld, Glasgow, Lanarkshire, G67 1NE
Tel: 01236 452123 Fax: 01236 452888

## *SALES INVOICE*

**Invoice number: 3**
**Tax point 04/01/2006**      **VAT Reg No**      **627 1329 84**

TO:

Special Breads                    Contact:
Unit 1                            Phone: 01236 328829
Little Drum Road                  Fax: 01236 590610
Cumbernauld                       VAT: 778 9940 92
Glasgow
G68 9LH

| Description | Quantity | VAT rate % | Unit price £ | Amount exclusive of VAT £ |
|---|---|---|---|---|
| Navman in-car GPS (portable) | 5 | 17.5% | 893.75 | 4,468.75 |
| Installation charge (per hour) | 3 | 17.5% | 70.00 | 210.00 |
| | | | | |
| | | | | |
| | | | | |

| | |
|---|---|
| Net | 4,678.75 |
| VAT at 17.5% | 818.78 |
| TOTAL | 5,497.53 |

# A-80 Ltd

18, Ettrick Walk, Cumbernauld, Glasgow, Lanarkshire, G67 1NE
Tel: 01236 452123 Fax: 01236 452888

## *CREDIT NOTE*

**Credit note: 4**
**Tax point 15/01/2006      VAT Reg No      627 1329 84**

TO:

Special Breads
Unit 1
Little Drum Road
Cumbernauld
Glasgow
G68 9LH

Contact:
Phone: 01236 328829
Fax: 01236 590610
VAT: 778 9940 92

| Description | Quantity | VAT rate % | Unit price £ | Amount exclusive of VAT £ |
|---|---|---|---|---|
| 2 x faulty Navman GPS devices | 2 | 17.5% | 893.75 | 1,787.50 |
| Installation refund (per hour) | 1 | 17.5% | 70.00 | 70.00 |
| | | | | |
| | | | | |
| | | | | |

| | |
|---|---|
| Net | 1,857.50 |
| VAT at 17.5% | 325.06 |
| TOTAL | 2,182.56 |

KAPLAN PUBLISHING

## DATA FOR TASK 8

| Cheques etc. | | | Brought forward £ | | | £50 | | |
|---|---|---|---|---|---|---|---|---|
| | | | | | | £20 | | |
| | | | | | | £10 | | |
| | | | | | | £5 | | |
| | | | | | | £2 | | |
| | | | | | | £1 | | |
| | | | | | | 50p | | |
| | | | | | | 20p | | |
| | | | Riddle | | | Silver | | |
| | | | Fencing | 8535 | 62 | Bronze | | |
| | | | | | | Total Cash Cardnet Cheques etc. | 8535 | 62 |
| Carried forward £ | | | Carried forward £ | 8535 | 62 | Total £ | **8535** | **62** |

Date        14/01/2006              500002                FOR A-80 LIMITED                                    277951673

| Cheques etc. | | | Brought forward £ | | | £50 | | |
|---|---|---|---|---|---|---|---|---|
| | | | | | | £20 | | |
| | | | | | | £10 | | |
| | | | | | | £5 | | |
| | | | | | | £2 | | |
| | | | | | | £1 | | |
| | | | | | | 50p | | |
| | | | | | | 20p | | |
| | | | Riddle | | | Silver | | |
| | | | Quickmet | 5493 | 13 | Bronze | | |
| | | | | | | Total Cash Cardnet Cheques etc. | 5493 | 13 |
| Carried forward £ | | | Carried forward £ | 5493 | 13 | Total £ | **5493** | **13** |

Date        19/01/2006              500002                FOR A-80 LIMITED                                    277951673

**DATA FOR TASK 9**

| PETTY CASH VOUCHER | | | |
|---|---|---|---|
| Authorised by | Received by | No PC001 | |
| Date | Description | Amount | |
| 9 February 2006 | Stamps | 32 | 60 |
| | | | |
| | | | |
| | | | |
| | | | |
| | Total | 32 | 60 |

| PETTY CASH VOUCHER | | | |
|---|---|---|---|
| Authorised by | Received by | No PC001 | |
| Date | Description | Amount | |
| 9 February 2006 | Tea, coffee | 53 | 46 |
| | | | |
| | | | |
| | | | |
| | | | |
| | Total | 53 | 46 |

| PETTY CASH VOUCHER | | | |
|---|---|---|---|
| Authorised by | Received by | No PC001 | |
| Date | Description | Amount | |
| 9 February 2006 | Stationery | 1 | 20 |
| | VAT | 0 | 21 |
| | | | |
| | | | |
| | | | |
| | Total | 1 | 41 |

KAPLAN PUBLISHING

# KEY TECHNIQUES ANSWERS

## UNIT 21

**WORKING WITH COMPUTERS**

### Chapter 1

△ **ACTIVITY 1**                                                        △ △ △ △

Disks are divided into folders and the folders contain a collection of files.

△ **ACTIVITY 2**                                                        △ △ △ △

A    The grandfather/father/son is a technique for maintaining back-ups.

△ **ACTIVITY 3**                                                        △ △ △ △

The operation of this method is shown in the following diagram:

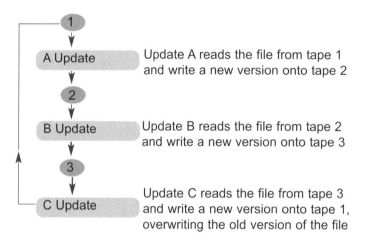

|  |  |
|---|---|
| 1 | |
| A Update | Update A reads the file from tape 1 and write a new version onto tape 2 |
| 2 | |
| B Update | Update B reads the file from tape 2 and write a new version onto tape 3 |
| 3 | |
| C Update | Update C reads the file from tape 3 and write a new version onto tape 1, overwriting the old version of the file |

The three versions of the file are known as grandfather, father and son. The principle of the system is that only two generations are on the computer at the same time, so that even if both are spoiled the file can be reconstructed from the third.

△ **ACTIVITY 4**                                                        △ △ △ △

The order would be (B) – AAT, Foundation level, Units 21, 22 and 23.

### Chapter 2

△ **ACTIVITY 5**                                                        △ △ △ △

There are several ways of minimising the risk:
·    Burglar alarms can be fitted.

·   Access to the building can be controlled.
·   Smaller items can be locked away securely. Larger pieces of equipment can be bolted to the surface.
·   The organisation can maintain a log of all equipment so that its movement can be monitored.
·   Disks containing valuable data should not be left lying around

## △ ACTIVITY 6                                    △ △ △ △

Examples include:
·   Theft of assets, e.g. computers, stock or software.
·   Theft of incoming cheques.
·   Invented personnel on the payroll.
·   Unauthorised discounts given to customers.
·   False supplier accounts.
·   Corruption and bribery, e.g. when selecting suppliers.
·   Abuse of organisation's credit card facilities, e.g. company car fuel allowance used privately.

## △ ACTIVITY 7                                    △ △ △ △

There is no printed answer for this question.

## △ ACTIVITY 8                                    △ △ △ △

The answer is (b).

## △ ACTIVITY 9                                    △ △ △ △

Using your Christian name may be the easiest way to remember your password, but it will also be easy for someone to gain unauthorised access to your files when you are not at your desk. Alternative passwords that are easy to remember are your mother's maiden name or a brother or sister's name. Try to add in a number e.g. year born, to make it even more difficult for someone to guess it.

## △ ACTIVITY 10                                   △ △ △ △

(iii)  Because the computers are only connected to a local area network they cannot receive e-mail from customers and suppliers.

## UNIT 22

**CONTRIBUTE TO THE MAINTENANCE OF A HEALTHY, SAFE AND PRODUCTIVE WORKING ENVIRONMENT**

## Chapter 3

### △ ACTIVITY 11                                           △ △ △ △

Details of the injured person (name, address, age, etc).

Injuries sustained.

Details of the accident (date, time, place, narrative, diagram if necessary).

First aid or medical treatment provided on site.

Names of witnesses (if any).

### △ ACTIVITY 12                                           △ △ △ △

(a)  It would include information on:
  (i)   the people in charge of health and safety within the firm and their specific responsibilities
  (ii)  safe operating practices (e.g. the operation of electrical equipment)
  (iii) the system for recording accidents in the accident book
  (iv)  details of first aid available, including the names of qualified first aiders and the position of the first aid box.

(b)  Adequate premises which are structurally sound, have adequate fire exits and safety equipment.

Suitable accommodation: suitable temperature, enough space for number of people, proper ventilation, blinds for windows, adequate lighting and safe floor surfaces in good condition.

Appropriate furniture: safety stools to reach items stored on shelves, adjustable chairs for VDU operators and filing cabinets in which only one drawer can be opened at a time.
Adequate toilet and welfare facilities.

Separate accommodation for noisy or dangerous equipment (e.g. photocopiers which give out fumes) or substances (e.g. cleaning materials).

Safe equipment which is serviced regularly by trained technicians.

### △ ACTIVITY 13                                           △ △ △ △

Most likely causes are:
(a)  people tripping up, slipping or falling off equipment or furniture

(b)   people being hit by falling objects or colliding with equipment, furniture or other people
(c)   people using electrical equipment incorrectly
(d)   people using equipment or materials incorrectly.

## △ ACTIVITY 14                                                      △△△△

(a) Discovering a fire:
   (i)     decide whether or not it can be dealt with using a fire extinguisher or fire blanket – these methods are only successful for small fires
   (ii)    ensure that no one else is in immediate danger
   (iii)   if the fire is in one room only, close the door
   (iv)    raise the alarm and follow company procedure on who must ring the fire brigade
   (v)     leave the building as quickly as possible – do not stop to collect any personal belongings.
(b) Hearing a fire alarm:
   (i)     close all windows and doors and leave the building as quickly as possible – do not stop to collect any personal belongings
   (ii)    remain calm and go to the assembly point
   (iii)   follow the instructions of your managers or the fire brigade officers – do not re-enter the building until you are authorised to do so.

## △ ACTIVITY 15                                                      △△△△

### ACCIDENT REPORT FORM

| | |
|---|---|
| Name(s) of injured person(s) | Vanessa Wilson |
| Date of accident | 9th April 2006 |
| Place of accident | Accounts office |
| Details of accident | Vanessa Wilson was carrying a large pile of papers and did not notice the waste paper basket that a colleague had left in the path between the two desks. She tripped over it and hurt her wrist. |
| Names of witnesses | |

| Completed by | Block capitals<br>A STUDENT | Signature<br>+A Student |
|---|---|---|

| | |
|---|---|
| First aid treatment given (to be completed by First Aid Officer) | |
| Action taken to prevent recurrence (to be completed by Safety Officer) | |

## △ ACTIVITY 16                    △ △ △ △

Fatal injuries and serious injuries involving admission to hospital for more than 24 hours require an immediate telephone report followed by a written report within seven days. Also applies to certain dangerous occurrences such as a pipeline explosion or the collapse of scaffolding.

Reportable diseases such as skin cancer require a written report.

## △ ACTIVITY 17                    △ △ △ △

A   The report covers employees and other people on the employer's premises and incidents away from the employer's premises if they occur in the course of an employee's duties.

## △ ACTIVITY 18                    △ △ △ △

# Fire action

**Any person discovering a fire:**

1. Sound the alarm
2. Receptionist to call fire brigade
3. Attack the fire if possible using equipment provided

**On hearing the fire alarm:**

1. Leave the building by nearest route
2. Close all doors behind you
3. Do not use lifts
4. Report to assembly point

Do not take risks
Do not return to the building
   until authorised to do so

KAPLAN PUBLISHING

# Chapter 4

## △ ACTIVITY 19 △△△△

A bomb threat checklist might include the following:

**Note:** the phone number of the caller if it appears on your display and whether the caller is reading out the threat or speaking spontaneously.

**Ask:**
· When is the bomb going to explode?
· Are you representing an organisation?
· Do you have a security code number?
· Where is it right now?
· What does it look like?
· What type of bomb is it?
· What will cause it to explode?
· Did you place the bomb? Why?
· Where are you calling from?
· What is your name?
· Where do you live?
· Exact wording of threat

**Caller's voice:**
Male/Female
Approximate age

**Characteristics:**

| Calm | Nasal | Slow | Soft | Deep breathing | Laughing |
|------|-------|------|------|----------------|----------|
| Excited | Rapid | Deep | Upset | Lisp | Angry |
| Disguised | Distinct | Familiar | Stutter | Clearing throat | Loud |
| Ragged | Cracked | Raspy | Normal | Slurred | Agitated |

**Accent:**

| English (Southern, Northern, Midlands, West Country) | European (French, Spanish, German, Eastern European) |
|---|---|
| Irish | Indian |
| Scottish | American |
| Welsh | Afro Caribbean |

**Background sounds:**

| Street noises | Factory machinery | Other voices | Children |
|---|---|---|---|
| Music | Office machinery | House | PA system |
| Radio/TV | Long distance | Motor | Animal noises |

## △ ACTIVITY 20 △△△△

Becoming familiar with the emergency procedures might involve:
· study of appropriate procedures manuals
· attention to explanations given during induction or later training
· attention to signs and notices displayed in the workplace
· studying evacuation plans, and allocating meeting places
· specific training relating to responsibilities for other employees in the event of emergency.

## Chapter 5

## △ ACTIVITY 21 △△△△

There is no printed answer for this question.

## UNIT 23

## ACHIEVING PERSONAL EFFECTIVENESS

## Chapter 6

## △ ACTIVITY 22 △△△△

In example A, because the flow of authority is shown as passing down from the production manager to the assistant manager and then on to the operatives. In example B the production manager can delegate to the assistant manager and to the operatives, but the assistant manager is not shown as having any authority over the operators.

## △ ACTIVITY 23 △△△△

Ensure that the following information is included:
(a) the full name and title of the person you intend or are required to see;
(b) the full and precise name and address of the relevant organisation;
(c) the telephone number of the organisation together with the area code (STD code) and the extension of the person you must see;

(d)   the time, date and anticipated length of the meeting;
(e)   the exact location of the meeting (eg which room on which floor in which block);
(f)   outline details of the matter to be discussed;
(g)   travel directions and details of entrance points and security procedures.

It is, of course, equally important for those details to be sent to people who may be intending to visit you.

## △ ACTIVITY 24    △△△△

C – Contact his supervisor immediately and explain the problem. He should suggest that he finishes what he considers to be the most urgent task first before starting one of the others.

## △ ACTIVITY 25    △△△△

The written instructions will give the standard sequence of steps or operations necessary to perform an activity – clearly indicating what is required to be done, when, where and how. This will probably be in loose-leaf form to facilitate any amendments. The contents might include:
(i)   an outline of the operation to be carried out within the procedure
(ii)   title of person with overall responsibility for the procedure (not the name of the person currently holding the post)
(iii)   systems or methods of dealing with the work
(iv)   the title and department of the member of staff performing each stage of the procedure (again not the individual by name)
(v)   sample forms and entries
(vi)   sample calculations
(vii)   timetable of various stages and cut-off dates
(viii) details of exceptions to be reported and methods of reporting these
(ix)   sample of any final output
(x)   distribution of final output
(xi)   methods of initiating changes.

Here is an example of a simple administrative procedure:
(i)   All cash receipts are entered in the cashbook.
(ii)   At the end of the day, the totals are added up.
(iii)   The addition is checked.
(iv)   The totals in the cashbook are posted into the main accounting records.

## △ ACTIVITY 26    △△△△

(ii) is not true because an organisation chart does indicate line authority within a business.

## Chapter 7

### △ ACTIVITY 27    △ △ △ △

The procedures manual should contain information on:
· health and safety procedures
· accounting and reporting procedures
· disciplinary and grievance procedures.

### △ ACTIVITY 28    △ △ △ △

Darren might be used to giving his staff this information (particularly as Fiona is a new employee) but on this day one of the following may apply:
(a) he is very busy himself
(b) he has personal problems.

He might expect all staff to look up information for themselves and several other people might already have asked him.

### △ ACTIVITY 29    △ △ △ △

Diana might:
(a) look away or out of the window
(b) play with a pencil or other item
(c) continue writing
(d) interrupt unnecessarily.

Her supervisor might assume that she is either not capable of doing the job or not interested. Her supervisor might decide not to give her some more interesting work as a type of punishment.

## △ ACTIVITY 30    △△△△

The advantages and disadvantages associated with the preparation of office manuals include:

**Advantages**

(i)     To prepare an office manual the systems and procedures must be examined carefully. This close attention can only benefit the organisation, in that strengths and weaknesses are revealed.

(ii)    Supervision is easier.

(iii)   It helps the induction and training of new staff.

(iv)   It helps to pinpoint areas of responsibility.

(v)    Having been written down in the first place, systems and procedures are easier to adapt and/or change in response to changing circumstances.

**Disadvantages**

(i)     There is an associated expense in preparing manuals both in the obvious financial terms and the perhaps less obvious cost of administrative time.

(ii)    To be of continuing use an office manual must be updated periodically, again incurring additional expense.

(iii)   The instructions as laid down in the office manual may be interpreted rather strictly and implemented too rigidly. Within any organisation it is often beneficial for employees to bring a degree of flexibility to their duties to cope with particular circumstances.

## △ ACTIVITY 31    △△△△

(i)     Your boss would look foolish and the customer will have a poor opinion of your organisation's efficiency.

(ii)    Without detailed and accurate information to base the discounts on, your boss may be forced to defer discussions until a later, and perhaps less opportune, occasion. Alternatively, he could concede an over-generous rate of discount to finalise the deal while he has the opportunity.

(iii)   Your boss will form a poor opinion of your abilities and reliability, with possible damaging consequences to your later career.

## △ ACTIVITY 32    △△△△

(iv)   A facsimile or fax is a facility for sending a duplicate copy of a document electronically.

## Chapter 8

## △ ACTIVITY 33    △△△△

There is no printed answer for this question.

## △ ACTIVITY 34 △ △ △ △

There is no printed answer for this question. The appraisal is important in staff coun-selling and development. This would involve such matters as:

· Feedback on performance and problems encountered – they establish an individual's current level of performance and identify strengths and weaknesses.

· Career development – they identify training and development needs.

· Identifying job interests and likely development areas – they can motivate individuals.

· Defining performance targets – they provide a basis for rewarding staff in relation to their contribution to organisational goals.

· Reviewing promotion potential – they assess potential and provide information for succession planning.

· Enabling individuals to appreciate where their jobs fit in the overall company scheme.

## △ ACTIVITY 35 △ △ △ △

(i) Possible sources of information include:

    (a) the bought ledger accounts of the two current suppliers

    (b) invoices from the two current suppliers

    (c) costing records showing purchasing costs over the last six months.

(ii) You should immediately contact the purchasing manager and explain the problem. It may be possible to take action to salvage the meeting by asking for help from someone who has not such a heavy workload. Alternatively, the meeting may be postponed.

# MOCK SIMULATION 1
# ANSWERS

**TASK 1**

The effect of concentrating on the screen for long periods has been found to be very tiring by many operators. Other complaints have been of headaches, back- and neck-aches, giddiness, nausea, irritability, anxiety and depression. In general these may be associated with the ergonomic design of some VDUs and unsuitable working conditions, which aggravate matters. Headaches may result from several things that occur with VDU work, such as:

· screen glare
· poor image quality
· a need for different spectacles
· stress from the pace of work
· anxiety about new technology
· reading the screen for long periods without a break
· poor posture
· a combination of these.

Many of these things can easily be put right once the cause of the problem has been found.

Some users may get aches and pains in their hands, wrists, arms, neck, shoulders or back, especially after long periods of uninterrupted VDU work. 'Repetitive strain injury' (RSI) has become a popular term for these aches, pains and disorders, but can be misleading – it means different things to different people.

A better medical name for this whole group of conditions is 'upper limb disorders'. Usually these disorders do not last, but in a few cases they may become persist-ent or even disabling.

Problems of this kind may have a physical cause, but may also be more likely if a VDU user feels stressed by the work. If you get aches or pains you should alert your supervisor or line manager.

Problems can often be avoided by good workplace design, so that you can work comfortably, and by good working practices (such as taking frequent short breaks from the VDU). Prevention is easiest if action is taken early, before the problem has become serious.

Eyestrain is probably the most serious problem which operators experience. Long spells of VDU work can lead to tired eyes and discomfort. Also, by giving your eyes more demanding tasks, it might make you aware of an eyesight problem you had not noticed before. You and your employer can help your eyes by ensuring your VDU is well positioned and properly adjusted, and that the workplace lighting is suitable. Ask for an eye test if you still think there is a problem.

**TASK 2**

| Fault | Probable cause | Action |
|---|---|---|
| No response from printer when command to print given | · No power to printer<br>· Printer not switched on<br>· Printer not connected to computer<br>· Printer not 'on-line'<br>· Wrong command given | · Check plug lead<br>· Switch on<br><br>· Check printer lead<br><br>· Press 'on-line' key<br>· Check manual |
| Print is gibberish | · Printer set in test mode<br>· Software and printer incompatible<br>· Printer lead faulty | · Set test mode to 'off'<br><br>· Call supervisor<br><br>· Test with another lead |
| Print quality poor | · Ink jet/laser – cartridge needs changing<br>· Laser – paper wrong specification or internal cleaning required | · Replace with new ink/toner cartridge<br>· Check printer manual |
| Print wrong size | · Printer 'remembering' command from other software | · Switch printer off and on again to clear memory |
| Paper jam – Document feed | · Wrong paper specification<br>· Inserted wrongly | · Change paper and reinsert<br>· Check document feeder instruction booklet |
| Paper jam – Tractor feed | · Printed/unused sheet 'backing up' into printer<br>· In-tray over full<br><br>· Paper specification wrong | · Stop printer and use paper release to unjam<br>· Clear area behind printer<br>· Reduce paper in the in-tray<br>· Change to correct paper<br>· Check printer manual |
| Print crooked on paper | · Tractor feed - paper dislodged from sprocket holes | · Stop printer and realign paper and sprocket holes correctly |
| Printing with incorrect pitch or line spacing | · Software over-riding printer settings | · Check printer manual |

**TASK 3**
· Fire alarms and sprinklers.
· Locks on doors.
· Security labels or the company's name etched onto the equipment.
· Proper environmental controls - not too much heat or humidity.

**TASK 4**
There are several inherent problems with passwords:
· Authorised users may reveal their password to a colleague: this may arise because allowing temporary access in this way may be perceived as being more convenient than going through the process of setting up the colleague with their own account.
· Many passwords may have associations with the user (e.g. son's name and age: Max14; house name and number: 17beehive) and these can be discovered by experimentation.
· Passwords are often written down close to the computer (e.g. pinned to the notice board inside the office), left on a yellow 'post-it' in a desk drawer or even attached to the terminal!

To protect passwords and user numbers against discovery, a number of precautions should be adopted:
· Users should be required to change their passwords regularly.
· Passwords should be memorable but not obviously related to a user's private life (common password choices such as children's or pets' names or birthdays).
· Users should be encouraged never to write down their passwords. Making up a phrase or nonsense sentence using the numbers and initial letters should be suggested.
· Passwords should be case-sensitive and passwords should be a combination of numbers as well as letters.
· There should be strict controls over passwords – they should never be 'lent' or written down where they can be easily seen.
· There should be automatic sentinel or watchdog programs to identify when a password has been keyed incorrectly.

**TASK 5**
It is standard practice to keep at least three generations of a file or database, the third providing a further level of security in the event that restoration is not achieved using the first back-up copy. The three versions of the file are known as grandfather, father and son. The principle of the system is that only two generations are on the computer at the same time, so that even if both are spoiled the file can be reconstructed from the third.

When an updating run occurs a new disk is written, combining the previous master disk and any updates and leaving the previous master disk unchanged. Both the previous master (now the 'father') and the new master (now the 'son') are retained, together with the actual transactions processed. In the next updating run, the 'son' disk is used as the master and a new (blank) disk is used to become the new master. At the completion of the second run the 'father' becomes the 'grandfather', the 'son' becomes the 'father' and the new disk becomes the 'son'.

KAPLAN PUBLISHING

The operation of this method is shown in the following diagram:

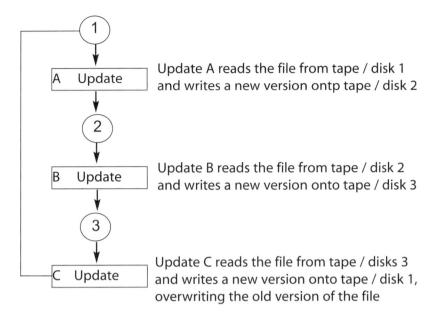

Update A reads the file from tape / disk 1 and writes a new version ontp tape / disk 2

Update B reads the file from tape / disk 2 and writes a new version onto tape / disk 3

Update C reads the file from tape / disks 3 and writes a new version onto tape / disk 1, overwriting the old version of the file

## TASK 6

Most computer systems allow the user to set up the following types of system:

· Directories – these can be set up to cover the main areas of work, for example a directory for word-processing and a directory for spreadsheets.

· Sub-directories – these are part of the overall parent directory, for example the sub-directories of the word-processing directory might include reports, memos, letters, etc.

· Sub-sub-directories – it is also possible for some systems to set up sub-directories within the sub-directories, for example if reports needed to be classified according to their nature or subject matter.

## TASK 7

There are two laws that will affect your actions:

(i) The Copyright, Designs and Patents Act is designed to protect both software and the manual associated with the software. The software publisher has the exclusive right to make and distribute copies – you are only allowed to make a copy for back-up purposes. There are steep penalties for companies prosecuted for software theft – unlimited damages, legal costs and the cost of legitimising the software.

(ii) The Data Protection Act protects data from being disclosed to others for any reason other than the reason for which it is held. The list of Turner's customers is not held for your friend to access and help him find some business. If the customer found out he/she may seek compensation through the courts for damage and any associated distress caused by the unauthorised disclosure of data about himself/herself.

KAPLAN PUBLISHING

# MOCK SIMULATION 2
# ANSWERS

**TASK 1**

You as an employee must:

·   behave as a responsible person
·   take care of your own health and safety in the workplace and do not endanger the people you work with
·   co-operate with anyone carrying out duties under the Act (including the employer)
·   make sure you know what the health and safety rules of your employer are and keep these rules
·   correctly use work items provided by your employer including personal protective equipment in accordance with training or instructions
·   never interfere with or misuse anything provided for your health, safety or welfare
·   inform your employer, or the person responsible for your health and safety, of any perceived shortcoming in safety arrangements or any immediate and serious dangers to health and safety.

**TASK 2**

The official sources of information include:

·   explanations during training – including induction
·   internal procedures manual
·   published emergency codes
·   contract of employment
·   signs and notices displayed in your organisation.

**TASK 3**

When you examine the first aid box, you find it contains:

·   20 Washproof plasters
·   2 Triangular Bandages
·   1 Large Wound Dressing
·   1 Pair Medium Latex Gloves
·   6 Alcohol Free Wipes
·   6 Safety Pins
·   First Aid Guidance Leaflet

Unfortunately, it contains no aspirin. You are allowed to carry aspirin, antiseptic creams and scissors around with you or keep them in your drawer at work, but they should not be given to others as first aid.

**TASK 4**

| ACCIDENT REPORT FORM | | |
|---|---|---|
| Name(s) of injured person(s) | | |
| Date of accident | | |
| Place of accident | | |
| Details of accident | | |
| Names of witnesses | | |
| Completed by | Block capitals | Signature |
| First aid treatment given (to be completed by First Aid Officer) . | | |
| Action taken to prevent ecurrence (to be completed by Safety Officer) | | |

**TASK 5**

| ACCIDENT REPORT FORM | | |
|---|---|---|
| Name(s) of injured person(s) | Joe Bloggs | |
| Date of accident | 1st May 2006 | |
| Place of accident | Accounts office | |
| Details of accident | Joe Bloggs stood on his chair to reach a box on top of the cupboard. The chair became unsteady and he fell and hurt his right elbow and the top of his right leg | |
| Names of witnesses | | |
| Completed by | Block capitals<br>CHARLIE SMITH | Signature<br>C Smith |
| First aid treatment given (to be completed by First Aid Officer) | | |
| Action taken to prevent ecurrence (to be completed by Safety Officer) | | |

**TASK 6**

Because it is a foam fire extinguisher it should not be used on the printer because it is not suitable for use on live electrical equipment. The extinguisher might have a warning sign on it as shown below:

SAFETY: Do **NOT** use on electrical fires, always read the instructions before use. Special foam is required to fight fires involving industrial alcohols.

What you should do, but only if you can do so safely, is to remove the plug for the printer from the wall. Then telephone the safety officer and explain what is happening. If taking out the plug does not stop the burning and if there is no suitable fire extinguisher available, you should follow your organisation's procedures for evacuating the premises safely. The safety officer will be able to deal with the fire or he/she will call in the fire brigade.

**TASK 7**

Matching the correct choice of extinguisher to a particular fire risk is of vital importance. Use of an inappropriate type of extinguisher may significantly increase the potential for personal injury and make the task of fighting the fire more difficult and hazardous.

**TASK 8**

You could check for the following:
· equipment that is wet or very dusty through being used in unsuitable conditions
· damage to the outer casing of equipment or obvious loose screws
· overheating e.g. burn marks or staining
· non-standard joints e.g. taped in the cable
· damage to the plug e.g. bent pins or casing cracked
· damage to the cable covering e.g. cuts.

**TASK 9**

There are many different types of answer for this question – depending on the type of job you have and the company you work for. If you handle cash then the security risk associated with the work is very high. The main health problems might include:
· stress
· lack of exercise and weight problems - due to sedentary work
· feeling drowsy - due to poor ventilation
· drinking too much coffee or tea with an excess of caffeine
· eye strain - due to close figure work
· back pain - poor posture.

**TASK 10**

The assets and their associated security risks will include:
· Cash/cheques and credit card slips may be subject to loss or theft by people from either within the company or from outside.
· Stocks may suffer damage or may be stolen.

KAPLAN PUBLISHING

- Equipment such as computers can be subject to theft, disk corruption or damage arising from inappropriate environmental conditions.
- Information on computer disks or on files may be subject to unauthorised amendment or theft.
- Trade secrets can be stolen or at risk due to careless talk by employees.
- Staff at Turner & Sons may be subject to attack by intruders and to emergencies affecting the buildings e.g. a bomb scare.
- Vehicles may be subject to theft or damage due to careless driving.

## TASK 11

Some or all of the following procedures and devices will be present in this type of organisation:

- Admission and exit controls e.g. voice recognition, badge readers, electronic keypads.
- Locks on doors, windows, filing cabinets and cash tills.
- Reinforced glass in doors and windows.
- Alarm systems on doors, windows and vehicles.
- Fireproof safe.
- Reception staff vet all visitors.
- Security guards in reception and patrolling building.
- Security badges with photos to gain admission to the building.
- Surveillance cameras.
- Stock control procedures for delivery of goods and equipment.
- Protective clothing e.g. helmets for security guards who carry cash.
- Procedures for accessing computers and confidential documents e.g. passwords.

You may have identified more (or different) security systems than listed here – obviously the methods and devices chosen will vary from one organisation to another.

## TASK 12

True or false?

(i)   Buildings can be evacuated for other reasons besides fire – *True* – there could be a bomb alert that would necessitate everyone leaving the building.

(ii)  All fire extinguishers are red – *True* – they have a label in another colour to identify the contents.

(iii) An employee who wedges open a fire door is committing an offence under the Health and Safety at Work Act – *True*.

(iv)  An employee who falls in a busy area should be moved immediately – *False* – you must wait until an expert is present before attempting to move someone after a bad fall.

(v)   It is essential you read the instructions thoroughly before operating a new piece of equipment – *True*

## TASK 13

The health and safety document should include the following information:

- Details of how accidents must be reported.
- Where the first aid box and the accident book are situated.
- Details of qualified first-aiders and safety training.

· The names and duties of the official safety representatives.
· The name of the manager in charge of overseeing the policy.
· Information on safe working practices throughout the organisation.

### TASK 14

She does not look as though she is working very efficiently because the files are in a mess and she has spilt her drink onto the saucer on top of the filing cabinet.

By adopting a neat and tidy approach to work the employee will find that in addition to a pleasing appearance, such an approach will aid efficiency.

It is very important to work in an orderly manner. You can find papers easily, answer queries quickly and have the most up-to-date information to hand. Inefficient filing causes delays, problems, annoyance and can cost money in lost orders and lost customers.

### TASK 15

Some practical tips for making yourself comfortable at work:
· Adjust your chair and VDU to find the most comfortable position for your work. As a broad guide, your forearms should be approximately horizontal and your eyes the same height as the top of the VDU.
· Make sure you have enough workspace to take whatever documents or other equipment you need.
· Try different arrangements of keyboard, screen, mouse and documents to find the best arrangement for you. A document holder may help you avoid awkward neck and eye movements.
· Arrange your desk and VDU to avoid glare, or bright reflections on the screen. This will be easiest if neither you nor the screen is directly facing windows or bright lights. Adjust curtains or blinds to prevent unwanted light. Adjust the brightness and contrast controls on the screen to suit lighting conditions in the room and make sure the screen surface is clean.
· Make sure there is space under your desk to move your legs freely. Move any obstacles such as boxes or equipment.
· Avoid excess pressure from the edge of your seat on the backs of your legs and knees. A footrest may be helpful, particularly for smaller users.
· Adjust your keyboard to get a good keying position. A space in front of the keyboard is sometimes helpful for resting the hands and wrists when not keying.
· Try to keep your wrists straight when keying. Keep a soft touch on the keys and don't overstretch your fingers. Good keyboard technique is important.
· Try not to sit in the same position for long periods. Make sure you change your posture as often as practicable. Some movement is desirable, but avoid repeated stretching to reach things you need (if this happens a lot, rearrange your workstation).

Most jobs provide opportunities to take a break from the screen e.g. to do filing or photocopying. Make use of them. Frequent short breaks are better than fewer long ones.

KAPLAN PUBLISHING

# MOCK SIMULATION 3
# ANSWERS

### QUESTION 1

(i) Most of the work done at Turner & Sons is not done in isolation. People rely on colleagues to provide them with certain information to get things done. When a piece of work is finished the results are passed on to other colleagues, superiors, customers or clients. Any delay by one person prevents others from getting on with their work. A person who does not produce a piece of work on time also gets a reputation for unreliability.

(ii) If someone is late in producing a piece of work then they will tend to hurry it as the deadline draws near (or passes) and its quality will suffer

(iii) Being late with one piece of work has a knock-on effect on the next because there will be less time than planned to spend on it. As a consequence, the following piece of work may also be late or below standard

### QUESTION 2

Work can be organised so that you meet your deadlines by:

· thinking through the entire task
· planning how to achieve it in the time specified
· scheduling routine tasks so that they will be completed at appropriate times
· handling high priority tasks and deadlines by working into the routine urgent tasks that interrupt the usual level of working
· arranging for any contribution required from others to be available in plenty of time and co-ordinating your efforts with them
· adapting to changes and unexpected demands
· monitoring your performance standards and progress.

### QUESTION 3

Confidential information could fall into three categories:

(i) Information of a personal nature e.g. personnel and payroll details and files relating to the credit status of customers.

(ii) Trade secrets e.g. customer database, product development plans, product designs and specifications and marketing initiatives.

(iii) Information where publicity would be prejudicial e.g. plans for expansion or going public and loan negotiations with the bank.

### QUESTION 4

Safeguarding confidentiality:

· Never leave sensitive files lying around. If you are not working with them, lock them away in a drawer or cabinet. When working on confidential files on the computer, make appropriate use of passwords.
· Check with your manager or supervisor before sending out information that may be confidential.
· Return confidential files as soon as you are finished with them and make sure you return the keys for the secure filing cabinet to the authorised holder.
· Make confidential telephone calls only where you cannot be overheard.
· If a letter contains sensitive information it must be marked 'confidential'.
· When faxing confidential information, check first with the recipient that they are ready to receive it.

KAPLAN PUBLISHING

**QUESTION 5**

Technical information would include:

· Reference books.
· Individual car manufacturer's models and specifications.
· Turner & Sons' catalogues and price lists.
· Suppliers' catalogues and invoices.
· Magazines or on-line information on price movements in materials.
· Product costing master files and current files.
· Budget forecasts and control files.

Organisational information would include:

· Organisation charts and list of contacts.
· Production processes and schedules.
· Stock reordering and materials delivery procedures.
· Procedures manuals for administrative tasks and for the budget preparation process.
· Time charts showing budget cycle.

Personal information would include:

· Contract of employment.
· Personnel records e.g. time sheets, expense sheet forms, holiday dates booked, performance appraisal results, portfolio showing evidence of competence at work and agreements for study time off.
· Details of work experience and courses attended.
· Diary and planning aids.

**QUESTION 6**

Planning aids include:

· timetables and diaries
· personal organisers
· time charts
· action lists and checklists
· action plans including time scheduling
· wall charts, peg boards, year planners and calendars for long-term planning e.g. holidays
· bar charts.

**QUESTION 7**

You would not analyse the individual employee's contracts when drawing up a staff planning chart

**QUESTION 8**

Copyright law does not cover business letters

**QUESTION 9**
**Task 1**

(a)  Mary should first check with her colleagues in production that they can do their input on the day planned and draw their attention to the deadlines so that any preparatory work that needs doing can be organised.

| Day | Job | Allocated to | Comments |
|---|---|---|---|
| Mon | Database extraction | Joe | Charlie not available |
| Tues | Database extraction | Joe | |
| Wed | Analysing information | Joe | Takes all day |
| Thurs | Review of Joe's work in morning | Mary | Half day |
| | Data entry in afternoon | Charlie | |
| Fri | Data entry | Charlie | |
| Mon | Data entry | Charlie | Half day |
| | Grouping results | Mary | Half day |
| Tues | Transferring to production schedule | Mary | |
| Wed | Report produced | Charlie | Takes twice as long |
| Thur | Report produced | Charlie | |
| Fri | Review of Charlie's work in morning | Joe | |

(b)  If Charlie is ill and not in work on, say, Thursday, the work will be delayed. Mary needs to mention the possibility to Mr Osmond, who may be prepared to revise the final deadline or arrange for help from another junior in the department.

**Task 2**

(i)  Arthur Barnes joins. This must refer to a new member of staff. Will you need to help out with his induction, and if so what tasks exactly will fall to you eg, tour of department, meeting with personnel, signing of forms? This will be an ongoing task, not just something that will take 15 minutes on Monday morning. Over the next few days you will need to schedule in 'looking after' Arthur – making sure he is given work to do, receiving on-the-job training and so on.

(ii) Check the status on the Jupiter account. It looks as though action is being considered if payment has not been received. Mary was due to meet the credit controller on Tuesday, perhaps you should contact him/her to explain Mary's absence, get the full story and find out what you should do.

(iii) You already know about the departmental meeting on Tuesday, but was Mary due to prepare any kind of report/notes for it that requires input from you? Joe is on holiday next week and Mary was considering a temp to cover for him. The diary entry was for Friday but you might need to consider this before then to allow time to organise this. Will you need to find out from Joe what his current and anticipated workload is?

(iv) Report due with Mr Osmond. What report is this? Is it definitely needed by Wednesday or could it wait until next week? Has Mr Osmond been alerted yet to a possible delay?

(v) Presumably the codes relating to existing products are about to be changed, or possibly some new products are about to be introduced. You will need to talk to Kathy to make sure that she will be providing the information required. Either way, the new codes will probably need to be entered in the sales order processing system because they are being sent to customers on Friday.

(vi) Review overdue accounts. This must be to initiate possible follow-up action against late payers. Have the overdue accounts already been identified or is further work needed?

(vii) Mary has made a note to send the updated product codes out. You need to know how she planned to do this - was it to all customers? – by e-mail or post? Can it wait until Monday?

# MOCK SIMULATION 4
# ANSWERS

Please note that in the following screen displays, the year is shown as 200X for illustration purposes only. Your answers will obviously show the current year that you are working in.

### TASK 1

Task 1 involves entering the standing details for a new company. If you have used the new company wizard, then you should have had few difficulties. Leave any choices that you are not sure about at their default values. You can always change them later if you change your mind.

### TASK 2

The initial journal will be:

|  | Debit £ | Credit £ |
|---|---|---|
| Bank account | 15,000 |  |
| Share capital |  | 15,000 |

In Sage, the journal looks as follows:

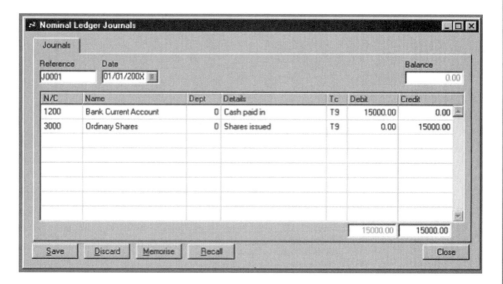

Press the **Save** button to post this journal.

### TASK 3

Task 3 involves inputting the standing data for suppliers. The wizard makes the process fairly straightforward. You can leave all the difficult-looking choices (discounts, currencies, etc) at their default values.

Once the five suppliers have been input, the list of suppliers should look as follows:

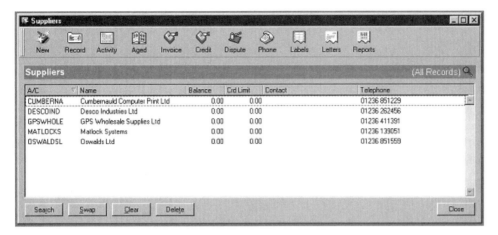

## TASK 4

Each of the five purchase invoices must be inputted. You must be careful with the nominal code that is debited for each invoice, since they are not all purchases of goods for sale. For example, the invoice from Desco Industries is for an item of machinery (a fixed asset) so must be charged to nominal code 0020 (for plant and machinery), as below.

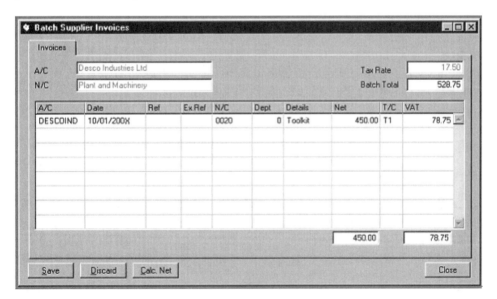

A further problem arises in the invoice from Matlock Systems. £1,274 of the invoice is for computer fixed assets, while £424 is for the cost of software (an expense). No obvious nominal ledger code exists for the cost of software, so a new account (e.g. number 7506) can be created for this purpose.

In summary, the five invoices will be charged as follows:

| Supplier | Nominal ledger account charged | Net £ | VAT £ | Gross £ |
|---|---|---|---|---|
| Desco Industries | 0020 | 450.00 | 78.75 | 528.75 |
| Oswalds Ltd | 7600 | 99.00 | – | 99.00 |
| Cumbernauld Computer | 7504 | 320.00 | 56.00 | 376.00 |
| Matlock Systems | 0030 | 1,274.00 | 222.95 | 1,496.95 |
| Matlock Systems | 7506 | 424.00 | 74.20 | 498.20 |
| GPS Wholesale | 5000 | 9,602.21 | 1,680.39 | 11,282.60 |

After all five invoices have been entered, the list of suppliers will look as follows:

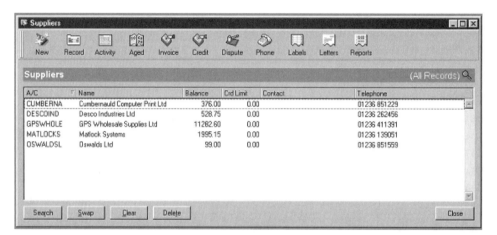

### TASK 5

Task 5 involves paying three suppliers as instructed. The cash at bank balance will fall to £15,000 – £99 – £376 – £528.75 = £13,996.25.

### TASK 6

Task 6 involves setting up the stock records with the items bought from GPS Wholesale Supplies Ltd. After following the wizard for each line of stock, the stock list should look as below:

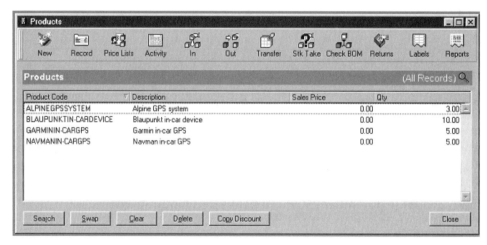

### TASK 7

First you must set up the customer standing details (with nil opening balances) and then post the three invoices and one credit note.

After setting up the three customers using the new customer wizard, the customer list should look as follows:

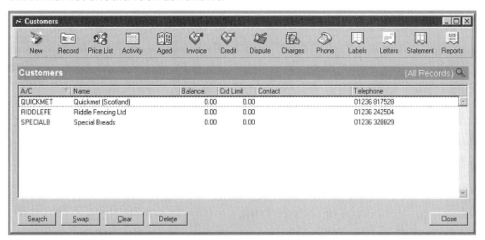

Each invoice is then entered in turn. For example, the first invoice is entered as below and then the **Save** button is pressed to record the invoice (but not yet post it to the ledgers).

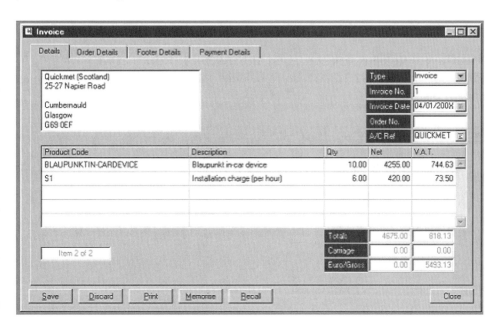

Once the three invoices and one credit note have been saved, the Update button is pressed for each line to post each item to the ledgers. Note how a 'Yes' is then shown in the 'Posted' column.

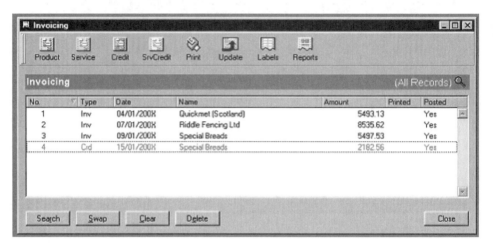

## TASK 8

Task 8 involves entering two customer receipts in turn, and clicking on Save to post them to the ledgers.

After Task 5 the bank balance stood at £13,996.25. Now that we have paid in £8,535.62 and £5,493.13, the bank balance stands at a total of £28,025, as shown below.

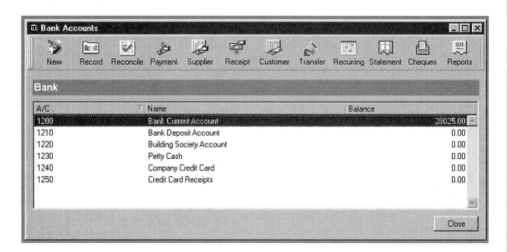

**TASK 9**

In Task 9, first the petty cash must be set up with an opening journal of £300, then the three petty cash vouchers must be posted.

The journal should look as follows:

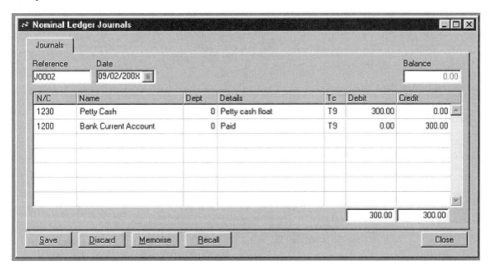

The posting of the petty cash vouchers should look as follows:

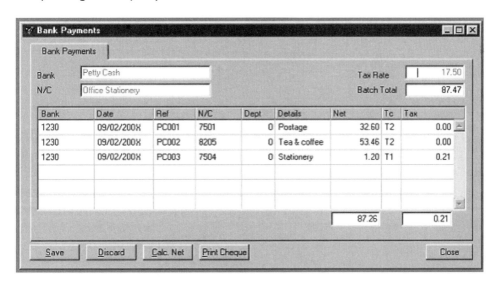

**TASK 10**

The final task simply involves pressing the right buttons to print out a trial balance and an audit trail at the end of the period.

Compare your result with the answer below.

Page: 1

**A-80 Limited**
**Period trial balance**

**To period:** Month 2, February 2006

| N/C | Name | Debit | Credit |
|------|------|-------|--------|
| 0020 | Plant and machinery | 450.00 | |
| 0030 | Office equipment | 1,274.00 | |
| 1100 | Debtors control account | 3,314.97 | |
| 1200 | Bank current account | 27,725.00 | |
| 1230 | Petty cash | 212.53 | |
| 2100 | Creditors control account | | 13,277.75 |
| 2200 | Sales tax control account | | 2,583.11 |
| 2201 | Purchase tax control account | 2,112.50 | |
| 3000 | Ordinary shares | | 15,000.00 |
| 4000 | Sales type A | | 14,760.61 |
| 5000 | Materials purchased | 9,602.21 | |
| 7501 | Postage and carriage | 32.60 | |
| 7504 | Office stationery | 321.20 | |
| 7506 | Office software | 424.00 | |
| 7600 | Legal fees | 99.00 | |
| 8205 | Refreshments | 53.46 | |
| | Totals | 45,621.47 | 45,621.47 |

**A-80 Limited**
**Audit trail (brief)**

| | | | | | | | | | |
|---|---|---|---|---|---|---|---|---|---|
| Date from: | | | 01/01/2006 | | | Customer from: | | | |
| Date to: | | | 31/12/2006 | | | Customer to: | | ZZZZZZZ | |

| | | | | | | | | | |
|---|---|---|---|---|---|---|---|---|---|
| Transaction from: | | | 1 | | | Supplier from: | | | |
| Transaction to: | | | 99999999 | | | Supplier to: | | ZZZZZZZ | |

Exclude deleted tran:                                No

| No | Items | Tp | Account | Date | Refn | Details | Net | Tax | Gross |
|---|---|---|---|---|---|---|---|---|---|
| 1 | 1 | JD | 1200 | 01/01/2006 | J0001 | Cash paid in | 15,000.00 | 0.00 | 15,000.00 |
| 2 | 1 | JC | 3000 | 01/01/2006 | J0001 | Shares issued | 15,000.00 | 0.00 | 15,000.00 |
| 3 | 1 | PI | DESCOIND | 10/01/2006 | | Toolkit | 450.00 | 78.75 | 528.75 |
| 4 | 1 | PI | OSWALDS | 10/01/2006 | | Legal cost | 99.00 | 0.00 | 99.00 |
| 5 | 1 | PI | CUMBERN | 10/01/2006 | | Stationery | 320.00 | 56.00 | 376.00 |
| 6 | 1 | PI | MATLOCK | 10/01/2006 | | | 1,274.00 | 222.95 | 1,496.95 |
| 7 | 1 | PI | MATLOCK | 10/01/2006 | | | 424.00 | 74.20 | 498.20 |
| 8 | 1 | PI | GPSWHOL | 10/01/2006 | | | 9,602.21 | 1,680.39 | 11,282.60 |
| 9 | 1 | PP | OSWALDS | 05/01/2006 | 1001 | Purchase payment | 99.00 | 0.00 | 99.00 |
| 10 | 1 | PP | CUMBERN | 05/01/2006 | 1002 | Purchase payment | 376.00 | 0.00 | 376.00 |
| 11 | 1 | PP | DESCOIND | 05/01/2006 | 1003 | Purchase payment | 528.75 | 0.00 | 528.75 |
| 12 | 2 | SI | QUICKMET | 04/01/2006 | 1 | Blaupunkt in-car devi | 4,675.00 | 818.13 | 5,493.13 |
| 14 | 4 | SI | RIDDLEFE | 07/01/2006 | 2 | Garmin in-car GPS | 7,264.36 | 1,271.26 | 8,535.62 |
| 18 | 2 | SI | SPECIALB | 09/01/2006 | 3 | Navman in-car GPS | 4,678.75 | 818.78 | 5,497.53 |
| 20 | 2 | SC | SPECIALB | 15/01/2006 | 4 | Navman in-car GPS | 1,857.50 | 325.06 | 2,182.56 |
| 22 | 1 | SR | RIDDLEFE | 14/01/2006 | | Sales receipt | 8,535.62 | 0.00 | 8,535.62 |
| 23 | 1 | SR | QUICKMET | 19/01/2006 | | Sales receipt | 5,493.13 | 0.00 | 5,493.13 |
| 24 | 1 | JD | 1230 | 09/02/2006 | J0002 | Petty cash float | 300.00 | 0.00 | 300.00 |
| 25 | 1 | JC | 1200 | 09/02/2006 | J0002 | Paid | 300.00 | 0.00 | 300.00 |
| 26 | 1 | CP | 1230 | 09/02/2006 | PC001 | Postage | 32.60 | 0.00 | 32.60 |
| 27 | 1 | CP | 1230 | 09/02/2006 | PC002 | Tea and coffee | 53.46 | 0.00 | 53.46 |
| 28 | 1 | CP | 1230 | 09/02/2006 | PC003 | Stationery | 1.20 | 0.21 | 1.41 |

# INDEX

KAPLAN PUBLISHING

KAPLAN PUBLISHING

KAPLAN PUBLISHING